INDUSTRIAL MARKETING

INTERNATIONAL ENCYCLOPAEDIA OF MARKETING SERIES

INDUSTRIAL MARKETING

Edited by
A. S. BHAMHRA
A.K.CHAUDHARY

ANMOL PUBLICATIONS PVT. LTD.
NEW DELHI-110002 (INDIA)

ANMOL PUBLICATIONS PVT. LTD.
4374/4B, Ansari Road, Daryaganj
New Delhi-110 002

Industrial Marketing

First Edition 1999

ISBN 81-261-0254-3

PRINTED IN INDIA

Published by J. L. Kumar for Anmol Publications Pvt. Ltd., New Delhi-110 002 and Printed at Mehra Offset Press, Delhi.

CONTENTS

PREFACE

The *Internaional Ecyclopaedia of Marketing* comprises of five volumes, the different core areas of marketing, narrates the business and its marketplace. Here the interaction of buyers and sellers establishes whether the business firm has successfully contributed useful goods or services. In competition with other sellers, each firm endeavours to meet more effectively the needs of buyers and thereby insure its survival. In the early 1950s, largely as the result of a shift from a World War II production-oriented economy to a peacetime market-oriented economy, the business community became increasing sensitive to the problem of interpreting conditions in the marketplace. Out of this era came the 'marketing concept', essentially the notion that a firm's future hinges on an integrated program designed to meet customer needs. Obviously, marketing management problems are broad in scope. Their solution calls for information and insights provided by production and financial management as well as marketing management. It is the particular responsibility of marketing management, however, to interpret conditions in the marketplace. These conditions include such factors as the changing attitudes and habits of buyers, the impact of government regulation, and the prediction of competitive tactics.

In approaching the study of marketing, we shall stress both the formal and informal role of executives. Thus, normative patterns of decision making and planning will be described. As human beings, we would hope that the marketing executive is sensitive to the social problems of our time. As an executive, he should be held responsible or the manner in which he performs his functions.

Editors

1

INTRODUCTION TO INDUSTRIAL MARKETING

What is industrial marketing? The first step in answering this question is to do define marketing. While there are about as many definitions of marketing as there are writers, the one adopted by the American Marketing Association (AMA) is appropriate for our purposes. This definition interprets marketing as the performance of business activities that direct the flow of goods and services from the producer to the consumer or user. Industrial goods and services, on the other hand, are destined to produce or become parts of other goods and services, or to facilitate the operations of business, public, and nonprofit enterprises. Goods which can be included in the production category are machinery, 'materials, and components. Paper, a seemingly indispensable supply item, is an example of a good which is utilized in the operation of all types of enterprises.

It follows then that a particular good may be either consumer or industrial, depending upon how the purchaser intends to use it. The nature of the good, while appropriate for some commodities, is not always a valid basis for making a distinction. The following examples will help to illustrate this:

1. Automobile batteries are purchased by both automobile manufacturers and car owners. In face, the use of a particular brand of battery by the manufacturer as original equipment is perhaps its strongest selling appeal in the replacement market.
2. Office furnishings, such as a desk or lamp, are frequently indistinguishable from those found in

homes. Often a store will number among its clientele both types of purchasers.

3. Trucks, until a few years ago, were considered as strictly industrial goods. This view has changed substantially with the development of the camper market.

Thus, the most workable definition of industrial marketing is based on the intended use of the particular good or service in question. Accordingly, industrial marketing is the performance of business activities that direct the flow from producer to user of goods and services which produce or become part of other goods and services, or facilitate the operation of an enterprise, either business, public, or nonprofit. Stated more succinctly, it is the marketing of industrial goods and services.

Types of goods and services

For purposes of convenience in studying, both goods and service can be classified into more definitive groupings. The use of classification, however, is subject to several qualifications, the most significant of which is the lack of mutually exclusive categories. As a result, it is not possible to classify all goods and services; some will be of a borderline nature. Industrial chemicals, for example, can be can material or supply depending upon the exact situation. The same ambiquity is encountered among some items of accessory equipment. Such items tend to exhaust their utility through use and are frequently discarded rather than repaired. Thus, these items of equipment could be easily confused with operating supplies. Another qualification is that specific use of a good may change over a period of time. Thus, its current classification may not be applicable a few years from now. Goods in the research category, when adopted, present a situation requiring reclassification.

Before proceeding with the descriptions of the various goods, consideration is given to the area of services. There are only two distinct types of industrial services: physical and advisory. Application of a physical service results in a change of form or composition. Wrecking or demolition is a service which brings about a very evident change. Other examples include electroplating, the polishing of metals, and the acid treatment of oil wells. Most of the firms performing this type of service are relatively small. An effort is usually made to locate as near the potential customer as possible.

Advisory service include geological and oceanology surveys, the x-rating of castings for flaws, and R&D contract programs for the government. They are performed by businesses, non profit organizations, foundations, and universities. Firms engaged in providing this type of service are frequently international in scope. Under contract from the United Nations, Aero Service made a comprehensive inventory of Surinam's mineral resources. Their most significant discovery has been a bauxite deposit valued at $350 million.

A recent development in advisory service is that provided by such nonprofit research corporations as Systems Development, Mitre, and Aerospace. What the Mitre Corporation does was briefly outlined by their officials.

1. Dispensing technical advice in evaluation concepts, proposals, and hardware for the Air Force.
2. Coordinating the project of military contractors and holding proprietary information the various companies will not share among themselves.

Machinery and equipment

Examples of machinery and equipment can be found almost anywhere. In the plant such goods as lathes, grinders, and stamping mills manufacture other goods and services without becoming part of the final products themselves. Machinery and equipment of a more administrative nature include such items as typewriters, postage meters, copying machines, and electronic data processing equipment.

Major equipment comprises those items of a high unit price which appear in the balance sheet as capital assets. Usually this type of good is marketed directly to the customer by the manufacturer. The feasibility of a direct approach is enhanced by the high unit price and the infrequency of purchase. Some use is made of functional middlemen by smaller firms who find themselves a considerable distance from the market.

Major equipment of a significant size, such as a blast furnace or a crude-oil distillation tower, is referred to as an installation. As part of the fixed plant, installations are closely allied with construction. Therefore, a more extensive market is involved because contracts must be maintained with architects, engineering firms, and consultants. By way of illustration, an engineering, purchasing, and construction of a liquid-fertilizer plant. In another situation, consulting engineers designed an oil refinery in conjunction with engineers from the oil company and then constructed the facility.

Accessory equipment is lower in unit price and is charged off to current operating expense or depreciated over a short span of years. Almost every conceivable marketing channel is utilized to distribute such equipment. If the marketer is large enough and has a fairly extensive line, he may even have his own sales branches. A part of any industrial distributor's line is accessory equipment.

Machinery and equipment can be further categorized as special purpose or multipurpose. A special-purpose machine is designed to perform a single operation. Often as not, it is built to customer specification, as is usual in the case of coal-mining equipment. The market for special-purpose machinery and equipment is ordinarily limited to a single industry or trade.

When machinery and equipment can be utilized with little or no modification by different industries, they are generally referred to as multipurpose. Among the items which can be classified thus are hoists, power wrenches, lift trucks, and hydraulic presses. Industrial distributors occasionally maintain a market for used goods of a multipurpose character. They may be forced to do this because of trade-ins. In many areas, however, local demand will far exceed the supply resulting from trade-ins. As a consequence, distributors have had to seek out sellers in other areas to replenish their inventories.

Raw materials

Raw materials can be defined as the unprocessed goods which come from mines, oil wells, forests, fisheries, and farms. In getting raw materials to market, two vitally important functions are transportation and storage. Transportation is important because raw materials often have to be shipped great distances. The following examples illustrate the shipping distances for two raw materials-lumber and copper. The Douglas fir region in the Pacific Northwest, which accounts for about 30 percent of the softwood consumed by the nation, is a considerable distance from all of the major urban areas with the exception of those in California. Forty-five percent of the copper in the United States is mined in Southern Arizona, but a large part of the nation's refining capacity is situated around New York. Raw materials are also bulky, so economical means must be found for moving vast quantities of the commodity. As an example, boats and pipelines, two of the lowest-cost forms of transportation, carry over 92 percent of the crude petroleum obtained from fields in the United States.

The bulkiness of raw materials also necessitates provision of extensive as well as economical facilities for storing raw materials. Buying and selling of raw materials are facilitated by the extensive application of standards. In the United States, the federal government through its various agencies has assumed much of the responsibility for control of standards. Agricultural materials have been standardized under the direction of the U.S. Department of Agriculture. The Commodity Standards Division of the U.S. Department of Commerce is interested in the development and control of standards for other types of goods.

The marketing of raw materials is not limited to the United States. American industry depends upon a number of foreign countries to supply its raw-material needs. Pakistan for jute, Katanga for cobalt, and Canada for uranium ore are but a few. Some of the major imports of raw materials are presented in Table 1.

The flow of goods from the raw-materials source, then through various production and marketing levels or stages to its final destination can be described as a vertical chain. Absorption or control of one level by another is called vertical integration. For the manufacturer of industrial goods, vertical integration may be backward toward the raw-material source or forward toward the end user. It is fairly common to find industrial-good manufacturers integrating vertically in the direction of the raw-material source. Among the major advantages sought through integrating the extraction of raw materials into a company are assured supply, desired quality, and lower costs. Examples of this form of vertical integration are the iron-ore mines, oil wells, and timberlands owned and operated by steel, oil, and lumber companies respectively.

Table 1. Imports of selected raw materials,

Rawmaterial	*Value*
Petroleum	1,187, 741.9
Iron ore	443,806.6
Sugar	440,502.0
Wool	278,480.6
Rubber	194,124.6
Bauxite	148,557.8
Cocoa	137.445.2
Tobacco	129,812.6
Manganese ore	110,280.2
Crude asbestos	70,457.2
Zinc ore	54,417.1
Lead	26,923.1
Cotton	26, 734.4

Even in agriculture, some tendency toward integration is noted. Poultry processors in the South have extended their operation to the raising of chickens, and canners of frozen juice own their own citrus groves. However, such integration is not without its disadvantages, one of the most significant being the reduced ability to adjust when changes occur in the demand for the consumer product.

Functional middlemen who do not take title to the goods in which they deal play an important role in the marketing of raw materials which are not controlled by firms that have integrated. For nonagricultural commodities, the two most important types are brokers and selling agents. Brokers are also involved in the marketing of agricultural raw materials. The selling of grain and livestock at terminal markets is usually handled by commission merchants.

Commodity exchanges provide markets for various raw materials, generally agricultural. The most prominent exchange is the Chicago Board of Trade, whose annual volume is normally in excess of $25 million. Cash and futures markets are maintained in wheat, oats, rye, cotton, corn, soybeans, soybean oil and meal, and lard.

Fabricated materials

Fabricated materials are those goods which have received some processing but will require even more before becoming part of the finished product. They frequently lose their identity in the finished product. Examples are tinplate, glass, plastics, corn syrup, cold-and hot rolled strip, and plywood. In the aluminum industry, both alumina and metallic aluminum can be classified as fabricated materials.

The physical properties of fabricated materials provide a wide range of application. The markets for certain industrial chemicals, commodities used by nearly every industry, are probably the most extensive. For some fabricated materials, such as aluminum, the range of possible uses is still expanding. In this stage of development, labeled "imitation" by Schumpeter, research is undertaken largely to discover new-product applications.

Marketing of fabricated materials which possess few unique features is highly competitive. Take, for example, the competition that exists between steel and aluminum. Steel, the more traditional material, is being actively challenged by aluminum in canning, automobiles, construction, and many other markets. The high degree of competition is evidenced by the advertising campaigns both types of industries have undertaken to get the ultimate consumer to appreciate and select those consumer goods made of their particular material. An important part of this has been the development of trademarks to assist in identification.

Large scale marketers sell all or a large portion of their output directly to users through sales branches. Metallurgists and architectural engineers as technical specialists support the sales force when and wherever needed. In the metals industry, there has been a tendency on the part of certain large firms to utilize fabricated materials in making consumer products such as foil wrappings, kitchen-ware, and furniture.

Direct sales, for the most part, are in large quantities. In the steel industry a carload lot is usual. Two thousand five hundred steel distributors are relied upon to take care of customers who need less than a carload. This channel accounts for 16 percent of the total steel shipped. The major products handled are cold-and hot-rolled sheets, standard pipe, and plates. Steel distributors tend to concentrate in those areas which have a preponderance of small manufacturers. A good example is Los Angeles, California.

Small-scale marketers may locate near customers to facilitate direct selling. Textiles, as an example of a fabricated material which is produced at some distance from its markets, are distributed by various types of middlemen. These include selling agents, brokers, an converters. From the standpoint of functions performed, selling agents can be considered the most important. In addition to selling, they provide their principals with advice on merchandising, prices, and future trends. Among the extra services offered are research, inventory control, designing, and credit and collections. Commission rates range from 2 to 5 percent.

Products which perform a specific function and do not require further modifications to be installed as part of the final product are classified as component parts. Vacuum tubes, diesel engines, automobile batteries, transistors, and ball bearings are but a few examples of what can be called component parts.

There are two markets for parts; original-equipment manufacturers and replacement or aftermath. Original-equipment manufacturers, after deciding on purchasing rather than producing the part, buy components for two reasons. The first and more compelling one is that the part is essential to the operation of the finished product. Examples would be a torque convertor and a clutch in the power shifting transmission for an earth scrapper.

The second reason is that the part enhances the finished product from an engineering or a marketing standpoint. In neither case, however, will the part be absolutely necessary to the operation of the final product. The addition of a counter to certain types of machinery and equipment is a good illustration of a engineering enhancement. A counter will allow the positioning of a table on a milling machine or similar equipment by digital readout instead of vernier dial. The quantitative output of a punch press can be measured with a counter. It should be noted, too, that improvements such as these which are basically, engineering in nature are used as marketing features.

Components are frequently added to increase the marketability of a product. This is the situation in the automobile industry. Power steering, air conditioners, radios, and countless other components have been added to cars for marketing reasons. Even in the truck industry, one company has designed a new driver's seat to improve the riding qualities of the heavy-duty truck. Most of the time, however, marketing components are used to heighten the attractiveness of consumer goods.

Many component parts are marketed directly to OEM accounts. In the automobile and aerospace industries, component suppliers have a tendency to locate their manufacturing facilities near major buyers. Much of the industry in the Detroit and Los Angeles areas is of satellite nature.

Large marketers have their own sales forces, whereas small firms, if they are geographically close, rely upon an owner, partner, or executive. A common arrangement is a partnership in which one partner sells and the other manages the plant. An unusual situation develops when the buyer franchises out the production of component parts to still another company. An example of this is found in the television industry. One West Coast firm pays a royalty under a licensing agreement for every part they have made by a Chicago manufacturer.

Both functional and merchant middlemen are retained by small marketers. Manufacturing agents or reps are used when there is no need for intensive coverage, the agents' established contacts are desired, technical knowledge is required in selling, and there is little need for warehouse or service facilities. Agents are also ideal for supplementing other methods of distribution. Industrial distributors handle more of the standardized parts, such as valves and fasteners, which are frequently purchased by the wide variety of manufacturers.

Two basic distribution systems are used to reach the replacement market. The first consists of channels controlled by the original-equipment manufacturer. The second, established by the part manufacturer involves all the middlemen who normally sell a particular part. Ideally, maximum use is made of both systems.

The replacement market for automotive components provides a good example. Briefly, more than 1,000 manufacturers distribute over $7 billion worth of parts through two channels. The first is labeled the manufacturer channel and is composed of franchised dealers and service organizations like the General Motors' United Motor Service Division. The second is an independent channel which contains autonomous warehouse distributors, jobbers, garages, and repair shops.

Research goods

Research goods are the tangible results of government-or industry-contracted R&D programs. Accordingly, goods in this category are closely related to the advisory service provided by R&D, and are most often found in highly technical industries such as electronics and aerospace. It is estimated that 83 percent of R&D monies are concentrated in the aircraft and electrical-equipment industries.

From a marketing standpoint, research goods differ considerably from other types. First of all, it is not the goods themselves which are being marketed, but rather the abilities and experience of the firm doing the R&D work. Secondly, many research goods are models, prototypes, or mock-ups. A third factor is that most R&D programs are heavily dependent upon government financing. Government expenditures account for about two of every three dollars spent annually for R&D. Finally, research goods are frequently employed in promotional campaigns directed at the ultimate consumer. All automobile manufacturers exhibit experimental cars from time to time to obtain some indication of public opinion.

Salvage goods

Material objects which are extracted from wreckage, destruction, or the like, and have further value and usefulness can be classified as salvage goods. Much of what is considered salvage has metallic content. Copper, gold, lead, iron, and aluminum are all reusable commodities.

Many salvage goods supplement the supply of new materials. The world's copper resources represent only fifty years' supply at the present rate of usage. This is not significant, however, when it is estimated that 60 percent of the copper put into use eventually returns as scrap. Almost one-third of all newly made steel in the world comes from scrap. The exact percentage will vary, depending upon the type of furnace used and the nation in which the furnace is located. Bessemer converters accept almost no scrap, but there is ready utilization of scrap by open-heart furnaces. Among the various nations, the amounts vary between Belgium, which depends on very little, to Italy, which uses over 80 percent scrap.

Supply and demand considerations play important roles in pricing salvage goods. The drop in price of steel scrap between 1956 and 1968 is a good illustration. In 1956, the average price per ton was $53.50. On September

25, 1968, the quotation for a ton, Chicago was $23.50. The contributing factors were a reduction in the amounts of steel scrap required in existing furnaces, the erection of new steel facilities with basic oxygen furnaces which use only 25 percent scrap, and the availability of more new ore from the exploitation of mines in other parts of the world.

The inability to supply the demand for used brick frequently results in its being priced higher than the new. An attractive product for home construction, used brick, in any appreciable amount, is difficult to extract from wrecking operations.

Salvage goods are marketed through two channels. In terms of number and sales volume, merchant wholesalers are the more significant. These middlemen, often criticized in the past for their high profit margins, are predominant in the distribution of iron and steel scrap. The Ogden Corporation of New York City is considered the world's largest, with 30 percent of its annual sales derived from scrap.

The other channel is made up of wrecking and salvage companies that obtain salvage goods in the course of their service operations. These wrecking firms vary in size from international corporations to proprietorship with no more than one or two employees. Many of the larger firms also handle new products to supplement salvage sales.

The largest wrecking company in the United States has added such lines as new kitchen equipment.

Operating supplies Supplies are goods that exhaust their utility or are used up in the production process or the operation of any enterprise. What purchasing agents refer to as MRO items are included in this category. Lubricants, drill, cleaning solvents, and abrasives are production supplies. In the operation of any business or public organization, paper in its various forms is undoubtedly the most necessary supply item. Other administrative supplies include ink, pencils, paper clips, fuels, and maintenance products. The use of supplies by many different industries results in their markets being more widespread than is normal for other types of industrial goods. In this respect, there is some resemblance to the marketing of consumer goods.

Supplies have a relatively low unit value and are usually purchased in small quantities. Wherever practical, the routine reordering of supplies has been automated with electronic data processing equipment. Some buyers, in an effort to reduce the frequency of purchase, have entered into a contract for specified quantities to be delivered during a given period of time, generally a year.

Price is the dominant buying influence to the extent that supplies are standardized. Other factors governing the choice of a vendor include the convenience of his location, his capacity to fill orders completely, and his reputation for reliability.

Supplies are distributed through almost every possible channel. The practice of manufacturers of machinery and equipment is to market supplies through the outlets used for their primary products. Such is the case with electronic data processing equipment and office machines. Very often more than one channel is employed to reach an extensive market. Paper is a good example of multiple-channel distribution. Manufacturers' sales branches, merchant wholesalers, and functional middlemen are all employed.

Wholesale sales of paper and paper products (not including wall-Paper) in 1963 were as follows:

	Number of Establishments	*Sales (in thousands)*
Merchant wholesalers	7,046	$4,714,610
Manufacturers' sales branches	2,646	8,562,090
Merchandise agents and brokers	443	835.033

Probably the most important middleman in the marketing of supplies is the industrial distributor. A survey of manufacturing plants disclosed that industrial distributors are the preferred source for many supply items.

Size of the industrial market

Up to the present time, there have been no concerted attempts to measure, either in terms of the value of goods marketed or the volume of trade, the magnitude of the industrial market. A number of authors have estimated that the industrial market accounts for approximately one-half the value of manufacturing shipments. There are a number of reasons which can account for the failure to take a measurement;

1. A consensus that demand which is derived rather than direct is not an indicator of economic activity. This, of course, completely ignores the multiplier effect of derived demand.
2. A lack of agreement as to the definition of industrial marketing.
3. A number of practical difficulties that would have to be overcome in the collection of data. One severe limitation is imposed by the fact that very few industries maintain records of shipments by class of consumer.

Some idea of the dollar volume of industrial transactions can be obtained by the statistics on cost of materials to manufacturers, capital expenditures for the various forms of private enterprise, and government purchases of goods and services.

The first relates to the quantitative significance of the industrial market. For Purely comparative purposes, the dollar volume of transactions in both 1964 and 1965 is equal to roughly two-thirds of the valuation placed on Gross National Product. Another impression of size can be gained from the fact´ that the industrial market very nearly approximates the combination sales of retail and merchant whole sale establishments.

2

CHARACTERISTICS OF INDUSTRIAL MARKETING

Demand for industrial goods and services

Demand is not inherent in industrial marketing as it is in consumer marketing. Rather, it is derived from the demand for consumer goods and services as well as the purchasing of governmental units at all levels. Industrial demand can also be distinguished as showing a wide degree of fluctuation, an acute sensitivity to buyer inventory policy, and a tendency to exhibit counter price elasticity initially.

Derived demand

The demand for industrial goods and services, being derived, is activated by ultimate consumer and government purchasing. The level of such transactions is translated into marketing activity not only for the firms making these products, but for their numerous suppliers as well. For example, a manufacturer of consumer products will buy industrial goods and services to implement and sustain his operation only if his own products are selling. Likewise, the suppliers of consumer-product manufacturers will in turn base their buying on what is sold. As this chain of sale and purchase lengthens, the influencing effect of derived demand weakens. Automobiles represent a product for which changes in ultimate consumer demand generate repercussions throughout much of the industrial market. According to the Automobile Manufacturers Association, the auto industry consumes over 20 percent of it's malleable iron, and over a third of its zinc.

Another way of looking at the industrial market is in terms of input-output data or the interindustry flow of dollar transactions for a period of time. It can be seen that total purchases or inputs equal total sales or outputs. This is basic assumption of input-output analysis. The rows of the table show how the output of one industry is distributed to other industry segments. The columns reflect the purchasing patterns of the industries. Thus, each statistics in the table is both an input an output for an industry segment.

Using input-output analysis, a manufacturer obtains a general picture of the market segments for the products of his industry-a general picture because the various market segments are defined as heterogeneous SIC groupings. This has resulted in some rather surprising findings, as, the fact that the food and kindred products industry has been shown to consume almost 2 percent of the communications industry output. Even so, input-output analysis contributed valuable information to the industrial-good manufacturer in planning market strategy.

Table Hypothetical Input-output Data

Industries producing	Industries purchasing A	B	C	Other	Total output (Sales)
A	10	8	5	2	25
B	6	2	6	4	18
C	7	4	1	0	12
Other	2	4	0	10	16
Total input (purchases)	25	18	12	16	71

The derived nature of demand causes it to have a multiplying effect on the volume of industrial trade. The following hypothetical example will help to illustrate this phenomenon. Suppose that company ABC, a manufacturer of consumer products, has a yearly sales volume of $1 million. Since it is essentially an assembler, suppose its cost of material amounts to 80 percent, or $800,000. Further assume that suppliers are arranged in three levels with each firm's purchases divided up among four vendors.

The total volume of industrial trade is 36 percent greater than the consumer demand from which it is derived. A still greater increase would have been noted if the allotted capital and supply expenditures for the eighty-five firms had been included. It is also noticeable that the extent of the increase has a direct relationship to the number of supplier levels and the relative costs incurred by individual suppliers for materials and capital.

The multiplier effect also increases the initial contract outlays made by the government to meet its obligations. In the aerospace industry, for example, about 100 prime contractors are supplied by over 100,000 "first-tier" subcontractors and some 200,000 "vendors".

Widely fluctuating demand

The derived nature of demand for industrial products causes it to experience a wide degree of fluctuation. Frequently, it can be said that industrial demand takes on the appearance of what might be described as a "boom or bust" cycle. This can be understood by looking at the market during prosperity as well as depression. During prosperous times, the manufacturers of consumer goods increase production. This accelerates the purchase of industrial goods and services. Industrial goods which become part of the final product are absorbed at a greater rate to meet current requirements and expectations of still further growth. Firms speed up the replacement and addition of capital items. Then, too, the amount of overall business activity causes an increase in the consumption of supplies. During this time the market gravitates toward the seller. Many of the buying considerations such as price and quality are outweighed by shorter delivery dates. If the seller's output is relatively limited, his problem is how to allocate it between old and new customers. New firms will spring up in those portions of the industrial market where entry costs are not formidable. One of the best examples of such a market is the one for gray-iron castings.

When consumer-goods demand slackens, the opposite situation develops with deceleration rather than acceleration and pessimism replacing optimism. Production of consumer goods is at a lower level, inventories of both consumer and industrial goods are reduced, and no new capital expenditures are made.

Often, too, expense-cutting programs are initiated to lessen such costs as those incurred by the use of operating supplies. Some retrenchment is also noted among consumer-goods manufacturers. Goods and services which were formerly purchased are now produced so as to sustain as nearly as possible the levels of employment. This, in effect, abolishes much of the supplier spectrum. The indirect suppliers in the lower strata are most acutely affected, often having to cease operations.

Some indications of retrenchment in recent years have been observed in the auto industry. A division whose sales are down will change over to the production of components for other more successful divisions. Another example is found in the military market today. The failure to obtain a contract or a cutback of a current project has brought more serious consequences for the subcontractors than for the major contractor.

Sensitivity of inventory policy

The demand for industrial goods and services is highly responsive to changes in customer inventories. These changes may be effected to adjust to new sales patterns or to modifications in general company policy. What happens may best be explained by the following hypothetical situation. A company operates on a two-month inventory of a component part, one part going into each final product. If there is a constant flow without time lags that occur under actual conditions, balance is maintained by purchasing the same amount as is sold every month. Suppose that sales increase 25 percent. To satisfy the expansion of both sales and inventory, purchases of the component part will have to be increased 75 percent-25 percent to allow for current sales growth and 25 percent for each of the two months of inventory. With future sales expectations bright, the amount of inventory might also be increased. If another month's supply were added, three times as many components as before would have to be purchased. Inventory buildups, for the most part, are gradual with purchases spread out over a number of months.

Now, suppose that sales have fallen off by some 25 percent. An immediate inventory adjustment will mean that the firm will need to purchase only twenty-five percent of the original order for the next thirty days. If a decrease in inventory requirements, say to a month's supply accompanies the drop in sales, nothing more need be purchased until the third month. Changes that occur in a declining market have a sense of urgency about them and tend to be abrupt.

Initial counter price elasticity

Elasticity is the responsiveness of demand to changes in price. Normally, the demand curve is pictured as downward-sloping. That is, as the price is lowered, demand increases. Conversely, demand will decline with a raising of price. Demand is elastic if the percentage change in quantity demanded is greater than the percentage change in price. For example, a 5 percent decline in price results in a 10 percent increase in demand. If in the preceding situation the increase in demand is less than 5 percent, demand is said to be inelastic.

Initially, the elastically of demand for industrial goods and services runs counter to this. A price increment brings about a growth in demand, whereas a drop in price is attended by a shrinking of demand. The reasoning behind such a response by industrial consumers is that any price change foretells greater movement in the same direction. An increase, therefore, will signify that prices will go still higher. In order to avoid even greater material costs, users commence to "load up", as it is usually termed in industry. The extent of the commitment depends on three factors-the relative cost of the material, the degree of price competition for the final product, and the financial capabilities of the purchaser.

When the price is cut, purchasers will surmise that it will fall even farther and will consequently refrain as much as possible from entering the market. How much they will have to purchase depends upon their inventory position at the time of the price decline and their present rate of consumption.

This abstaining action, if taken collectively by a major portion of the market, will in effect drive the price even lower. This is especially true when the suppliers have a relatively high and unavoidable fixed-cost burden. In recent years, remarkable progress has been attained in alleviating such marketing hindrances. Much of this can be attributed to increased accuracy in sales forecasting and market analysis. A notable example is a West Coast cement company whose research objectives are slanted toward the prediction of long-range sales trends. Sometimes, not only the buying requirements of immediate customers are studied, but those of their customers as well. One steel company states with a great deal of pride that its research department forecasted a slump in automobile sales much before the automobile manufacturers themselves.

Another approach that has been used successfully by some firms is the attainment of greater manufacturing flexibility. One major steel firm can operate profitably at a much lower rate of capacity than was ever thought possible. Facing the rigidity of vertical integration, another firm has found it profitable to channel off some of its un needed iron ore to Japanese concerns.

Market characteristics

Generally speaking, there are two types of industrial markets-vertical and horizontal. Narrow markets which involve a particular trade or industry are referred to as vertical. Distribution tends to be intensive in that almost every market segment will possess a need for a particular good or service. Notice, too, that the market represented by what is defined as mineral industries is even more restricted when only mining establishments with twenty or more employees are considered.

Horizontal markets involve those goods and services whose use is not confined but rather extends to all kinds of firms in many different industries. Most multipurpose equipment and operating supplies fall into this category. A good example is sulfuric acid, the market for which is so extensive that its rate of consumption has often been used as an indicator of general industrial activity.

Other distinctions that can be made between the industrial and consumer-goods markets are the geographic location of customers and the process of arriving at a purchasing decision. How the industrial market tends to localize is considered first.

Number of Mineral-industry Establishments, by Geographical Division, United States, 1963

Geographic Division	Industry		Oil and Gas Extraction	
	Total	20 or more Employees	Total	20 or more Employees
New England	349	57		
Middle Atlantic	4,072	516	932	40
East North Central	4,743	574	2,230	124
West North Central	3,547	398	1,877	175
South Atlantic	4,433	807	1,080	39
East South Central	3,336	569	1,051	101
West South Central	12,131	1,726	11,362	1,552
Mountain	3,656	511	1,820	254
Pacific	2,370	332	885	155
Total	38,637	5,490	21,237	2,440

Geographical concentration

In following the same geographical pattern as its largest customer, the manufacturer, the industrial market gravitates toward urban areas and certain regions of the United States. Its density is highest in and around major metropolitan areas. Measured in terms of value added by manufacturing, the degrèe of urbanization is vividly demonstrated by the following:

	Percentage of the total value added for the state
Arizona;	
Phoenix	69.5
California:	
Los Angles-Long Beach Orange Couhtry	53.5
San-Francisco -Oak land San Jose	21.9
Michigan:	
Detroit	51.1
Texas:	
Dallas-Fort Worth	25.1
Houston-Galveston	27.1
Wisconsin:	
Milwaukee	41.7

Number of manufacturing establishments, by geographical division, United States, 1963

Geographical division	Establishments Total	20 or more employees
New England	24,650	8,677
Middle Atlantic	81,707	28,526
East north central	63,092	22,320
West north central	20,668	6,257
South Atlantic	35,546	11,809
East south central	14,196	4,939
West south central	20,237	5,920
Mountain	8,527	2,022
Pacific	43,307	11,813
Total	311,930	102,283

Probably the most important industrial region is the one which extends from Pittsburgh to Chicago and from Cincinnati to Milwaukee and Detroit. The value added in the Chicago-northwestern Indiana area alone is greater than that recorded by 45 states. The largest single concentration in terms of value added is the New York northeastern New Jersey area with over $19 billion.

Additional evidence of the high degree of geographical concentration in the industrial market is provided by comparing for five states the shipments of gray iron and the number of foundries with the number and the sales of retail establishments.

The trend toward industrial decentralization may have only limited disruptive effects on the time-established patterns of concentration. The auto and meat-packing industries provide two examples which seem to support this observation. In neither case have a substantial number of suppliers moved to be geographically decentralized with their customers. Much of this apparent inertia may be attributable to there being no reason for the marketer to be convenient. Another explanation may be the deep-rooted relationships suppliers have with those firms who in turn provide them with goods and services. The experience of a manufacturer of speciality lacquers and varnishes is contrary to this. To retain the volume of business they had been doing with the automobile firms, they were forced to locate near the assembly plants. Special orders, it seems, are the rule rather than the exception for this group of products.

Rational buying motives

Industrial buying is substantially rational in nature. A careful and frequently exhaustive study of all the objective factors is the basis for buying a product from a particular vendor. This should not be interpreted to mean, however, that emotional motives involving the images of the salesman and his company do not influence the final decision. They most assuredly do, particularly among products and vendors that are fairly competitive in price and quality. One major detriment to a favorable image in the eyes of most buyers is the supplier's small size. At the risk of overgeneralizing, it can be surmised that emotional buying motives become more important as the degree of similarity of quantifiable factors among products and vendors increases.

The industrial buying process starts with the anticipation or recognition of a need and ends with the placement of an order with a vendor. The buying process may be new in that it represents the initial purchase of the item in question, or it may be a repurchase to replenish inventory or replace equipment. Informational requirements of the purchasing influences will vary in direct relation to the newness of the purchases. The newer the item is in regard to purchasing experience, the greater the extent of the need for information.

The informational dimensions of the industrial purchasing decision are quality, price, and vendor. While the definition and the relative influence of quality and price will vary from situation to situation, the usual approach is to obtain the lowest price consistent with minimum quality standards. This was aptly and succinctly expressed by the chief design engineer for a manufacturer of portable industrial equipment. Reflecting his company's interests in both cost and weight, he said, "Our rule of thumb is a dollar a pound."

Since the early sixties, the technique of value analysis has played a prominent role in the cost-reduction programs of industrial buyers. The organized approach to cost reduction is a systematic way of determiny the most economical means of reliably performing a function. This is called the value of the function. The crux of value analysis is the evaluation of an item's function or use parameters.

The concept of value analysis is particularly applicable in purchasing components because it implies that the minimum standard of one vital part determines the maximum for all those related to it. For example, there would be no need for transistors which have longer life than the system of which they are a component. Value analysis has also encouraged the expanded use of materials which are lower in cost and perhaps more suitable than the more traditional ones. One company, by way of illustration, was able to achieve substantial cost savings and a reduction in weight by substituting anodized aluminum for stainless steel.

Industrial consumers conceive of quality in terms of their products and manufacturing processes. How will it affect performance? Does it extend the life of the final product? Is servicing made any easier? These are but a few of the questions which might be asked about goods and services which become part of the final product. For machinery, equipment, and supplies, the considerations include possible savings in labor costs, improvement in output performance, and reductions in maintenance expense.

The importance of price for goods and services which become part of another product is relative to their position in that product's cost structure and the degree of price competition confronting the product. If the cost position is proportionately high, purchasing will tend to be highly specialized and concerted efforts will be made to minimize the market risks incurred by unfavorable price fluctuations. As an example, a flour miller will have a separate department may be as high in the company's hierarchy as a vice-president.

Three basic approaches are taken to secure added protection against unfavorable price fluctuations of a major component or material. The first is exhaustive study of the market. With adequate information the reactions of the market can be predicted with more surety. A second approach is to integrate vertically in the direction of the supplier. All too often, however, this will reduce the flexibility of the firm to adjust to changes in demand. One more obstacle to integration is the substantial amount of capital that has to be committed for such an undertaking. Hedging, the third approach, is often resorted to when commodity exchanges furnish continuous cash and futures markets in the particular commodity. Briefly, what happens is that the purchaser takes positions in both the cash and futures markets to assure his operating profit regardless of future price fluctuations.

The more competitive the market is for the final product, the greater will be the pressures on all suppliers for price reductions. Purchasers will apply pressure in an effort to gain more leeway in their own pricing or to maintain a specified profit position. Even those who supply goods and services which constitute a relatively insignificant part of the cost structure are subjected to some form of stress. The reasoning is that collectively such reductions may be noteworthy and the purchaser's bargaining position is usually more formidable to many of these suppliers.

For machinery, equipment, and suppliers, the question of price revolves around the attainability of savings-how significant and when. Today's purchasers are also concerned with their capital position. The present burden, which would necessarily be increased, as well as their status i regard to depreciation, is carefully reviewed. Such considerations may have been the major cause for the soft-drink bottlers' postponing or at least slowing down the changeover to canning, an operation which has countless product and process advantages.

The third informational approach to the purchasing decision is an appraisal of all potential suppliers or a vendor analysis. This appraisal is divided into two parts. One part has to do with rating vendor performance. Although the definition of vendor performance may vary from firm to firm, most plans rely on three factors-quality, delivery, and supplier relations. Once ratings are arrived at for each performance factor, they are combined into a composite index for the individual supplier.

The quality rating depends on the relative number of defective items received from a supplier. This, in turn, is weighted by the disposition of the defectives. If the defectives can be used as they are, the weighing is not as adverse as it would be if the cost of reworking the defective had to be absorbed. The delivery rating is determined by comparing the promised delivery data with the actual delivery date The resultant rating may be modified by a quantity factor and/or an expediting factor. The purpose of the quantity factor is to penalize the supplier for failure to deliver the exact quantity specified. It is felt that the supplier who makes several smaller and unscheduled shipments is not doing as good a job as the one who delivers the specified quantity as promised. The expediting factor penalizes the supplier for more than a routine number of contacts by the purchaser. The greater the number of excessive contacts by the purchaser, the higher the affixed penalty.

Supplier relations are services other than quality and delivery. Among the services considered are before and after-sales service, technical counseling, prompt supply of requested documents, salesman calls, and cooperation. Needless to say, supplier relations are difficult to quantify.

The other part of the vendor analysis is the evaluation of vendor capabilities. All potential suppliers are appraised in terms of their R&D, manufacturing, service, financial, and management capabilities. One very large aerospace firm has specifically assigned this responsibility to the purchasing department. Initial evaluation is performed by survey teams, which are composed of an engineer, cost analyst, and representatives from manufacturing, reliability, quality control, and purchasing. The person from purchasing is charged with the administrative function. All reports on experience with the suppliers are filed for future reference in a library maintained within the company.

Among the more significant factors influencing the selection of a supplier are:

1 Price including transportation charges

2 Terms of sales

3 Maintaining quality standards

4 Dependability, particularly in meeting delivery schedules

5 Reputation for integrity

6 Availability of servicing facilities

7 Keeping customers informed

8 Efficient handling of requests

Businesses and governmental units, in ever-increasing numbers, are utilizing computers in the purchasing process. There appear to be three broad levels of application. Undoubtedly the widest application has been in automating the repetitive, routine clerical tasks such as those found in placing the purchase order. Another application has been in the repurchasing of such items as operating supplies at regular intervals. In such situations the purchasing decision rests with the purchasing department and the requirement for new information is minimal. The third application is in supplying purchasing-information. In addition to providing up-to-date and comprehensive data, the computer can provide new facts never before available to the purchaser.

Other factors which have to be considered in the buying process are testing and design cycle. For a new product, the buyer relies initially upon the laboratory and field testing the marketer has done. The results of these tests are usually contained in a specification sheet. Credence is placed on past experience for more mature goods and services. After deciding on the basis of the evidence thus presented that the good or service is worth further appraisal, the buyer requests samples so that he can proceed with his own testing. This may take anywhere from a few weeks to a year. Small firms have a tendency to accomplish the necessary testing in a shorter period of time. Their lack of complexity often facilitates faster action. This is demonstrated by a small manufacturer of cement mixers who fieldtests with customer permission a component in the final product less than a month after receiving the samples. Too, the good or service may be of greater significance to the small firm; for example, a quarry operator, with a large impending gravel order, had to test a number of loaders during a two-week period.

Design cycle, the other factor, is defined as a sequence of events necessary before a fabricated material or component part appears in the final products which roll off the assembly line. The cycle starting with testing runs about a year in most industries. When the final product has a yearly model changeover, the design cycle can extend over an even longer period of time. In the automobile industry, production of parts starts about ten months before the introduction of new models. In a Twelve-month design cycle, testing would have to commence almost two years before the part appears in the final product. Complete redesign of the final product is effected in stages and stretches over a considerable number of years. A manufacturer of industrial equipment estimates that it takes about ten years to accomplish this in his line.

Two of the more commonly found general purchasing policies are order splitting and reciprocity. Many companies divide up their purchases among all approved suppliers. There are at least three reasons for such a policy. In the first place it prevents any one vendor from becoming too important. Secondly, this policy has been found to be a highly effective method of creating goodwill. A third reason is that a greater diffusion of reciprocal influence can be obtained.

Reciprocity, almost a standard operating procedure in many portions of the industrial market, is another policy that plays an important role in supplier selection. Its significance tends to be greatest for large firms and for buyers and sellers who are able to use each other's products in worthwhile quantities.

Reciprocity

Reciprocity, or in less maligned terms trade relations, is the practice of extending purchasing preference to those suppliers who are also customers. So called primary reciprocity involves a direct arrangement between a buyer and a seller who have reciprocal product needs. A simple illustration of this is as follows: Company B, a manufacturer of office equipment, agrees to buy steel from Company S if the steel producer, in turn, purchases its equipment. If Company S represents a fairly small potential for office equipment. Company B may decide to divide up its purchases among other firms (S_1, S_2, and S_3). The amount purchased from each will be in proportion to the business done with him. One of the basic tasks of the purchasing agent is to compile summaries of the business done with each supplier.

Often as not, however, reciprocity is more indirect. Through integration and diversification industry has become increasingly complex. An inevitable result has been the amplification of possibilities for reciprocity requests. Such arrangements are usually referred to as secondary and may involve any of the myriad subsidiaries, divisions, customers, and suppliers who are associated with either the buyer or seller. As an example, a glass-container corporation will exert pressures upon those chemical companies from whom it purchases soda ash to buy corrugated cartons from its paper-box subsidiary.

Enforcement of reciprocity agreements takes two forms. One is reprisal in the form of a decrease or discontinuance of orders as soon as it is practical. The other is more casual in nature and not quite as drastic. The purchasing agent or a salesman from the firm contacts the supplier to express the company's displeasure over the recent action. Such a tactic is generally reserved for small suppliers and those which do not represent much or a potential market for the buyer's products.

Purchasing influences

Most industrial purchasing decisions are influenced by a number of persons within the organization. Specifically who is involved will depend upon the good or service being considered and company policy. Only rarely will one person make a decision without consulting others. It is hard to imagine even the owner of a small machine shop not seeking the advice of his employees before purchasing a new item of equipment. The usual role assigned to the purchasing agent is a facilitating one. What influence he seems to have is confined to the selection of suppliers, especially for highly standardized items. It is generally conceded, however, that to ignore him in making the sales contact is a serious tactical error.

This multiplicity of influence creates a major problem for the marketer. He must ascertain who are the most influential individuals concerned with his product. While some reliance can be placed on past experience, much of the evaluation will have to be accomplished through trial and error. This is further complicated by the ambiguity of title nomenclature. It is little wonder that the selling process is apt to be lengthy.

To help in understanding the influences on purchasing, a number of periodicals have undertaken studies of a particular industry or product. One such study by University Research Associates for Electronic Design surveyed the purchasing influences in 133 electronic companies for 24 product categories. To indicate clearly the nature of a person's influence, the purchasing task was broken down into specific actions as follows;

1 Establish need for product type

2 Develop specifications or standards

3 Locate potential suppliers

4 Evaluate suppliers' products for performance and reliability

5 Select and specify brand

6 Approve purchase expenditure

7 Place the purchase order

Summarizes the findings on the actions of establishing product need and brand selection for three selected electronic-product categories. As might be expected, engineering exercises the greatest purchasing influence in the technically oriented electronics industry. The influence of both administrative and marketing officials is more apparent in establishing need than it is in brand selection. The purchasing agent's influence appears to increase as the products become more standardized.

Influence of the government

Government's participation in the economy has a tremendous impact on the functioning of the industrial market. To understand this more readily, it is necessary to consider both the direct and indirect relationships between the industrial market and the complex of local state, and federal governmental units.

Direct relationships

The buyer-seller relationships where industrial markets and the government deal directly with each other are undoubtedly the most significant. Government represents the biggest single customer. In 1967, federal, state , and local expenditures for goods and services amounted to about $139 billion. The rate of growth of government spending since 1958 nearly parallels that attained by the Gross National Product during the same period of time.

Of greater import, however, is the appropriation of total government monies. Many decisions have political overtones. Witness the controversy over the awarding of the TFX contract, the basing of numerous political campaigns on the theme of more government spending in a given area, and the direct appeals to Congress when it is felt that a designed share of business has not been forthcoming. Other relationships that have a direct effect are government doctrines on antitrust and pricing. To gain economies of scale, industrial marketers frequently resort to the merger process. Today such economic reasoning is viewed as irrelevant by the courts. Even conglomerate mergers (between parties that are neither competitors nor related as supplier and customer) have not escaped legal challenge. An injunction was entered against Ingersoll-Rand restraining the contemplated acquisition of three manufacturers of underground coal-mining machinery and equipment.

In setting prices, industrial marketers must operate within an enforceable framework of government regulations and scrutiny. The most important and at the same time most heatedly debated statute is the Robinson-Patman Act. This law prohibits price discrimination between buyers of commodities of like grade and quality. The government can also bring action under its antitrust powers when pricing policies are used to restrain competition. This was dramatically demonstrated in the 1961 suit against seven manufacturers of electrical equipment.

Another factor which has a measurable effect on pricing is the mindfulness of government regarding the industry to which the firm belongs. Industries which produce basic commodities are particularly susceptible to this form of possible intervention. This was made apparent by the pressure placed on twelve steel producers to rescind their 1961 price increase. Finally, firms should realize that in all direct relationships, the government can utilize public indignation to strengthen its position. The glare of adverse publicity was quite harmful to the public images of the electrical and steel companies involved in the situations cited previously.

Indirect relationships

Included within this group are foreign policy, taxation ruling, depreciation allowances, and government subsidization of special interests such as small business. They may or may not affect a particular firm's operating environment.

One relationships industrial markets are not fully aware of its their role in the nation's foreign-policy commitment. For example, business has been made a full partner in the Alliances for Progress program for Latin America. The goods and services required by these needy nations at their stage of economic development will be predominantly industrial in nature. Then, too, trade is becoming increasingly important as a tool of foreign policy. Businesses are being called upon more and more to make short-run sacrifices, such as an unfavorable tariff position, to further international cooperation and respond to the economic challenge of the communistic world.

Another indirect relationship for marketers of

machinery and equipment is the possible acceleration in sales from liberalized depreciation allowances and the tax credits for capital investment. The effect of these will vary from firm to firm and from industry to industry, the greatest sales increases occurring where customers now are able to fully utilize their present capital and a speedup in cash flow is imperative.

3

CONTROLLING INDUSTRIAL MARKETING

The essence of the control process lies in seeking to answer the question: How are we doing? The question is closely related to setting objectives and making plans. In fact, we can do little in the direction of measuring how well we are doing something until we know clearly what it is we want to do and how we propose to do it. So it is that controls should grow out of plans, which, in turn, derive from the objectives sought.

The control process has three phases.

1. Setting standards of performance. Because the nature of marketing work is so intangible and the marketing of many industrial products requires so much preliminary development work, setting standards for it is very difficult.

2. Measuring performance against standards. The two phases of this operation are often done together. One consists of collecting information about what is happening; the other involves comparing this with the standards.

3. Correcting failures to perform to standard. This involves the analysis of such failures to find out why standards were not met, sometimes making plans to rectify the failures, and taking the necessary executive action to prevent their recurrence. When a standard is new and its validity uncertain, or when the conditions that governed its setting are found to have changed, corrective action may involve changing the standard.

Standards of performance

Too often, standards of performance for marketing, as for the other functions of business, are set entirely on an accounting basis or are borrowed from published or privately reported sets of marketing controls used by other firms, or are suggested by the people who write books on the subject. Such standards and the control instruments that implement them are apt to be unrealistic when applied to the marketing activities of any one industrial goods house.

The marketing control standards of a company should grow mainly out of two things-the conditions under which the firm's marketing work must be done and its marketing objectives. For example, a new firm in a field needs to apply marketing performance standards that are different from those of a well-established one. In marketing a new product, a wise manager will apply standards that differ from those he uses in the distribution of one that is mature. Since an objective is what you want to get done, and control is an attempt to measure how well you are doing the things you set out to do, performance standards should bear a close relationship to objectives. This percept is so simple that it seems childish nonsense to state it, but it is also so commonplace that setters of performance standards tend to overlook it.

Since no two firms are likely to have the same marketing objectives to operate under identical market conditions, we will confine our discussion of marketing performance standards to those of wide application and general use.

The marketing plan is rapidly gaining importance as a standard of marketing performance. Since it should include a detailed statement of objectives and the steps the marketing organization proposes to take in order to achieve them, the plan seems to be a good device for measuring actual operations and results. The chief drawback to its use is that it offers no standard against which to measure the adequacy of the objectives or of the plan itself. This is not strictly true, because the objective is not likely to be achieved if the marketing plan is inadequate. But this means that the objective, and not the various parts of the plan, is being used as the real performance standard. And the system offers no means of checking the adequacy of the objectives. On the other hand, if the marketing plan and the objectives contained in it are carefully drawn, they represent the best judgment of the firm's marketing executives, at the time of preparation, as to what can be achieved with the resources available and how it can be achieved.

Short-run marketing plans are much more useful as control standards than are long-run plans. The maker of a long-run plan can only try to forecast what conditions will exist in his market 5 or 10 years ahead, to determine what future position he proposes to occupy, and to prepare a general program for capturing that position. A marketing plan covering a period of 5 or 10 years cannot realistically be prepared in detail as great as one for the coming year or half or quarter of a year. It can merely be sketched out with enough exactness to indicate the future profit possibilities, to suggest sales and cost objectives, and to guide financial and general management in forecasting the firm's future needs for resources, financial and otherwise, and in planning to provide them.

It is especially hard for the industrial marketer to make the long-range increases that is basic to a long-range marketing plan. In order to forecast, he must deal with three major variables: the demand for the end products his goods are used to make, the technology of the industry that makes them, and the technology of his own industry in making his products. All these are highly uncertain.

As a result, long-term marketing plans are not generally used as standards of performance for control. The technique of long-range forecasting has not yet been perfected to the point where its results are exact enough to serve this purpose. Then, too, the longer the larger period of a forecast, the more numerous and greater become the variable factors that may upset it and invalidate the plans based on it. Partly because of these factors, long-range plans usually are so general that they lack the necessary detail for use as standards of marketing performance. So most firms that use marketing plans for performance standards employ the short-run variety year or less.

If the short-run or project marketing plan is properly drawn it includes a statement of the objectives we propose to gain, together with a list of the things we intend to do and the resources we expect to use in the process of achieving them. These may be arranged into a schedule by the addition of the time element. This affords us four checkpoints for control work as the operation proceeds: (1) Have we done the things planned? (2) Have we used the resources committed? (3) Have we done these things on time? (4) Have the objectives been gained or how far along are we toward attaining them?

The marketing plan may be broken down by products or groups of products, by customer groups, by geographical divisions, or by functional activities. This affords the same control checkpoints for each subsidiary operation.

As a system of control standards of performance, the marketing plan has the same general advantages and disadvantages as objectives. It is better than objectives in that (a) the items in it are much more specific (b) most of the items can be checked during the course of the operation, while objectives are usually achieved or lost only when the operation is complete or, in some cases, long after its completion. Checking performance of the marketing plan is thus much easier and more namely. But both suffer from the same weakness in that they offer no standard against which to measure the excellence of the objectives or the plan.

Marketing budget

The marketing budget probably constitutes the most widely used standard of marketing performance for both industrial and consumer goods. If a budget is realistically prepared on the basis of marketing plans from which its dollar figures are drawn, it forms a logical and useful set of yardsticks by which to measure the effectiveness of marketing activities. When the budget is the result of a guessing process, without detailed marketing plans to assure its realism, it is probably worse than no standard at all. As a control standard, the budget presents about the same elements of weakness and strength as does the marketing plan.

Past sales records

Another very widely used standard of performance is the past, sales record of the firm. Sales this day, this week, this month, or this year to date are measured against sales during the same period last year, or several previous years. The same technique may be applied to the several categories of marketing expense. To some extent, this is a process of measuring the garment of today against the pattern of yesterday. It is sometimes assumed that as long as improvement is demanded the method may be regarded as a good one. This is not necessarily true, since the method takes no account of the effect that changes in general business activity or in trade conditions may exercise on the sales of a firm. For example, a decline in sales that is less than the industry average may present good performance, while an increase that leaves the firm with a shrunken market share or decreased profits can hardly be so regarded. Because of the unusual sensitivity of industrial goods demand to changes in business conditions, this method is probably less useful as a measure of performance in marketing industrial products than selling consumer goods.

Activision

In some cases, standards may be set in terms of activity-for example, sales calls made, technical service rendered, catalogs distributed, or distributors' salesmen trained-rather than interms of dollars. This sort of standard is especially useful in industrial goods marketing because so much of the work of promoting sales must be of a developmental type, which cannot be expected to bring immediate results. If an activity quote is used as a means of setting sales tasks, it may also be employed with reasonable effectiveness as a standard of performance.

Market potential

A more fundamental standard by which to measure marketing performance, and one that is neither the product of a firm's managerial plans nor the outcome of its past activities, is the market potential. The market potential is the total amount of a product that may reasonably be expected to be sold by all competitors distributing it in a market. It is volume of rules of a product that a firm would have if it got all there was to get. A market potential may apply to the entire country or to any portion of it, such as a district, a division, a salesman's territory, a product or product group, or a customer or class of customers.

The market potential for some products can be constructed from actual sales figures. This technique applies to such products as gasoline or liquor, which are subject to special taxes posted in public records on a local basis, or automobiles or trucks, which must be registered before they can be used. The seller of such a product can find out for any period of be taken as the market potential for the potential for the period. Very few industrial goods are of this type.

Market potentials for most industrial products must be estimated on the basis of fragmentary facts. Such estimates are made by two chief methods. One employs statistical indexes or series that are found to be indicative of the product's sales or indexes, a reasonably reliable system of market potential figures can sometimes be built up. This method is of use chiefly in the consumer goods field, but it may also be applied to the development of potentials for some industrial goods, such as certain supplies or materials but have a horizontal market. The indexes or series most often used for this purpose are the Federal Reserve Board index of industrial production, electrical power consumed, number of man-hours worked in manufacturing establishments, number and value of building permits issued, and others applicable to specific industries.

The second method for arriving at an area or customer market potential figure is estimation of the product's total probable consumption by each possible user and addition of all these estimates to make up the area or market potential. This method is especially applicable for use in preparing market potential for industrial goods bought by limited numbers of users. For example, if a product can be sold to only a few hundred or even to a thousand customers, a manufacturer who has developed the proper contacts with his trade should be able to make a shrewd guess about the Product's total possible or probable consumption by each one. The accuracy known to buy all or certain percentage of their requirements from firm. By using this means, he is likely to obtain a final total figure much note accurate than one he could compute by employing any combination of available indexes or statistical series.

For example, a chemical house that makes a material used by pharmaceutical firms in producing certain drug products sold under their own brands estimated its potential as follows. The total number of units of the end products made and sold was computed from figures supplied by a marketing research firm that reports product sales of a representative sample of drugstores. From information on end product labels, the amount of the material used per unit of each end product brand was computed. By a simple process of multiplication and addition, the chemical maker then arrived at the total amount of the material used by each pharmaceutical house. This figure was then checked against an analysis of information fragments gathered by its salesmen through conversation and observation during their calls.

Once a market potential has been computed, the actual sales performance of a firm can be measured against it, and the percentage of the potential volume the firm is getting in any area can be computed. In this way, management may ascertain what part of the total marked it is getting, and what part of the total market it is thus has a measure of the effectiveness of its performance on an overall basis and in each sales territory.

A well-constructed market potential is by all odds the best standard of sales performance available. Each of the other types suffers from the difficulty that in one way or another it grows out of the plans or activities of the firm itself. If the plans are too timid or inept, or the activities are ineffective, the standard will not be high enough to afford a true as reliable measure of the quality of the sales job being done. The rub comes in computing an accurate potential figure.

The market potential is not a static thing but is constantly changing, As a Result, it should undergo constant revision in order to keep it up-to-date. This is probably much more true of industrial goods as a class than of consumer goods, such as population and purchasing power, or even consumer goods. Changes in the basic factors that underlie demand for consumer goods, such as population and purchasing power, or even consumer attitude, usually occur slowly in an area; the opening or closing of as quick and drastic shift in his potential sales. The development of a new material that is a substitute for an old one, or of a new process this increases the yield from a material, may be highly expensive. If he can not afford to keep them currently accurate, he cannot afford to use them.

Marketing cost analysis

A highly important means of checking sales performance, which has been developed during recent years, is the analysis of distribution costs through the application of cost accounting techniques.

A study of 74 concerns making industrial goods, picked at random from Moddy's Industrials, show's range in costs of selling and general administration from 1.6 percent to percent of total sales, with an arithmetic average of 11.8 percent and a median of 12.7 percent. The figures for 32 companies making consumer goods picked in the same manner, showed a range from 6.1 percent, and a median of 20.2 percent. A number of the consumer goods firms reported marketing expenses separately ;from general administration costs, and in each cases the marketing cost figure was used in making the comparison. Industrial goods makers combined the two types of cost in one figure at their reports, so their percentages are some what inflated relatively.

This difference in distribution costs is to be expected, and arises from differences in the essential nature of the two types of goods and in the conditions under which they must be marketed. Industrial goods are brought by experts who can be influenced to a relatively small degree by persuation; consumer goods are bought largely by nonexperts who are exceptible to the arts of persuasion through salesmanship and advertising. The purchasers of most kinds of industrial goods are concentrated within a small area; the buyers of consumer goods are scattered throughout the action. The average industrial buyer purchases in relatively large lots; the percentage buyer of consumer goods, in small lots. All of these factors tend to cause the manufacturer's cost percentage of distributing industrial goods to be less than that of marketing consumer goods.

There is considerable variation in manufacturer's costs of distribution among the various types of industrial goods. Among firms included in the above analysis, the average cost of selling and general administration for concerns making machinery was 11.5 percentage of sales; for firms making equipment, the percentage was 19.0 percent; for manufacturers of supplies, it was 14.8 percent; for makers of fabricated components, it was 10.4 percent and for producers of packages and packaging materials, it was 8.4 percent of sales.

At the wholesale level, this relationship between the costs of handling are two types of goods is reversed. In 1963, the average operating cost of trade groups of wholesalers handling mainly consumer goods was 15.7 percent of sales; the median figure of the group was 15.1 percent; for manufacturers of suppliers, it was 14.8 percent; for makers of fabricated components, it was 10.4 percent; and for producers of packages and packaging materials, it was 8.4 percent of sales.

At the wholesales level, this relationship between the costs of handling the two types of goods is reversed. In 1963, the average operating cost of the trade groups of wholesalers handling mainly consumer goods was 15.7 percent of sales; the median figure of the group was 15.1 percent. In the distributors was 19.1 percent of sales; their median was 21.1 percent.

This higher cost of industrial distributors may be due to the fact that several slowly. In general, though, the stocks of industrial distributors are probably no greater in relation to sales than are those of wholesalers handling consumer goods. The difference in cost is more likely to be explained by the fact that many industrial distributors perform function in the industrial field closely akin to those of the consumer goods results. They must sell many items in very small lots; they must usually rends technical services that the consumer goods wholesaler does not supply their salesmen must have at least some technical training and experience and, in consequence, must be paid more than the less expensively trained representatives of the consumer goods wholesaler.

However, the amount of the costs of marketing industrial goods, either actual or expressed as a percentage of sales, fails to complexly measure the importance of their proper management as a factor in the process of marketing such goods. Distribution costs that are too high can either remove a manufacturer from price competition or, if he sells as competitive prices, force him to be content with an inadequate margin of net profit. But by far the most important benefit to be gained by the guidance it may give in making managerial decisions on planning products, programming production, selecting marketing channels, determining marketing policies, and checking performance.

Cost allocation: In analyzing distribution costs, for either consumer as industrial goods, the first step is usually that of determining what express to include. A fairly sound procedure is that of including in this category all expenses incurred after the goods leave the machines that make them. This is likely to be more important for industrial than for consumers goods, because industrial goods must often be packed to suit the buyer's specifications as to size, materials, and methods used in packing.

The various types of technical help, advice, and service rendered to the industrial goods buyer are expensive phases of the marketing process this are not usually found in consumer goods marketing process this are not usually found in consumer goods marketing. It is also especially goods be included in marketing costs, because these activities usually affect the service element, which is one of the most important factors determining the patronage of the buyers of such products. This element is not so important in consumer goods.

It is highly important that the work of analyzing marketing costs has done by someone whose judgment the marketing executives have complete confidence in, and that it be carried on in close cooperation with those executives. The average marketing is vitally interned is sales volume. When a distribution cost analysis project is proposed, the chief outcome he visualizes from it may be the discovery that many of his customers and products are unprofitable and will be dropped from the catalog or account list, with resulting loss of volume. Therefore from the time the project is begun he must be sold on the idea that its primary purpose is not to take business away from him but to enable time is manage the firm's marketing work more efficiently and to change—items and customers into profitable ones.

It is also quite necessary that the work of allocating costs be done in the cooperation with the marketing executives of the firm, because in the process of making such allocations many assumptions about where particular cost items logically belong must be made. The validity of such temptations often depends on a knowledge and understanding of the details of the marketing process. The analyst who attempts to do this work without such knowledge is likely to produce a system of location that will be unrealistic at so many points that it will not command the support and confidence of either the top executives, who was approve it, or the marketing executives, who must use its results if it is to be effective. Also, a long-standing axiom is that often the best way to a project to a man is to get him to help carry it on.

The method used in allocating distribution costs depends to a very great extent on the type of cost results sought. Three basic types of cost results may be obtained from cost analysis -costs by product, by customer, and by transaction. From these can be derived costs by product or customer groups, by channels of distribution, by salesmen, and by territorial, branches districts, or regions.

One problem encountered in almost every distribution costing project is that of how far one should go in allocating costs. For example, is it desirable to allocate general overhead, research expenses, advertising, and general marketing overhead? The case for including advertising and general marketing overhead seems fairly clear. They are definitely a part of the marketing effort of the company. They vary to a considerable extent to the selling emphasis varies.

Marketing overhead is like general overhead in that: (1) there is no method of allocating it, except volume of sales, volume of other costs, or a study-bound to highly inaccurate-of the ways marketing executives second their time; (2) the deletion of a product from the line, or the dropping of a customer, will in no way change its total amount. If these costs, often so large that they constitute a significant portion of the total marketing expense, are allocated, they tend to distort the results so as to obscure the cost effect of activities whose amount and direction are subject to managerial control.

For this reason, it is sometimes good practice to exclude from the analysis all cost items for which there is no logically defensible method of allocation, or those that arise from activities not subject to the control of marketing management. This would exclude all general overhead, research, and in some cases, general marketing overhead and advertising. The final results of such an analysis would be expressed as the contribution of each customer, product, or transaction to general overhead and no profits-not as its contribution to net profits alone.

On the other hand, the inclusion of all cost factors in the analyses results in a job that has the appearance of greater completeness and field. It must be admitted that this appearance is often spurious, sometimes misleading, and often handicaps management in the use of cost results as the basis for decisions, when it should facilitate or lend soundness to such as. But if cost results are to be used in checking the profit performance of the firm may wind up with a mix entirely or largely composed of products that contribute to overhead without adding to net profits.

What we have said about the practicability of allocating overhead come to products applies with even greater cogency to their allocation is customers transactions. All overhead costs must be distributed on the basis of sales volume or volume of other directly allocable costs-even most of the advertising. In distribution costing work for consumer good advertising expenses can often be allocated directly to customers become such products are often promoted by means of local advertising, paid for jointly by the manufacturer and the retailer. This is rarely done is industrial goods advertising.

In his cost results, the marketing cost analyst must constantly compromise accuracy with the expense of getting it. When a few cents in the one way or the other will make the difference between product. A spending dollars to obtain complete accuracy. The product or the customer merits managerial study in any case. If distribution cost analyses whose stories are written in red ink on the company books, it has achieved human resources without adequate return are equally deserving of executive study and action.

It will serve no useful purpose here to enter into a detailed discussion of the methods used in allocating distribution costs to products or customers. It will be sufficient to indicate the general method employed and some of the problems encountered in the process.

Activity classification: The first step in allocation is to classify the firm's marketing activities into several homogeneous groups. The classification most generally used include: personal selling, advertising, stockcarrying, order handling-both paper work and physical order filling transportation, and supervisory work. Other classes may be used to fit the marketing conditions and methods of operation of the firm.

The second step involves segregation of the costs that apply to each of these activities. In doing this, it is necessary to divide such traditional accounting classes as rent and wages and salaries into several parts, and began each marketing activity its proper share. In and industrial goods firm, the portion of the total marketing costs assigned to advertising and personal selling is likely to be considerably smaller than that in a consumer goods firm; the order-handling costs are apt to constitute a somewhat larger portion.

The third step involves the allocation of each activity cost to products, customers, or transactions on some basis that is sound and logical, or as early so as possible. It should be pointed out again that in order to produce cost results useful to management it is not necessary that every sense classification be allocated or that complete accuracy be attained.

The cost of personal selling, which includes all payments made to salesmen fore salary, commissions, traveling expenses, maintenance expense, and entertainment, may be allocated to products, or groups of products, on the basis of a sort of time and motion study. A cost analyst accompanies a sample group of salesmen in the field and observes the amount of time each spends in selling each article or product group. This is often unsatisfactory because such a large part of the salesman's time is spent in general sales work not directly involving any one product. Then, too, a salesmen is very likely to depart from his normal behavior when he is under observation. The method is also very costly. About the same results will probably be obtained from a series of conversations with salesmen. The analyst then tries to appraise the relative emphasis the salesmen puts in the several products or product groups, on the theory selling time function of emphasis.

The techniques of time and motion study may also be employed in allocating the cost of personal selling to customers and transactions. This may be done either by traveling with the salesmen in the field or by requiring them to submit daily call reports in which they include a time schedule to their activities. Traveling expenses and the cost of salary time sent in travel may be allocated on the basis of mileage between call pints. All this these expenses on the basis of an average cost per call for each salesmen, computed by dividing his total costs by his total number of calls made during the period under consideration.

When advertising features specific products, its cost may be allocated directly to them. But much industrial advertising merely features the same and reputation of the firm. This cost may be allocated on the basis of the relative dollar sales volume of the several products, or according to the relative amounts of advertising cost that can be allocated directly to them. Either method is unsatisfactory, although the cost of advertising usually constitutes so small a proportion of an industrial goods manufacturer's general marketing cost structure that errors made in allocating is are not too serious.

The process of allocating advertising costs to customers and transactions is more difficult than that of distributing them among products. While the consumer goods manufacturer often engages in cooperative advertising with his dealers, which renders allocation easy, this is not often done by the industrial goods maker. Very rarely is an advertisement for and industrial product directed at, or for, the benefit of any specific customer. If the advertiser sells through distributors, the cost of trade journal advertising may be spread among distributor-customers according to the circulation of the journal among their user-customers. This may not be entirely sound, since, to a large extent, the advertisement is probably directed to prospective, as well as actual, customers. The bulk of the average industrial goods manufacturer's advertising expense must be distributed among customers on the basis of either sales volume or the amount of advertising cost, sometimes relatively small, that can be directly allocated on some logical basis. It is sometimes relatively small, that can be directly allocated on some logical basis. It is sometimes possible to allocate advertising expenses to customers by first allocating them to products, computed as a definite charge per unit per dollar sold, and then to customers through the application of this factor to the number of units or dollar worth of each product bought by each purchaser.

The financing costs associated with work of

marketing are usually two-discounts for prompt payment, which may be treated as a cost of deducted from gross sales to get cash billings, and the cost of financing finished goods stocks held to service sales. Since discounts for cash are usually expressed in terms of a percentage of selling price, and since they must be credited to each customer's account, it is not difficult to allocate them directly to customers. If a firm has a large number of small customers, so that the work of checking cash discounts taken will be too expensive and time-consuming to be worthwhile, it may be possible to compute an average percentage taken by customers, and then use that figure across the board, expect with the larger buyers, who may be expected to consistently take their discounts. For example, one firm that gave 2 percent, 10 days, net 30 days terms found that the average discount taken was 1 percent.

This cost may be allocated to products on the average percentage basis, unless it seems worthwhile to analyze invoices by item extensions which is apt to be exceedingly expensive. The result would probably be somewhat more accurate for both customers and products if the consistent discount-taking customers were segregated and charged directly with their discounts taken, while the others were treated on an average percentage basis. In the course of this process, products and transactions could be treated in the same manner.

The cost of fining finished goods stocks is often treated as a part of the general expense of carrying them. This method is probably more logical and convenient than treatment as separate operation; so we will defer it.

In an industrial goods firm, the expenses arising from the orderhandling routine are likely to be a more significant portion of the total distribution cost structure than they are in a consumer goods business. The emphasis industrial buyers put on delivery service quality as a factor influencing patronage causes vendors to emphasize it as an activity and leads to greater expense. Such expenses naturally fall into two classes-those arising from the paper work involved and those growing out of the work of physically handling the merchandise in assembling the order and preparing it for shipment.

Two factors influence the amount of paper work involved in servicing either a customer or a product. One is the number of orders handled; the other is the number of line extensions handled. A line extension is one line on an order including, at least, the number of product units, the description or designation of an item, the unit price, and the total price for the amount of the item bought on the order. In the course of the usual order-handling routine, certain operations must be performed on an order regardless of whether it has 1 line extension or 100, or totals$ 1 or $ 10,000. The remaining paper work operations in such a routine usually vary according to the number of line extensions on the order.

The process of allocation, therefore, is carried on by ascertaining a cost per line extension and a cost per order, counting the number of orders and line extensions for each customer or each product, and multiplying. Such per unit costs may be obtained by mans of time and motion studies that yield none too accurate results. A time and motion study may ignore the effects of alternate periods of intense activity and waiting time in order handling, which result from the normal ebb and flow of orders through order-handling group to determine what proportion of his working time is taken up with activities arising from the number of line extensions. On the basis of this data and the costs originating from the work of these persons, it is possible to compute and average cost per order and an average cost per line extension, including waiting times. When machine bookkeeping is used, these will be an average cost per customer care and per commodity or transaction card handled.

The cost of the physical handling of goods in filling orders may be allocated on the basis of the units in which they are handled. A material or supply is likely to be handled: (a) in car-or truckloads; (b) in bulk containers; (c) in the individual packages into which it is put for use, such as bottles or boxes; and (d) in the standard cases or cartons into which these individual packages are put for storage and transport. Small tools, fro example, are likely to be handled a piece at a time or in cartons or cases containing tens or dozens or multiples of tens or dozens; a fine chemical may be handled in 50-pound or 100-pound bulk drums, in 5-pound, 1-pound or 1/4-pound bottles, or in cases containing a dozen or a multiple of a dozen such bottles; a heavy material is likely to be handled in carloads or truckloads.

If, in the process of filling orders, goods are handled in bulk, in cases, and in loose pieces, the cost analyst may seek to establish an average or normal cost form handling each unit. To compute this cost, he can make a time and motion study or a study of the operations of the average person engaged in order-filling work to determine how much of his working time and motion study or a study of the operations of the average persons engaged in order-filling work to determine how much of his working time he spends in handling each type of unit and how many units he 56 cents each; case lots, 40 cents each; and loose pieces, 12 cents a piece. By counting the number of each type of units supplied a customer or handled in delivering a product over a period of tim, and multiplying by the appropriate cost factors, a reasonably accurate allocation of these costs can be achieved. With machine accounting, this is not too expensive.

The cost of packaging may or may not be regarded as a part of distribution expense. In most cases, it is probably more convenient and less expensive to treat packaging expense the distribution cost analyst must consider is that of putting loose pieces into shipping cartons, which can be allocated as a part of the physical order-handling expense. When the customer demands a special put-up, its cost should probably be regarded as a distribution expense, but is can be allocated to products in the same manner as other production expenses. If packaging costs are treated as a production expense, they are allocated to products and so to customers and transactions as part of the cost of goods sold. If , one the other hand, they are regarded as part of the costs of distribution, they must be allocated to products by the use of production costing technique, and thence to the customers who buy the products.

Stock-carrying expense is a function of two factors-space and time. It includes the cost of funds invested in inventory and the expenses arising from maintenance of the space in which the inventory is housed, plus certain incidental outlays such as insurance. By dividing the number of usable square feet in a warehouse not needed for aisles, etc., into the cost of maintaining the warehouse, the analyst may obtain a cost per square foot of usable space. He may then compute the average number of square feet set aside to house the stocks of a given product, and by multiplying these two will derive a total space occupation cost fro the product over a period of time. Dividing this figure by the total number of units of the product passing through inventory during the period, the analyst obtains a space-occupation cost per unit of the product handled. When an article as of such a nature that it can be stacked from floor to ceiling, it may be more realistic to compute a cost per cubic foot.

The cost of the funds employed in carrying the inventory may usually be computed as the interest at a reasonable rate on the capital invested in the inventory during the time it is held. Probably the most convenient method of allocating this cost to products is to compute total interest amount by the number of units of the product passing through inventory during the period, and thus obtain a financing cost per unit.

While stock-carrying costs can be allocated more or less directly to indirectly by adding the stock-carrying costs for each product to its cost of goods sold, or by charging against the customer the appropriate goods vendor sometimes agrees to carry a specified stock of his product earmarked for a specific customer. In such a case, of course, inventory-carrying costs must be allocated to the customer by a special technique suited to the circumstances.

When industrial goods are shipped by common carrier, the cost analyst can allocate transportation costs on the basis of published freight tariffs or freight bills. A company's products are likely to sufficiently homogeneous so that all or large groups of them take the same freight rate. If this is the case, the entire freight bill for the company or for the product poundage shipped. If this is not the case, the entire freight bill for the company or for the product group can be divided among the various products on the basis of the poundage shipped. If this is not the case, a more laborious and costly method must be followed in making the allocation. Transportation costs freight bills, or they may be computed less accurately and less expensively on the basis of the poundage shipped to the customer times a zone freight rate. The method to be used depends on the bulk of the products, the number and variety of them sold, and the importance of transportation freight equalization, the allocation of transportation costs can become almost impossibly complex.

Some sales supervisory costs can be allocated directly to products as groups of products, or to groups of customers. Very few can be allocated directly to individual customers. The costs arise from the activities of executives and supervisors who are responsible for overseeing the work of selling specific products or product groups, or to groups of customers. These expenses can probably be best allocated to individual products and customers within a group on the basis of the volume of other directly allocable sales costs assigned to them. The same is true of expenses of the firm's general marketing executives; any attempt to divide their total costs among product or customer groups is rarely worth the expense involved.

Uses of cost information: Cost information has such important uses in that it seems desirable to discuss them here instead of in the general section on the uses of control information.

Marketing cost analysis is worse then wasted unless its results are used by executives in making managerial decisions. They will not be used for this purpose unless the executives who make the decisions are convinced of the value of the entire project and of the validity of its results. For this reason, the cost analyst must at all stages of the process constantly seek to sell the analysis and the facts it discloses to the responsible marketing executives of the firm. This has already been pointed out, but it is of such paramount importance that the admonition cannot be too often repeated.

While the analyst should, during the early stages of a distributive cost out to obtain, he should be alert at all times throughout the process to discover by-product results not contemplated in the original plan. Such results often appear and are sometimes fully as important as those be sets out to find.

Selecting channels: A cost analysis may be of value to a firm's executives in selecting the channels of distribution to be used. A company that made a chemical product used by many small processors was selling direct to user-customers. A cost of distribution analysis showed that the firm's business with most of these customers was in the red. It was apparent this if the firm dropped all its losing customers, the remaining volume would be so small that it could no longer produce under favorable cost conditions. It was found that these small customers were served by distributors who sod them other materials, supplies, and equipment. While the grow margin it was possible to allow distributors on the product in question was not enough to net them much if any, profit, it was found that in the process of selling equipment and other materials on which they enjoyed a satisfactory gross margin they felt the need of making regular and fairly frequent calls on their customers. The product in question would both give an excuse for making such calls and pay the cost of making them.

Customer slection: The results of a cost of distribution analysis may provide a basis upon which a firm's sales executives can select customers to be dropped from the customer list. This does not mean that all customers whose business is not profitable should be dropped. Nor does it mean that a customer's profitability should be the only factor, or even the primary one, to be considered in deciding whether to retain or drop him.

Unprofitability simply indicates that the customer's

the problem of an unprofitable customer is what, if anything, can be done to make the firm's business with him profitable. It may be that the salesmen are calling on him oftener than he should. It may be possible to correct some or all of these cost-generating mistakes.

Other factors should be considered before deciding to drop an unprofitable customer. He may also be a supplier from whom the firm buys materials or equipment that it could not get on equally satisfactory terms elsewhere. It may be that he has connections in the trade whose patronage be that while he is now a small buyer whose business is not large enough to be profitable, his potentialities for growth are such that he is likely to become a highly profitable account. Some years ago, a chemical house sold direct to small buyer whose processing operations were carried on in a garage. Other houses refused to service him direct because his future was justified in later years when his purchases from the friendly house varied between $ 500,00 and $ 1 million annually, and he would buy from no other.

Some industrial goods manufacturers follow the policy of selling to certain customers direct and relying on distributors to serve others. Usually, the distinction is made on the basis of volume of purchases. The profitability of the account may offer a better guide in choosing customers to be granted direct status, which often carries at least a small price advantage as compared with the figure at which the distributor must sell. While cost analysis results should not be the only factor to be considered in selecting customers for direct selling status, it should be an important one.

Customer emphasis: In the administration of customer relations, marketing cost analysis results may serve an important purpose by offering a basis upon which sales emphasis may be varied among customers. This type of analysis often discloses that much sales effort is being wasted on customers who are not profitable and give no promise of ever becoming so. For example, one cost study disclosed that a customer whose business would have been unprofitable without any personal selling expect charged against it was visited 26 times during a year by a salesman assigned to the account-the same number of calls he bestowed on his highly profitable customers. Nor was there any indication of the existence of future sales potential that might justify the selling attention through possible future profits. The firm that wants to stagger its salesmen's calls by varying the number of their visits to different customers will find a customer cost study a most helpful factor in arranging such a schedule.

Pricing: The use of cost analysis results in pricing has already been discussed. Of course, the most important part of the cost structure of almost all industrial products is composed of production or materials expenses, but marketing costs usually possess sufficient significance so that their improper allocation to products or product groups may cause a firm either to sell without profit or to price itself out to the market. Adequate marketing costing can be a very real help in price administration.

Product deletion: An industrial goods concern with an extended line of products may find the results of distribution cost accounting a great help in administering its product deletion program. Such a firm must be constantly alert to add to its line new products that give promise of profitability, and to delete old ones that have outlived their usefulness. When applied to new products, of course, marketing cost analysis must be so largely guess work that it is of limited value. But in dealing with old products, the situation is different. Presumably, any article in the line that every such item should be deleted, but it does mean that the justification for its continued existence as a part of the firm's product line should be carefully examined. Distribution cost analysis can be of very great importance as a guide to product deletion work.

Packaging: A by-product result of distribution cost analysis may consist of the information it discloses about the packaging work of the firm. It may show that packaging materials or supplies to the customer's specifications is too expensive to justify continuance. It may indicate that certain products in small demand are being packaged in job lots that are too small.

For example, a firm's long line of a certain type of materials included many bought in very small lots and infrequently. It packaged, in runs of 7 units at a time, an item of which 50 units were sold annually. A distribution cost study indicated that this item was one the company lost money on, even though other sizes of the same article were profitable. A further analysis to determine the reason disclosed that the cost of the item was out of line because of heavy packaging charges per unit. Examination showed that the bulk of the packaging charges of 95 cents a unit were the result of makeready and cleanup time in the packaging process. As a result of packaging a year's supply instead of 7 units at a time, the packaging cost was reduced to about 20 cents a unit. Even with the addition of 2 percent of month for stock-carrying costs, the saving was enough to change a loss item into one on which the company enjoyed a profit. The discovery of this minor loss product led to a search for other similar items, which, in sum resulted in substantial savings throughout the line.

Direction of sales effort: A knowledge of the distribution costs of specific products enables a firm's marketing managers to direct sales effort so as to emphasize the products with greater profit possibilities and thereby to maximize earnings. In some cases, marketing cost analysis by products may indicate that the expenditure of greater sales effort on some of those not showing adequate profit results will increase volume and turn losing items into profitable ones. Much may be gained by a proper direction of sales emphasis; marketing cost analysis may be of great help in guiding the direction of such emphasis.

By combining the marketing cost results of customers, a picture of the profitability of a salesman's efforts may be obtained, making possible a more intelligent direction of his activities and affording a measure of their effectiveness. A further combination of the cost results for salesmen into cost results for a branch, district, division, or region may afford the same type of managerial benefits.

Order size: Marketing cost analysis may disclose that below a given size are without profit. For example, a firm found that when one of its products was ordered in less than 250 - pound lots the transaction was in the red. Since this article was usually bought alone and not in combination with others, it was apparent that any customer who habitually purchased in less than this quantity was a losing one. Such buyers were referred to distributors who, because they handled other products made by other manufacturers and sold to the same purchasers, were able to serve buyers of smaller lots without losing money on the business.

Those who make decisions on the basis of marketing cost analysis results must always bear in mind that within wide limits many such costs behave like overhead. Consider, for example, the expense of the paper work involved in handling orders. In a firm of any size, the orderhandling routine is a sort of production-line operation in which each of a number of people perform a single function on each order. Once such an operation is set up and staffed, the volume of orders it can handle is subject to very wide variation.

For example, it may be economical to set up and staff a unit to handle 300 orders a day, but the same staff may be able to process twice that number of orders without expansion. If the volume of orders increases to more than 600 a day, the division of work must be reorganized and more people added. This means that if the order-handling routine of a firm is set up on a 300 order-per-day basis and is actually handling 450 orders there will be very little, if any, saving enjoyed by reducing orders to 400 perday.

To a considerable extent, the costs of personal selling behave in the same manner; several other important types of marketing costs follow the same pattern. Therefore, efforts to control distribution costs are sometimes regarded as bootless. On the other hand, the firm that labors to keep expense-generating factors trimmed within reasonable proportions will find itself able to respond to changes in its volume of business without excessive additions to cost when volume increases, and without drastic personnel changes when business declines. Moreover, its marketing costs will always be somewhere near what they should be, and are not likely to affect its competitive position adversely.

Marketing managers who rely on cost analysis results in making their decisions must also constantly bear in mind that it is sometimes good business for a firm to lose money on some of its operations. This loss may be justified on the ground of customer service and goodwill, the future possibilities of profit from those operations, and other like factors. For example, so long as its total business with them is profitable a concern may be willing to sell certain customers money-losing items that the customers to supply products that are cats and dogs may find it difficult to win patronage on items that are profitable. It is no business crime to loss money on certain items. The crime consists in not knowing why it is worthwhile to continue handling them without profit.Marketing cost analysis discloses such losses and often supplies a clue to whether they are worthwhile.

Checking performance

The process of checking performance against standards involves selecting, analyzing, and studying information about the firm's marketing activities and their results. This done chiefly by two methods observation and reports, mainly statistical.

Observation

For this purpose, observation is much less useful in marketing than is production, and it is less applicable to industrial goods marketing than to consumer goods. Unless his span of authority is very broad or his plans are widely scattered, a production executive can, by walking the shop, have a chance to see what practically every man under him doing. Many marketing executives would spend months visiting and observing all the men under them. The executive in charge of marketing consumers goods can observe how a part of his operation is working every time he visits a retail store that can handle his product, views or listens to a TV or audio program, reads a newspaper or a magazine, or talks with his friends are neighbors. The industrial marketer can observe his advertising and talk with his customers at trade gatherings.

Aside from this, his observation of performance is largely limited to traveling with his salesmen, who are very likely to perform differently when he is with them than when they call on customers alone. If he or his salesmen command the confidence of his distributors, he can often secure permission to examine their stocks and thus judge the adequacy and representatives of their inventories. In spite of its situations, personal observation is useful to the industrial marketer in checking the performance of at least part of his marketing organization.

Statistical analysis The operating records, particularly of sales, expenditures, orders, shipments, and inquires, supply very useful control information if properly analyzed.

Sales figures may be broken down by products or product groups, customers or groups of customers, salesmen's territories or other geographical areas, or on any other basis that promises to be useful. These classifications can then be compared with performance during past period, such as last year or several preceding years, last month or last week, at the same month or week last year. The consumer goods marketer may even find it useful to compare today's sales with those a year ago today. This is usually not worthwhile for the industrial goods marketer, because his sales occur in much larger lots and much more irregularly. Actual sales figures may also be compared with planned sales and with potential are desired market share.

When orders are taken mainly for future delivery, it may be worthwhile to analyze shipments and unfilled orders so that they can be against the same standards as those suggested above for sales. It may also be helpful to analyze orders by size and the manner of their receipt, through salesmen, by phone or mail.

It may be worthwhile to analyze inquiries on the bases of the types of firms they come from, the functional area or executive level that originates them, or the factor, such as and advertisement or trade journal article, that generates them.

Marketing expenditures should usually be analyzed so that they can be compared with past outlays or with budgeted expenditures. For example, to date we have spent 10 percent more of our advertising budget the same date last year, but 15 percent more of our advertising budget remains unspent todays than remained at this time last year. In managing advertising, it may be worthwhile to make similar comparisons of commitments to spend.

Reports

All these analyses result in reports. The matter of reports should probably be viewed from two standpoints. How many and what kind of reports should operating personnel be required to submit? How many and what kind of reports should be supplied to management?

The factors governing the answer to the first question are fairly simple. Operating people hate to prepare reports. While they are preparing reports, they are not operating. So the reports required of them should be as few as simple and as easy to prepare as possible, but still supply the information management needs to make decisions and guide action. It is amazing how much information can be reported by making check marks on a form in the first place. It is also true that operating people usually talk better and more comfortably and willingly than they write. Sometimes, money spent on providing dictating equipment-to salesmen, for example-will be more than repaid in the completeness of their reports and is their more cheerful acceptance of the idea of making reports.

No item of information should be required that is not used. And operating morale is lifted if those required to report information are told how it is used, especially if its use makes their own work easier or more effective.

Control reports prepared for management are as various as the executives a that use them, and they should be. A system of control reports should be built for the men who are to use it, for the conditions that govern the business they run, and for the methods they use in running. It should supply the information they consider important, and that information should be arranged and analyzed in each report in the manner most convenient and immediately useful to the men who must makes executive decisions based on it. Such control reports usually contain daily, weekly, monthly, quarterly, yearly, or yearly-to-date sales figures, activities of salesmen; advertising expenditures or commitments; inventory position; price relationships; and other similar data.

Certain general principles may be laid down to govern the preparation of marketing control reports.

1. Any one report should not contain too much information. The executive to whom it goes may become so enmeshed in detail that is overlooks salient facts or relationships. It is a good idea to construct each report so that it deals with one subject or small number of related subjects.

2. All significant relationships should be computed and included in the report in the form of percentages or ratios. The report that must be sadied with a slipstick is a time waster and often fails to call the executive's attention to the facts that really count.

3. The report should contain no facts or figures that are not used. The report constructor should always remember that when people compute figures and put them down on pieces of paper it costs money, and that in the course of a year or several years the compilation of unused information may became exceedingly wasteful. That information should be used but is not has no bearing on the subject; if the person supposed to use it does not do so, it is a waste of time to supply it to him.

4. The report should be so constructed that important facts or relationship stand out and call attention to themselves. This usually results from placing related items of information near each other on the report form. If a figure in one part of the form has to be compared with another remote part or it, the comparison may not always be made.

Use of control information

The uses of marketing control information are as varied as marketing situations and operations and the ways in which they can go wrong. They all mainly into six general classifications, however.

1. It can be used to spot things that are going wrong so they can be remedied before the process has gone far enough to cause serious loss. For example, and advertising campaign may be designed to bring in inquiries. If the first few issues fail to generate a satisfactory volume of inquiries, the nature of the campaign can be changed or it can be abandoned. This is one of the two most constructive and fruitful purposes to which control data can be put.

2. It can be used to spot things that are going wrong and to guide marketing executives in picking up the pieces and trying to cut the losses resulting from failure. This happens when the debacle has gone so far that it is reversible until it has run its course-for example, sales below the planned volume. In such a case, management may cut production and reduce inventories, cut price, increase advertising or sales pressure, modify the product, or take other remedial or salvage action.

3. It can be used to determine just how and why failure has occurred, and to suggest what steps may be taken to prevent its recurrence. Fop example, a firm analyzed several past failures in introducing new products so find out why they occurred. The same mistake was found to have been a causative factor in a number of them. This also is highly constructive use. Mistakes cannot always be avoided, but they need not by repeated.

4. It may be used to find out who is to blame for failure. In general this is the least constructive of its uses. If it is consistently employed for this purpose, the people controlled become afraid to decide or to act. They develop the habit of wasting time and effort in thinking up excuses and in trying to conceal failure. A favorite concealment method is no operate in a way that permits one to blame failures on

someone else if they occur. This leads to cumbersome operation and destroys the cooperation and mutual coordination of effort so vital to successful marketing work. Often, people become highly skilled at covering themselves, which tends to defeat the constructive purposes of the control system. A scared begets error. If a marketing control system is administered in the spirit of "Who is to blame?. " it is apt to do more harm than good. If administered in the spirit of "What's going wrong, what can we do about it, and how can we prevent its happening again? it may be highly constructive part of a system of marketing industrial products as well as any other kind of goods.

5. If a control system is properly conceived and administered n the right spirit, it is apt to induce an attitude of self-examination in the operating executives. They study their failures more assiduously than their operations are going. They study their failures more assiduously than their successes, the end that in the future they may avoid the mistakes that caused them. Controls can build men's self-reliance and initiative as well as destroy those qualities.

6. Control information can be of inestimable value in planning marketing operations. Basically, control work is an attempt to measure the effectiveness of marketing tools and activities in the situations to which they are applied. From it may come a better understanding of the jobs for which specific tools and activities are suited and an ability to forceps what their results will be if applied in the future.

4

INDUSTRIAL MARKETING PLANNING

Marketing management, stripped to its essentials, is much the same as the management of other business functions. It consists of making plans, carrying them out, and controlling them by measuring what is done against suitable standards and then rectifying failures. The essence of planning is an organized thought process before taking action.

Although the essential elements of marketing management are the same as those for other business functions, the process of planning for it is more complex than in other functional areas because in much of his work the marketing manager must deal with customers, prospects, distributors, and competitors, operating within a constantly changing technological, social, and political environment. He is concerned primarily with people and ideas, and only to a minor degree with physical things. His relationship with people outside the company is basically of a persuasive character, with little, if any, possibility of direct control through authoritative sanctions. Furthermore, there is inevitably some degree of conflict of interest in business relationships with distributors and customers, as well as with other groups in the market complex.

This indicated that in planning the marketing manager must cope with a dynamic and volatile environment of great uncertainty and difficulty that makes it hard or impossible to forecast the results of particular marketing efforts. All of this represents a real challenge to competent management. Success depends not only on skillful and aggressive adjustment to shifting market forces, but also on bold innovation that can itself change the market environment. Because of the lead time that must elapse between concept and fruition in most product and marketing programmes the industrial marketing manager in his analytical and decision-making processes must learn to live in the future, despite all its frightening uncertainties.

The three most important areas of general marketing decisions are: What should be the product mix and the effort put behind each product line? What markets should be cultivated and with what intensity. What mixture of the tools of marketing should be used an in what proportions in order to bring products and markets together to yield desired objectives? Actually, decisions in the first two areas are necessarily merged, since products cannot be considered without relation to particular groups of customers or markets., and markets are meaningless except in the framework of their expected consumption of specific products. Thus, what is really involved is an extensive series of product-market combinations, which are either presently in existence or represent feasible objectives for the company. Overlaid on these product-market combinations are the selling methods that are in use or might be used.

From this complex of facts and relationships, decisions concerning the most desirable allocation of company resources must be reached. The first two of these areas are ultimately matters of top management decision although the marketing manager and his staff must do much of the primary work of exploration fact-finding, analysis, and recommendation. The thirds is apt to be largely or entirely within the marketing department's area of decision, with top management's role largely confined to criticism and approval.

The problems of managing industrial marketing vary with the different types of operations involved. In later chapter, we will analyze the product mix and the various components of the marketing mix. This chapter will be devoted to a general consideration of the role of planning in the total marketing management process.

Only within the past few years has the need for emphasis on marketing planning begun to be widely recognized. In part, this is a result of the increase in the number of firms that have adopted the market concept wholeheartedly and have become customer-oriented in all of their operations to a degree only rarely true 15 to 20 years ago. Effective adjustment to present and future needs of customers requires careful consideration both of the direction and scheduling of many types of activities. Compensation has become keener, the technological revolution has produced more and more products with a faster pace of change, vastly improved data processing systems are being widely adopted, new industries are developing, the technical content of products has increased and become more complex, and new types of management decision aids have become available.

All these factors add up to more complex marketing operations, higher costs, and increased uncertainty. Greater emphasis on the planning function in terms of more detailed plans, better information on future trends, more complete integration with company objectives and total operations, and forms of organizing that will assure planning a continuously high urgency rating, offer industrial marketing management important tools to cope with its increased responsibilities.

BASIC CONSIDE-RATION

Perhaps our study of planning for industrial marketing may be more realistic if we first emphasize a few platitudes so commonly accepted that people tend to forget them. Plans deal entirely with the future. The future may be good or bad, pleasant or painful, but it is always and forever uncertain and, therefore, fraught with risk. Planning is an attempt to reduce its uncertainties and protect against its risks. Therefore, the essence of planning lies in an attempt to foresee the area of uncertainty, to appraise the chances or probability of the occurrence of various possible events within those areas, and to plot a course of action that will take advantage of the beneficial aspects of those events most likely to occur and avoid or minimize their damaging features. It is also designed to cause certain things to happen that will be beneficial to the company.

Marketing planning for industrial goods is much more difficult and, at best, is much less exact than that for most consumer goods. The demand for consumer goods depends on people in the mass, their income, and their willingness to spend it. Population changes tend to occur slowly, and since they arise in part as a result of shifts in the birth rate many of them can be foreseen before their influence becomes effective in the marketplace. Income shifts also tend to occur gradually and to conform to trends that are often discernible. Willingness to buy is a more volatile element, but even here consumer purchasing behavior for most products tends to change slowly over relatively long periods.

Since the demand for industrial goods is derived from that for consumer goods, it is subject to all the uncertainties that beset consumer purchasing performance. In addition, it suffers from factors of risk that do not affect the market for consumers goods, or influence it only mildly. The total demand for a material, component, supply, or piece of equipment may be changed profoundly and abruptly by changes in technology.

For example, an improvement in the technique of making castings may increase the demand for casting and reduce that for machined parts and the equipment that machines them; technical developments in making and using plastics may take business away from metals; electronic transistors largely destroyed the market for tubes; the development of synthetic fibers invades the market for textiles; if Du Pont's synthetic leather proves itself in use, the tanner's market will suffer.

This uncertainty of total demand is augmented for the individual firm by the fact that most of the volume of an industrial product is usually bought by a small number of large users. A shift of patronage by any one of them is apt to subtract heavily form the sales volume of one supplier and add greatly to the total sales of another. Thousands or millions of ultimate consumers shift their collective patronage slowly. By a single act any one of a dozen or half-dozen industrial goods buyers can significantly change the patronage balance in the typical trade.

THE END RESULTS OF MARKETING PLANNING

Logically, it might seem that we should discuss the end products of marketing planning at the close of this chapter after we have examined the process itself. We have chosen to treat the subject briefly here on the theory that we can better understand the process if we first gain responsibly clear notion of what it is intended to accomplish. We can better if we know what we are shooting at.

In discussing the operating end results of marketing planning, we will move from the very general to the highly specific in much the same way the process itself must progress—objectives, policies, procedures, programs, schedules.

Marketing objectives

An objective is an end or goal that is sought. The marketing objectives of a firm must grow out of its general overall objectives. In theory business concern has but one objective- to make as much profit as possible, to maximize profit, as the theorists state it. Really, it is probably rare that this is the sole objective of a firm, or even its primary goal. This is not to deny that profit is almost always a prime objective, but it does not raise the question of how much profit the average management sets as its goal.

Theoretically and legally, top management should set goals that are for the best interest of the firm. Practically, it is inevitable that personal or group interest gets mixed into management thinking about company objectives. This is especially true with respect to profits. Management almost always has a profit goal, but how near this target approaches the maximum that can be made depends on the need management has for profits.

This varies with different companies, but certain elements are almost always present. Top management almost invariably keeps control of the company through the votes of the stockholders, and it needs profit sufficient to be able to pay dividends beg enough to keep them reasonably happy and quiescent. It needs enough profits to build up a surplus as a reserve against bad periods, so that the firm can pay dividends consistently in lean years as well as fat. It need enough profits to finance new ventures and planned growth, either out of retained earnings or by borrowing on terms made favorable by an earnings record attractive to lenders. Whatever the profit goal may be, it vitally affects the planning of marketing activities.

Almost every management has as one of its most important goals the survival of the firm. This objective may be diametrically opposed to that of maximizing profit. Over considerable periods such objectives as expanding the firm's share of the market, entering a new market and establishing a position in it, developing or maintaining a full product line, or creating a company image may command the central place in management thinking. Keeping on the legal side of the various governmental regulations is always a highly influential objective and one that often demands a limited profit goal.

In planning the activities of his area, the marketing manager must understand the overall goals of his company and the emphasis top management attaches to each one. Then, for his own department he must translate this understanding into a set of objectives that comfort to the broader goals and are designed to aid in achieving them.

How ambitious should objectives be? Within the limitations of the company goals, the industrial marketing manager may have considerable leeway in picking his targets. The maxim, "Hitch your wagon to a star," is not always a sound guide in making this choice. A target that is manifestly impossible challenges only the rare person; it discourages others and tends to become meaningless.

On the other hand, a goal that is too low supplies no incentive, offers no challenge, and is likely to lead to complacency and a false sense of security. Probably the desirable compromise is to shoot for a target that can be achieved but that will strain the muscles and test the will of the organization in its attainment. This is a nice problem in managerial judgment.

Policies

A marketing policy is a course of action established to obtain consistency of marketing decisions and operations in recurring or essentially similar circumstances. It is a guide to specific decisions within an area. Example are: to emphasize quality as our primary appeal, to rely on manufacturer's agents as our sole outlets, to market through only one outlet in each marketing area, to be competitive in price but not a price leader.

Marketing policies, like marketing objectives, should be consistent with an implement companywide policies. The marketing manager plays a dual role with respect to them. He must see to it that marketing plan conform to long-standing policies. It is also part of his job to examine these continuing policies from time to time to make sure that the situations that gave rise to them have not changed so as to render them obsolete; if they are, he must move to revise them. An outworn policy deadens executive ingenuity and fetters management in attempting to meet new obstacles and exploit new opportunities. In addition, he is expected to develop policies to cover new recurring situations in which they can be useful. Policies thus play a dual role in the process of marketing planning; they both guide it and are an end result to it.

A companywide policy is usually started in very general terms; other wise, it may tie the hands of operating executives in handling unusual situations. This means that as it moves down the managerial hierarchy, it must be interpreted in terms of the operating conditions and problems of each level. In the process, it tends to become more specific and, all too often, twisted from its original meaning and purpose. This throws on the marketing manger a dual responsibility to see to it that company policies are accurately reflected in the policies of the marketing area and to make sure that as departmental policies are transmitted down the line they are properly interpreted and understood. This duty is especially important in the industrial goods field because success is so dependent on close cooperation among the several units in the marketing area, and between the marketing department and other functional areas of the business.

Procedure A procedure is an item-by-item description of who is to do what, and often of when and how he is to do it, in carrying out a recurring process. A routine for handling orders is an example. Another at a somewhat higher level is a listing of the things that are to be done, the decisions, that are to be made, and who is to do what in the course of deleting products from the line. A procedure, like a policy, is a continuing pattern that may last through many marketing plans-for example, the routine by which budgetary marketing plans are drawn. Unlike a policy, a procedure is strictly nuts-and-bolts affair.

Adequate procedures are necessary if recurring operations are to be carried on effectively. They are vital in attaining a long-term objective implementing a continuing policy, or carrying on a recurrent operation that involves the concerted action of a number of persons or divisions of the business, especially when the action required of each is not a primary part of his job. A procedure is often not thought of as a plan; but if it is not made a part of the planning machinery, even the work of planning is not likely to get done, for it fits the above description pretty snugly.

Programs and schedules These are the planning process results the operating people live with most intimately. Only rarely is long-range planning carried to the point where its results are expressed in the detailed lists of things to be done that constitutes a program or, if the element of timing is added, a schedule. Most short-range and project plans are cast in the form of such programs or schedules. The most familiar of these is the budget or, rather, the background documents from which the budget is drawn. The budget is simply an expression of the dollar costs of the things we propose to do in carrying out our plan and of the dollar results we expect to obtain by carrying it out.

If a marketing plan is to be really effective, the programs and schedules expressing it must be very detailed. For example, the work of each salesman may be planned to the point of indicating the number of calls he is expected to make on each customer or prospective customer, and perhaps a rough approximation of the time he expects to spend on each products or group of products. The advertising plan may detail the space or time to be used in each publication or station or network, together with a listing of the implementing activities involved in getting the space or time and filling it. This may be broken down by products or groups of products or by groups of customers. The marketing plan for a large company may constitute a sizable volume or series of volumes. It may represent weeks or months of work on the part of the marketing staff.

This is a process that can be easily overdone. It can and sometimes is carried to such detail that the time and money spent on it exceed any possible value that can be gained from it. One industrial marketing manager was heard to remark in the midst of his budget planning season, "I have to spend so much time planning around this place that I can't get any work done". He is not alone in that feeling, and perhaps the opinion is justified.

The general theory that should govern this matter is simple and easy to state. The work of planning should be extended to, but not beyond, the point where an additional dollar spent in planning will add something more than a dollar to the income from its cost. This principle is easier to state than to apply in specific cases. But the mere process of thinking in these marginal terms is apt to cause the manger to discard habitual planning activities that are of doubtful effectiveness and may even lead him to introduce new planning features whose value has not been previously appreciated.

SPECIFIC PURPOSES OF MARKETING PLANNING

Our broad statement at the beginning of this chapter, outlining the purposes of marketing planning, covers the waterfront but leave much to be desired in the way of specifics. Our understanding of the process may be enhanced by an examination of the detailed used that various parts of the business may make of a well-constructed marketing plan.

Coordination of effort

One way to run a business might be everybody's pitching in and doing the best he can in his particular job without too much regard for what anybody else is doing. In fact, when our whole economy and the various business units in it were smaller an simpler, that was approximately the accepted theory of management. If the marketing department sold all it could, and production turned out the largest volume it could at the lowest cost it could achieve, and finance conserved every penny as carefully as possible, success was assumed to be the outcome.

The vast increase in the scale and scope of business operations, the extensive development of complex and specialized technology, and the constant growth in the dynamic character of business enterprise made this theory no longer workable. It is vital to the success of the modern firm that the activities of the various functional divisions be coordinated. This can be accomplished best by planning. Through the relation of the marketing plan to the overall plan for the firm, top management can to some extent coordinate marketing activities with those of other functional divisions.

But the principle goes farther than this. The marketing manager himself finds that he must direct the activities of a variety of specialists, some of whose functions are highly technical and whose special interests are often in conflict. He, too, needs a plan to give some assurance that all units of his department work together for the benefit of the whole. This is especially necessary in the industrial goods business, because in this field technology is most important and change is more than ordinarily rapid.

Help to production planning

It once was the job of the marketing department to sell what the production department could make. With the shift from a sellers's to a buyer's market, it has become more nearly the job of production to make what marketing can sell. But in businesses that manufacture to stock, production can do this properly only if it knows what marketing will sell long before the sales are made. Even when goods are made to order production must be able to plan its needs for materials, facilities, and manpower ahead of the time when orders are received.

So it is that before production can plan what to make and when to make it, marketing must plan what it will sell and when the goods will be needed for delivery to customers. One of the chief purposes of marketing planning is to provide a guide to production planning.

In general, the consumer goods marketer can do this better than his industrial good alter ego because he can forecast his sales more accurately. This average consumer good is ultimately bought by hundreds of thousands or millions of people, whose buying habits change slowly and no one of those purchases looms large in the total. On the other hand, most industrial goods are bought by only a few customers, and usually the bulk of the volume of any one article is taken by a couple of dozen firms at most. They can change their patronage very quickly, and a shift by any one of them drastically upsets any forecast made by the supplier in reliance on its business.

Planning equipment and facilities

When a manufacturer considers buying a piece of equipment, he must be assured of a need for the productive capacity it will provide during the period of it amortization. Otherwise, its purchase price can not be recaptured out of its earnings. Therefore, he must ask: Can marketing sell what this machine can make during its operating life? If equipment and facilities are to be bought intelligently, marketing must plan far enough ahead to indicate whether they will be needed to make the products required to service sale profitably.

Aid in planning finances

The financial executive is charged with the job of providing the working capital investment in inventories and accounts receivable, and the fixed capital sunk in equipment and facilities. If the marketing manger can plan his activities far enough ahead to indicate with accuracy that X years from now sales volume will require certain specific additions to equipment, the financial manager can start making arrangements to have the money ready to buy the added machines. When capital, especially of the long-run type, must be raided on a crash basis, it is usually pretty expensive, and the extra expense lasts over a long period.

If the marketing manager can plan his annual sales by months, the financial executive can foresee how much capital will be needed in inventory to service each month's sales and how much will be tied up each month in outstanding. He can also forecast monthly needs for materials and wages. He is able to construct a chart showing when and in what quantity funds will flow out of cash, and when and how much money from sales will flow in to replace it. This enables him to foresee the need for bank loans and to provide for them ahead of time.

Short-range marketing plans

The short-term marketing plan consists of a volume of sales and sometimes of other objectives the firm will try to achieve during the coming operating period as well as a schedule of the activities it will carry on in order to reach the objectives. Often this is set out in great detail. When sales are priced out and the activities are costed, the result becomes the marketing part of the company budget, a statement of planned cash inflow and outflow for marketing costs.

To be most useful, the marketing plan should be expressed at least initially in physical units-pounds or tons or machines to be sold on the one hand and man-hours of work, pages of space, and minutes or hours of air time to be used in selling and delivering them on the other. These can then be translated into dollars on the basis on forecasted process and rats. If the process is short-cut by making the estimates initially in dollars, the planning process may be perfunctory and unrealistic and may lose much of its usefulness as a tool of management.

The short-term marketing plan may serve a number of managerial purpose if it is carefully done. If forecasts are properly made and alternative possibilities thoroughly considered, many matters can be decided in relatively relaxed atmosphere that would otherwise assume the proportions of crises. The net effect may be to change the daily business life of the operating marketing executive from a succession of major and minor crises into a series of minor crises, but with resulting improvement in the soundness of major decisions.

It also facilitates delegation of authority and responsibility. Once the marketing plan is set up in some detail, the manager can delegate to his subordinates the job of carrying it out, and he must intervene only when significant departures from it become necessary or when it is not going properly.

This suggests a third major use of the short-term marketing plan as a tool of control. It constitutes a statement of things we propose to do and events we will try to make happen. This is a way of describing a standard of performance. By checking what is actually done and achieved against this standard, management may be alerted to the need for reconsideration, decision, and action.

Project plans Project plans are sometimes also called special purpose plans. They deal with special problems or objectives that may be very important for a time but are not likely to recur. Their period of importance may be a few months or a number of years. The activities and costs they generate and the results they promise are likely to be closed into and made a part of the overall plans and budgets of the firm or department. But management may find it desirable to keep the plans for them separate in preparation, execution, and control.

Consider the case of the firm that added a new product to its line of industrial materials. Potential sales of it were estimated to be about $10 million annually. But management foresaw a five-to seven-year period of market development, during the early part of which yearly sales would probably be only a few hundreds of thousands of dollars and cost half a million or more. The new products was assigned to a marketing manager, whose departmental sales of other products were about $20 million a year.

After two years, management became dissatisfied with progress. A study of the situation showed that the marketing manager was not spending enough money on the new product's development, because the cost of doing this work was closed into the general budget for his department and made its profit result look bad. His attitude changed when he was asked to prepare three marketing plans and budgets, one covering his operations without the new product, one for the new product, and one combining the two. In its review and control work, management dealt with each of these separately.

The moral of the incident is that special projects are not apt to receive the attention they deserve unless they are set apart in planning and control. Of course, only those projects of considerable significance in relation to the welfare or objectives of the company should be treated in this manner.

MARKETING FORECASTING

Since all plans are made for an uncertain future, a vital part of planning is the attempt to forecast with reasonable accuracy those future events that will make up the environment within which the plans must be carried out. The most important elements that must be forecasted in preparing the marketing plan are dollar sales and marketing costs. In order to estimate dollar sales, the planner must forecast physical units sold and price per unit during the planning period. To arrive at a cost figure, he must determine the things that must be done to carry out the plan and the cost of doing each one. He can usually estimate costs much less volatile than prices and customers' buying behaviour.

Long-range forecasting tends to be much less accurate then short-range. The farther the forecaster tries to peer into the future, the hazier its outline becomes. The long-range planner in the industrial good field must try to foresee the behavior of consumer demand for the end products made from or by his goods during the next 5 or 10 years. He must also attempt to foresee the changes that will occur in the technology and competitive relationships in his industry and in customer industries as well as what the trend of general business conditions will be during the period. He must then try to appraise the effects of these changes on the need for his products and on his competitive position in his industry.

For example, during the late 1950's a fine chemical company, which make medicinal materials sold to proprietary and ethical drug houses for compounding and resale under their own brands, tried to forecast its business during the 1960's and 1970's. Its managers studied population trends and forecasts-noting that during these years the over-60 and under 7 age groups promised to constitute a larger than usual percentage of the total population-income trends, and trends in people's attitudes towards expenditures for health. They also examined the trend away form druggist compounded prescriptions toward the count-and-pour type, and the development of socialized medicine, medical service plans, such as Blue Cross and Blue Sheld, and group medical plans. They took account of the tendency of proprietary houses to make their own ingredients and of fine chemical firms to get into the compounding business. They tried to foresee the area in which technological breakthroughs were most likely to occur during the 20-year period. They looked into the political glass darkly to discern probable changes in governmental attitudes and actions with respect to public health. They examined trends in the operations and influence of retail and wholesale druggists in the business. On the basis of all the forecast resulting from these studies, they constructed a picture of the environment within which they thought their company would have to operate during the period.

A firm that makes and markets a basic material such as steel and steel products must try to project trends in gross national product, particularly in heavy metal-using industries such as the automobile, construction machinery, railroad, airplane, steamship, and communications, businesses. The firm would also try to foresee in these customer industries technological developments that might affect their use of steel products. It cannot afford to neglect a careful study of the possibilities for development of additional uses for steel substitutes, such as aluminum, plastic, glass, and perhaps new materials now in the test-tube stage or merely an idea in chemist's mind. It must also try to foresee in the steel industry itself technological breakthroughs that may adapt steel to new uses. Nor can steel firm forget the inroads that usage during the 20-year period are likely to make on the reserves of iron ore. It must estimate the effects this depletion may have on the costs of steel and thus on the prices of steel products, on the competitive position of steel in relation to other materials, and on company volume and profits.

As you can readily see, the work of planning these explorations into the future, summarizing their findings, and drawing conclusions from them essentially a function of top management and top management staff. It is equally apparent that much of the information sought lies in the marketing area, and that marketing personnel is likely to have the background needed to make intelligent estimates of many factors vital to long-range forecasting. Consequently, the work of assembling much of the material, analyzing it, and drawing initial conclusions from it is likely to fall on the marketing manager and his staff.

Making long-range forecasts is a relatively new activity for most firms. Comparatively few have been doing it in any systematic way for very long. On the other hand, many concerns have for many years made forecasts of sales and costs for periods of a year or less. As a result, the techniques of short-run forecasting are somewhat more highly developed than those used in long-range planning. All forecasting methods are based primarily on the technique of projection. It can hardly be otherwise. Inevitably, what will be grows largely out of what was and what is.

Whether we use the newest and keenest tools on the

statistician's kit or rely on less systematic methods- even on judgment or hunch-we start our forecast by projecting the trends of the past and present into the future. This is done in two chief ways, by means of statistics and by the use of imagination and judgment. By one approach, we build from the general (an overall industry estimate) to the particular (an estimate for the firm and its division); by the other, we move from the particular (an estimate for each potential customer) to the more general (an estimate for the firm).

The statistical approach

In using the first approach, we seek one or more statistical series that seem to be indicative of sales for all industry or for our particular industry. The types of series most commonly used for industrial goods are:

Gross national product.

The Federal Reserve Index, of Physical Production.

Personal income,

Inventories, wholesale, retail, manufacturers'.

Construction contracts awarded.

Car loadings.

Price indices.

Corporate profits.

Durable goods orders received.

Unfilled orders.

By statistical methods, chiefly the correlation method, we analyze the past behavior of one or more of these series, seeking to observe patterns of behavior that conform to and, if possible, lead in time and pattern of sales in our industry. By a further use of statistical tools, we project these predictive series into the future to establish an estimate of future sales for the industry. We then determine the probable share of the market for our firm on the basis of past performance and our proposed plans for the period. Finally, this can be broken down into estimates by products, geographical areas or other divisions of our company.

There is no need for us to detail the statistical techniques used in this work of analysis and projection. In books on statistics, they can be and are treated much more completely and competently than we can possibly do here. It is enough that we understand the conceptual basis underlying the task.

This essentially statistical approach has certain elements of strength and weakness. Its greatest strength probably lies in its almost complete freedom from the bias that inevitably colors all forecasting attempts that lean heavily on human judgment. By the same token, it is less subject to the reasonable doubt and criticism that is almost certain to attach to any forecast that is the result of opinion. The probable sales figure is like the traditional horse race in that there is always room for legitimate differences of opinion about both.,

A statistical forecast is based on an observed and proven tendency of sales to vary long with, and perhaps somewhat after, some other statistical series or combination of series in the past. It may, in addition, be grounded on a distinctive pattern observed to be characteristic of the behavior of sales or of the related series in the past. Even the part of the forecast that depends on the effect of our planned marketing efforts can often be developed from a pattern derived by observing and measuring changes on the behavior of sales when efforts of similar kind and intensity have been applied in the past. In this process, the only matter of opinion that opens the door to the frailty of human bias is the assumption that because certain patterns of behavior and relationship have prevailed in the past they will continue in the future. The statistical method has about it an aura of science and certainty, which lends a feeling of confidence to those who use its results.

One of the great weaknesses of the method lies precisely in this basic assumption that the pattern of the past will project itself into the future. The assumption gains soundness if a causal relationship can be proved to lie at the basis of the pattern- that is, if can be shown that changes in the predictive statistical series or combination of series cause changes in reasonably sure to operate in the future. Too often, this can be done only or largely by eliminating all other factors that might have caused the pattern. This can readily become a tenuous and highly uncertain process.

In the industrial goods field, the process of proving the assumption is especially difficult and its results less reliable, because the chain of causation must run through so many levels form ultimate consumer end product demand, through the highly dynamic environment of technology and operating methodology, to the demand for materials, components, or equipment. When we seek to pin it down further in forecasting the sales of a single firm, its validity is even more thinly diluted by the big-three or four or-five characteristic of the average customer industry. A change of patronage by one big using firm, which may result from numerous unpredictable factors, including many entirely within the buying firm (shifts in intracompany political influence, changes in top management personal or policy, death, promotion, or retirement of a chief purchasing officer or even of a buyer), may upset the most carefully calculated statistical forecast for an individual supplying firm.

When an overall statistical forest for a firm is broken down among its customer groups or geographical divisions, it tends to lose its soundness, since a market is not a monolithic solid but a fluid body with innumerable eddies and currents characteristic of its several customer or geographical parts. These often not significant enough too have much effect on the total figure, especially since they may offset one another, but they may cause the breakdown to be entirely unrealistic in specific areas.

For this reason, salesmen often display little or no personal acceptance of or commitment to territorial sales estimates arrived at by the statistical method; they tend to dub them "home office whiz-kid stuff." This tendency is emphasized in the industrial field by the fact that the average salesman's volume, like that of his firm, is heavily concentrated in the hands of a few customers. This lack of personal commitment on the part of the men in the field tends to subtract heavily from the usefulness of the statistical forecast as a tool for planning and controlling field operations.

The judgement approach

The other approach to forecasting sales depends largely on human judgment and imagination. It may be applied on at least two levels within the organization-the executive personnel and the field force.

Jury of executive opinion. When this method is used, several executives, whose background or job assignments may be assumed to equip them with some market familiarity, are asked to estimate what sales will be during a coming period. This may be done in one of two ways. The group may meet in conference and discuss the matter until an overall figure or a figure for each product or customer group or geographical area is agreed on.

This is a relatively inexpensive speedy method of forecasting. Aside from executive time, it usually requires only assembling past sales figures—sometimes past marketing cost figures-with general summary description of business conditions and apparent trends, and making this background information available to the participating executives to guide their deliberations.

On the other hand, it is no improvement on the statistical method in achieving acceptance and personal commitment on the part of the field force. The men in the field are apt to feel that they are at least as well qualified as their bosses to guess what the future will be in their respective territories. Who can deny that their feeling may be justified.

Furthermore, the method may posses either a considerable element of built-in bias or carelessness, according to the process used in carrying it out. If the executives meet in conference to make their estimates, the opinion of each man is almost certain to be subjected to considerable pressure of intracompany politics, with the effect that the estimates finally agreed on can hardly be said to be unbiased or systematic. On the other hand, if each member be said to be unbiased or systematic. On the other hand, if each member of the group set down his own estimates and submits them to be averaged, he knows that he will not have to defend them before his fellows, but that they will be hidden behind the anonymity of an average. The probable result is that only the most conscientious among them will devote to the estimating process the careful analysis and study that its significance deserves.

This method also suffers a loss of accuracy when its results are broken down by products, customer groups, or geographical areas- perhaps to a lesser degree than does the statistical technique, but still to an extent that is significant. While the men in the office, as part of their jobs, try to keep informed about conditions in the field, they are inevitably insulated to some extent against the impact of purely local factors that affect the volume opportunities of individual salesmen. This is even true of the executives in the marketing area. They may be told about such factors by the men in the field but are often at a loss to know whether they are hearing reasons or merely excuses for failure.

The jury of executive opinion method of forecasting is apt to be a none too satisfactory compromise between the costs of getting a reasonably high degree of accuracy and the dangers of planning without it.

Grass roots method. What might be called the grass roots method of forecasting relies on the use of the salesman's intimate knowledge of the needs, attitudes, and intentions of his customers. It is the most expensive technique, but also often the most useful in the industrial goods field.

One firm implemented the methods about as follows.

1. About the middle of August each salesman received from the home office a sheet. All the columns reporting past performances were filled in at the home office. Those involving plans were blank.

2. The salesman also received a summary statement of top management's expectations of general business and industry conditions, expected price changes, planned product line changes, and general advertising and promotion policies during the coming year. Copies of all these documents went to the field sales supervisor.

3. Between the middle of August and the middle of September each field supervisor spent about a day with each of his men, preparing a sales estimate and selling plan for each man's territory. In the course of this session, they discussed each customer and prospective customer and set down an estimate of sales of each product or product group to him. They also decided what field action, in the form of sales calls, etc., would be required to achieve this objective.

4. As these estimates were received at the central office, the marketing executives reviewed them. Those that did not seem to make sense were questioned, and the field men were called on to explain them. For example, a salesman who during the first 7 months of the current year had sold 600 pounds of a material to a customer whose annual take had never been more than 1,000 pounds estimated that during the coming year he would sell this same customer 6000,000 pounds. When questioned, he reported the according to his information the customer was about to introduce a new end-product which, if successful, would increase his total annual in-take of the material to about 1 million pounds. Of this amount, the salesman expected to get 6000,000 pounds, since he had worked with the customer during certain stages of the development program.

5. After all adjustments were made, the individual estimates were priced out and summarized by products or product groups, customer groups, and in total. The summary was the forecast.

One big advantage of this methods lies in the high

degree of personal commitment it achieves among the men on the field. Since a man sets his own objective, he will leave no stone unturned to achieve it. The plan will work out if he can possibly make it do so. This is a matter of high significance. No amount or quality level of control supervision or leadership can get out of the field force a performance that even approaches one resulting from the enthusiastic devotion of the men themselves to objectives they have had a hand in setting.

The grass roots procedure, if properly carried out, has an advantage in that, in the course of it, a detailed plan of work can be prepared for each field salesman, and this plan is directly related to the needs and problems of each customer. In fact, it and the sales objectives are the result of an analysis of the probable requirements of the customer, made primarily by the two people in the marketing firm who are closest to him and should know most about him-the salesman and his immediate supervisor. This is a plan that grows out of the conditions in the territory and should be realistic in relation to those conditions if it is nothing else.

On the other hand, the method is expensive. It uses up at least one selling day for each man on the force. In addition, it claims at least as many days of the supervisor's time as he has salesmen under him, not to mention the time he must spend in planning the individual sessions and reviewing their results. If the scheme is to work, one or more home office people fairly well up in the marketing executive hierarchy must review the objectives very carefully. All this adds up to a lot of company employee time and money.

This matter of cost is much less a drawback to the industrial good marketer than to consumer goods manufacturers. A firm that markets direct to tens of thousands of retail stores through a sales force of the thousands men is apt to find its cost prohibitive. We have pointed out that prospective buyers of many industrial products number only a few hundred or, at most, a thousand. The number of salesmen needed to serve them is likewise small, and the cost of the grass roots forecasting procedure is modest. This is less true or not true at all of some maintenance, repair, and operation supply items that are bought by many firms in many industries.

The firm that sells through distributors is not likely to find the method particularly useful. Its salesmen contact the distributors, and their knowledge of the users' operations and intentions is, at best, secondhand. The whole success of the procedure depends on that knowledge being intimate and detailed. This drawback is especially characteristic of the business in supplies.

If a firm markets through manufacturers' or sales agents who do not carry stocks, some modification of the methods can be used. Since it ships direct to user-buyers on orders received through the agents, the marketing manger is in a position to know who these buyers are and how much each has taken. The agent's knowledge of his customers probably reasonably complete. Considerable difficulty maybe experienced in getting the cooperation of agents because of a the time element involved, for each agent may represent 10 or dozen manufacturers, the necessary disclosure of information they consider confidential, and the fear that the results may be used against them when the time comes to negotiate renewal of the agency. It is not impossible for a firm that has built a record of cooperation and fair-dealing with its agents to overcome this reluctance.

By no stretch of the imagination can a grass roots forecast be said to be unbiased or free from the influence of personal interest or opinion. The smart salesman might even be expected to manipulate the process for his own benefit and at the expense of the accuracy of the forecast. For example, he might consistently underestimate expected sales, with the result that the forecast for his territory would be too low and he would look good to his management when his actual sales exceeded the forecast.

Experience with the method indicates that this defect is more apparent than real. The average salesman is an optimistic, self-confident soul who tends to plan more than he can do. Sales executives have found that individual estimates must be pruned just about as often as they must be padded to approach realism. Then, too, an observant field supervisor should know enough about each salesman's territory and the customers in it to be able to spot serious over or underestimates and ask embarrassing questions about them. The home office reviewers also are able to question individual customer estimates that are too far out of line with past performance trends. Most of those who have used the grass roots method have not found underestimating a serious drawback.

The grass roots method of forecasting is used very widely in the industrial goods field. The relatively small number of customers who comprise the market for many industrial goods products and the direct contract between producer and user that this characteristic makes possible and that the technical nature of many such articles demand tend to make this technique applicable in planning their marketing.

Some firms combine the statistical approach with either the executive jury or the grass roots method, checking the results of one against those of the other. If they agree, the executives can feel that they are planning on fairly sound grounds. If discrepancies appear, the planners then explore the specific areas in which differences occur and try to uncover reasons for them so that they can be reconciled into a reasonably realistic figure. Probably a little of this goes on in all forecasting work for industrial goods. Even though a firm is devoted to the statistical approach, its planners probably can not afford to neglect attempts to make special checks on the expected operations and buying intentions of very large customers. If the grass roots process is to produce realistic results, it must go on in the expected atmosphere of general business, industry, and customer trade conditions as forecasted by methods that are largely statistical.

Almost every forecast involves an effort to foresee

two things; what sales will be if we drift with the tide or continue to do what we have been doing, how this figure will be modified by changes we propose to make in our production and marketing activities. During recent years it has become the fashion to call these activities the "marketing mix". Let's explore some of the problems involved in planning the marketing mix.

PLANNING THE MARKETING MIX

The components of the marketing mix are certain to vary from company to company according to each firm's objectives, competitive position, strengths and weaknesses, and personnel skills. The elements almost always present in the marketing mix of an industrial goods company are:

Advertising Delivery service
Sales promotion Special jobs or putups
Personal selling Quality
Technical service Price

The use of any one of these to gain sales volume cost money. The central problem in planning the marketing mix is to find the combination that will result in the maximum net cash inflow, that is, cash inflow minus cash outflow.

In principle, the answer to this problem, is very simple. It involves the application of marginal analysis; that is, the use of each component should be pushed to the point where the return from an additional dollar spent on it exactly equals the return from an additional dollar spent on any one of the others. A top limit is placed by the maximum amount of money the firm can afford to spend or by the point at which an additional dollar spent on any one or all of the components will not bring in a cash flow of more than a dollar; usually, it is the former. While this principle is simple, any attempt to apply it is bound to be infinitely complex. This complexity arises not so much from the mathematical problems involved as from the difficulty of forecasting results of the use of the different components. If the results of applying each element in the mix could be accurately foreseen, a mathematical formula could be developed that would make the principle readily workable.

But it is very difficult to forecast the results of the future use of a tool unless its results can be measured once it has been used. This is now possible with only a few of the tools we have mentioned, such as direct mail advertising or promotional material designed to bring in orders of inquires. With most of them, though, the measurement of results is at the present time largely a process of more or less intelligent guessing and the exercise of seat-of-the pants judgment. In spite of the lack of adequate means to forecast the results of marketing action or even to measure them, the marketing manager cannot avoid trying to do so. Unless he does, he cannot plan. During recent years, much study has been devoted to attempts to improve both measurement and forecasting in this area. We may expect that during the company years, these efforts will be continued and probably intensified. Students and practitioners of marketing will be wise to keep themselves aware of the direction and progress of such efforts.

At this point, we might suggest what seems to be the most promising approach to the problem. Much of the work that has been done has been devoted to measuring what might be called preliminary or intermediate rather than the end results of marketing effort.

For example, most attempts to measure the effectiveness of magazine and trade journal advertising have sought to discover whether a given advertisement was noticed, read, or remembered; the radio and TV rating services report the number of people who listened to or viewed a program. This is only the beginning of the story. In order to be an effective marketing tool, a piece of advertising copy must call attention to itself so that prospective customers or persons who influence buying will read it or listen to it; it must get its message across to the buying or influencing group; it must convince them; and it must motivate them to adopt a pattern of thought or action desired by the advertiser. A certain conviction or action is the end objective of the advertisement. But none of the usual tests of effectiveness even approach this point.

Part of the reason for this lies in the fact that the end objectives of many advertising pieces and campaigns are not clearly stated or even envisaged by those who prepare them, or if they are, the goal of each advertisement differs somewhat from every other, which makes it impossible to measure all of them with single tool. The measurement of effectiveness of a marketing tool is a job that each marketing manger must do or have done for himself.

This suggests that the job measuring the effectiveness of an advertisement- or, for that matter, the use of any other marketing tool-must begin when the use of that tool is planned. For example, if when we plan an advertising campaign we set down its objectives in the most specific terms we can command, in the form of numbers. If possible, we can then seek to develop some method of checking its results after publication.

Suppose a campaign has as one of its objectives attracting inquiries. We might ask ourselves: How many inquiries are we shooting for and how many dollars of business do we expect to get from them? We must have some such figures in mind when we decide whether the campaign will be worth its cost. It should not be too difficult to set up a system of records and analysis that will tell us how near we come to our goal.

Consider a less tangible objective, creating or changing a customer attitude or company image, for instance. When we decide to do this by an advertising campaign, we must believe that the attitude, once achieved will be worth more dollars to our firm than we propose to spend for the advertising. Why not divide what we think the change really will be worth to us? Then, by attitude surveys we can check the degree to which we actually achieve the desired change and what return we really get on the money spent. It is true that all these dollar value appraisals would be made on very nebulous bases; but the fact is that we must make such an appraisal, usually subconsciously and on much more nebulous grounds, every time we make a decision about such advertising. The appraisal is apt to be more careful and accurate if we bring it out in the open and set it down on paper as part of our marketing plan. Industrial Marketing, May 1966, reports such an operation. A firm that makes electrical fixtures checked the effect of an advertising program on customers' attitudes toward the company. The study showed the following percentages of favorable attitudes toward several patronage factors;

	Percent favorable		
	1961	1964	1965
Product quality........	40	44	54
Product development.......	40	49	56
Product style............	.39	50	59

Once we build a background of experience in this area, we should find that it has predictive possibilities and that we can plan with more precision and confidence. Some such concept as this seems to offer possibilities for applying the marginal analysis to the problem of determining the marketing mix with results that will not be completely accurate but should be practically useful. But until we can measure, we cannot predict; until we can predict with some rough approach to accuracy, we cannot plan with confidence or soundness.

STEPS IN MARKETING PLANNING

For purposes of discussion, we may find it convenient to divide the planning process into several steps or stages. The divisions we use here are not necessarily standard or universal. Other writers and practitioners may prefer other breakdowns perhaps as good or better than the one we find most convenient. It should also be recognized that the chronological implication of the list of steps we shall use is largely false. In a typical planning operation, a number of them may be going on simultaneously and at least one of them-the collection of marketing information-must go on all the time if it is to be done properly.

Nor is the planning process itself so distinct from operation in either timing or nature as our treatment would imply. While carrying out the current plan, the marketing manager must be preparing others for the future and, at the same time, making such amendments to the current one as may be demanded by changing conditions and newly discovered information.

Collecting information

Before you can do much intelligent planning about a thing you must know about it. This is true of even the simplest situation. The more complex the problem, the more complete your information about it must be if your plan to solve it is to be realistic and sound. The technical nature of most industrial goods and the derived character of their demand cause the problems of marketing them to be naturally complex. The increasingly dynamic character of our technology and the growing interdependence of the different parts of our economy are constantly increasing the complexity and thereby multiplying the information needs of the marketing manager of industrial goods.

When we think of information, we normally think of facts. But the marketing manger must broaden his concept of the term to include opinions, attitudes, and even rumors; what people think or feel is true or even suspect or fear may be true often influences their buying behavior more than what actually is true. This is less the case in the field of industrial goods than in the consumer goods market, but the industrial marketer who ignores the emanations of the trade grapevine is courting trouble.

All planning must deal with the future, and the future grows out of the past and the present. Thus, it is helpful to the planner to know what was and is, it is much more vital to him to have some ides, however incomplete, about what will be. Therefore, the most useful kind of information for the marketing planner is the on-going kind that indicates is at a particular time without indication of the direction in which it is moving or the speed of its motion. Trends are usually the most important form of marketing information.

Information about what? Of course, the marketing planner needs to know all he can learn about the market, its extent, its geography, its depth, the people and firms in it, trends within it, its purchasing power, and any other items of information about it that he can use in his conscious analysis of it or that will add breadth or depth to his understanding of it.

It is especially important for the industrial marketer to know every scrap of information he can get about his product, what it is used for, the techniques of its use, the difficulties its users encounter in their operations and the methods they have found overcome those difficulties, its weaknesses and its points of strength. It is particularly important that he keep up to trade with respect to changes in the technology of the using industry that may affect the applicability or performance of his product.

He needs to know as much as he can find out about the channels or outlets through which he can move his goods to market. Changes constantly occur in the marketing services rendered by individual outlets or types of outlets, and in the struggle for power and influence that incessantly goes on among them. In this area, he cannot be content with knowing general trends, but must extend his information service to cover the behavior and fortunes of individual outlets.

The industrial marketing planner, much more than his consumer goods counterpart, must know his customers. It is not enough for him to be customer firm, he must ferret out the individuals who exercise buying power or influence, and must learn the selling appeals that are apt to motivate them. He is likely to find it worthwhile to study even the internal politics of important customer concerns to discover shifts in power and influence that are taking place or are likely to occur. An especially important area of customer information is that of new end products in the planning or development stage which may, in due course, cause a demand for new materials or equipment.

He needs somewhat the same kind of information

about his competitors, particularly about the men who make or influence marketing and pricing decisions. In addition, he must find out all he can learn about their present products vis-a-vis those of his own firm to discover where his competitive product advantages and weaknesses lie. An especially difficult area within which to obtain competitor information is that of product planning and development, but it is necessary if we are to avoid being outgunned in product quality, uses or appeal. A knowledge of a competitor's delivery and service performance and of his reputation for being helpful to customers and keeping his promises is very much worthwhile.

Of course, an elementary kind of information, which is usually much easier for the industrial marketer to get than for his consumer goods counterpart, is his own sales. For the many industrial goods houses that sell direct to users, getting this information is merely a matter of arithmetic analysis. It is simply a process of putting the raw data of the accounting records into usable form by classification according to customers products, areas, etc., and discovering relationships between them. When agents are used, the same is true since shipments are generally made direct. When a firm markets through distributors, the process is much more complicated and difficult, and the resulting data are much less complete and reliable.

The marketing planner must at all times keep abreast of changes in general business conditions and of shifts in the business climate or weather within his own and customer industries. This is usually not too difficult, since many publications and commercial services make their first order of business. The trick is to decide which items from among the welter of reported fact and opinion are significant and worthy of reliance.

Sources of marketing information. Some marketing information is to be found inside the firm or can be picked up in the course of the normal contracts of the people in the firm. Some must be obtained from outside the company.

Outside information comes from two sources. Much material about the average industry is published. Some must be gathered and analyzed by marketing research. Both these sources will be discussed in the chapter on marketing research, so we will not treat them further here.

Most marketing managers recognize that outside marketing research must be planned and organized. Not so many of them realize that the same is true of information gathering within the firm. Most management maintain a unit to analyze sales; many organize the analysis of marketing costs; but very few set up and administer any organizational unit or system for mobilizing and analyzing the flow of marketing information that more or less auto magically enters the average business concerned various points from president to office boy. Fewer still seek to stimulate and train the company personnel with public or trade contracts to observe and report the fragments of marketing information that naturally come before their eyes or into their ears.

Salesmen, repairmen, technical service men, researchmen, purchasing department people, public relations men, and executives at all levels are naturally exposed to fragments of information that, collected and fitted together, might present a fairly complete library of marketing information. An executive in one industrial goods company remarked. "Somewhere in this company there is somebody that knows anything we need to know about customers, competitors, products, and the market, but how can we find him when we want him?? His statement, iike the fabled hoop snake, had a sting in its tail. The organization problem involved in mobilizing this widely scattered and fragmented internal information is monumental, and very few firms have found even a moderately satisfactory solution. In fact, only a few firms have tried to organize it. More might find it worthwhile to do so.

A second step in planning marketing is the setting of objectives or goals for the marketing activity. We have already pointed out that, in the main, the goals of a firm's marketing division should grow out of and be designed to contribute to the achievement of its overall objectives. It is usually not a good idea for the marketing planner to be content with setting general objectives for the entire marketing area. He should go further and see to it that these are broken down into goals for different parts of functions of the total marketing activity, such as geographical divisions, products or product groups, customers or customer groups, advertising, personal selling, and even individual salesmen.

Once the marketing manager knows what he wants to accomplish, he usually finds that there are several ways of trying to do it. Usually, not all of these are obvious. Sometimes, the best ones must be sought in the imagination of the planner or in his creative analysis of the situation. Usually, each method consists of a certain combination of the tools of marketing, such as advertising, sales appeals, personal selling, the various sales promotion devices, pricing, delivery, credit, technical service, and the various other customer services all used in a certain pattern-a marketing mix. The number of marketing mixes available to achieve a given objective is limited only by the inventiveness and ingenuity of the planner in conceiving different proportions in which the marketing tools may be used or variations in the methods of their use. The crux of his problem is to find and choose the best one or, at least, one that is better than any of his competitors may hit on. This is certain to be more or less a hit-and-miss operation that depends heavily on executive judgment and feel until methods can be developed to measure and so to forecast the efforts of the use of the several marketing tools. So far, this has not been done satisfactorily. In the section dealing with forecasting, we have suggested a possible methods of approach to the problem.

Before a marketing plan can be considered complete, it must be implemented in the form of a program or list of very specific actions to be taken or things to be done and, usually, of when they are to be done. This process of implementation does not necessarily wait until selection of the marketing mix is completed.

5

INDUSTRIAL MARKETING AND THE INDUSTRIAL CUSTOMER

Industrial marketing is the marketing of goods and services to commercial enterprises, governments, and other nonprofit institutions for resale to other industrial customer or for use in the goods and services that they, in turn, produce. By contrast, consumer-goods marketing is the marketing of goods and service to individuals and family units for personal consumption and to wholesalers and retailers in the distribution system.

Hence, the distinction between industrial and consumer-goods marketing is made primarily in terms of intended customers. It is essentially the differences in the nature of the customers that give rise to the characteristically different problems and marketing approaches one encounters in the study of industrial marketing.

Secondarily, industrial products are, for the most part, distinctively different from those that are purchased by consumers for their own use. The types of products that businesses and other institutions buy include *heavy equipment*, such as machine tools, trucks and tractors, and blast furnaces; *light equipment*, such as typewriters, portable power tools, and measuring instruments; *construction*, such as factories, office buildings, docks, and communication towers; *component parts* such as motors, gears, pumps, and semiconductors; *raw materials*, such as coal, iron ore, and limestone; *processed materials*, such as steel plate, plastic sheeting, plywood, and chemicals; *consumable supplies*, such as cutting fluids, small tools, electricity, and paper towels; and *services*, such as repair and maintenance, design, and consulting services. It is important to recognize that not all goods and services can be classified as either industrial or consumer. Some products fall in both categories: typewriters, hand tools, automobiles, floor polish, sandpaper, and lawn tractors, for example. Marketing approaches for products such as these, however, are greatly different for industrial and consumer customers.

INDUSTRIAL MARKETING STRATEGY

Strategic Variables in any marketing scheme include *product planning, pricing, distribution, advertising and promotion,* and *selling*. Depending on the nature of the product, the market, and competition, there may be a good many other strategic variables, such as *plant and warehouse location, technical service, product service,* and *sales-financing* schemes. Strategic planning involves making choice in each of these areas and in allocating resources-manpower, dollars, and physical facilities to such elements of the marketing program as new-product development, field sales, advertising, and maintaining inventories.

As a broad generalization, proportionally more resources are committed to the field-selling and technical-service elements in industrial-marketing strategy, and proportionally less to media advertising than in consumer-goods marketing. This is because industrial customers for any given product are often (but not always) limited in number, readily identifiable, and more economically reached directly and personally. Another consideration is the nature of the communications that are required. Industrial customers may need technical education in the use of the product. In addition, industrial sellers need continuing and detailed feedback direct from customers on problems of product quality and performance.

By contrast, product information and buying appeals for consumer goods are communicated to a much large extent through newspapers, magazines, radio, television, and direct-mail advertising, as well as retail-store promotions. Media advertising may serve completely to "pre-sell" the consumer customer, to at least to get him or her into a retail outlet where the salesclerk can provide additional information. And market feedback on the quality of consumer product may be gathered from statistical data on the incidence of product failure and repair records and through the use of consumer panels.

If any general statement can be made regarding characteristic difference between industrial and consumer-goods marketing strategy, then, it would stress the relative emphasis on technical service and field selling for the former and on media advertising for the latter *Within* the several elements of strategy, however, there are marked differences between industrial and consumer marketing problems. We might briefly consider some of the different kind of problems the industrial-marketing manager typically encounters in the key areas of product planning, pricing, distribution, advertising and promotion, and customer relations. The treatment at this point is for illustrative purposes. A more detailed consideration of each area is reserved for subsequent chapters.

Product planning

Industrial-goods producers often face basic policy decisions regarding product/market level. Are they to function as suppliers of materials, components, or end products-or all three? Pulp and paper companies, for example, may and often do-function as supplier of pulpwood, paper, and corrugated boxes. A railroad-equipment manufacturer may produce the motors and generators that are used as components in the locomotives he builds; he may also sell these components to competing manufacturers of locomotives.

The manufacturer who operates at more than one market level is said to be "competing with his customers." Although this is not an untenable position, it introduces conflicts of interest in strategic planning between one market level and the other. Efforts to strengthen competitive position in, say, the locomotive market may adversely affect marketing efforts for locomotive components.

Pricing Certain pricing conventions used in industrial marketing also serve to distinguish this field from consumer-goods marketing. For example, competitive bidding is widely used in industrial marketing on large construction projects. Heavy equipment, supplies, and materials. Bids are based often on specifications issued by the purchaser and, under the rules of the competition, nay be opened publicly at a predetermined hour and the order awarded to the lowest qualified bidder. Alternatively, the initial bid may serve only to narrow the field of potential suppliers, and negotiations between competing sellers and the prospective buyers may proceed from there.

It follows, as well, that many contracts are individually priced. Except for commodity like products (relatively undifferentiated among different suppliers), orders often have unique design, delivery, and quality characteristics requiring that prices be set order by order. This poses some interesting problems for the industrial marketer, both in cost analysis on his own products and in market intelligence to determine competitors' prices.

On standard items, list prices are usually used, with discounts indicated for size of order and class of customer (user-customer or distributor) and price extras noted for such factors as freight and type of packaging.

Finally, price negotiation tends often to be an important part of the industrial buying/selling process. Here, the relative skill and purchasing power of large and small industrial customers are factors to be taken into account in coping with the market environment.

Distribution A characteristic problem of industrial-goods manufacturers has to do with conflicts that arise in selling to the few very large customer on the one hand and the many relatively small accounts on the other. It may, and usually is, most economical for a manufacturer to sell to the large buyer directly. It may be important to sell direct for other strategic reasons as well, such as developing strong customer relations. Small buyer, on the other hand, may be most adequately served through agents or distributors who carry local inventories, provide immediate delivery service, have broad product lines, and extend credit.

Because any market is far from being in a steady state, and because legal constraints prevent the manufacturer from limiting in any way the accounts the distributor solicits, manufacturers and their distributors not infrequently find themselves competing against each other for larger accounts.

The basic problem arises because markets are in a constant state of growth and change. The distribution system that may have been developed for one stage of market development may not be appropriate at another. The system planned for one market segment may not be competitively effective in another where buying behavior is entirely different. Yet distribution systems represent tremendous fixed commitments and are not easily changed to adapt to changing market conditions.

Advertising and promotion

Although media advertising may play a somewhat smaller role in industrial marketing than in consumer-goods strategies, it poses interesting problems and opportunities. It is often used to develop a favorable corporate image with potential buyers and the general public. It may serve to create a favorable environment for the company's field representatives as they call on purchasing managers.

Advertising may be used to develop product "pull-through" by being directed at the consumer markets in which the product is ultimately used. Thus, for example, Du Pont may promote Orlon and Dacron in consumer media advertisements that feature high-fashion clothing made with these synthetic fibers. Since du Pont does not make and sell these *end products,* its purpose is to develop brand recognition at the consumer, retailer, and clothing-manufacturer levels for the quality of its trademarked *materials.* In this way, it is hoped, fabric weavers may be persuaded by their customers to favor du Pont fibers over competing products.

Some industrial marketers will feature in media advertising the end products their customers make from materials they-the industrial marketers-supply. Such a strategy is aimed at building stronger positions as suppliers to large and important customers.

Customer relations In industrial marketing, buyer/seller relationships tend to be both continuing in nature and complex. They go well beyond sales transactions and very often involve technical assistance to customers, joint product-development efforts, and product service. Advertising on behalf of customers, financing their purchases, and entertaining key managers in customer companies are all tactics intended to put sellers in a favorable competitive position. Trade relations, or reciprocity, may also be involved in the buyer/seller relationship. Reciprocity has to do with buying from a supplier who buys from you. The firm's purchasing power is used, then, to persuade its suppliers to buy from it.

Clearly, industrial buyer/seller relationships involve many people on both sides procurement managers, field salesmen, technical service representatives, engineers, financial managers, R&D technicians, and top corporate officers. The relationships are difficult to control and even more difficult to appraise in terms of strategic effectiveness. But they are critically important. The development of strong, multidimensional, and constructive working relationships with one's customers is the key to industrial-marketing success.

We have looked at characteristic industrial-marketing problem areas. Those mentioned above by no means constitute an exhaustive listing. They simply serve to illustrate the range of matters that must be considered in any study of this field.

It will be useful now to try to understand and industrial customer. In the remainder of the chapter, we will consider, first, some different ways of classifying industrial customers. Then we will look at the range of factors that tend to influence industrial buying behavior. Finally, the chapter discuss factors and effect the relative bargaining power of industrial customers in buying situations.

Customer-classification schemes

Traditionally, industrial customers have been categorized as users, OEMs (original-equipment manufacturers), and dealers and distributors. The *user* customer is one who buys a product (such as a turret lathe or a grinding wheel) to use in his business. The *OEM* is one who buys a product to incorporate into what he in turn makes and sells. For example, a television-set manufacturer, buying electronics components to put in the sets the makes, would be classified as an OEM customer. Finally, *dealers and distributors* are those who buy products from manufacturers to resell in essentially the same form to users and OEMs Mill-supply houses, paper jobbers, steel warehouses, machine-tool dealers, and chemical distributors, for example, fall in this third category.

This is a meaningful classification scheme, because it has to do roughly with the purpose the product serves for the customer, and that in turn will shape the way he buys. Moreover, the terms *user, OEM,* and *distributor* are part of the language of industrial marketing.

For strategic planning purposes, however, this classification doesn't cut deeply enough. What is needed is a market-segmentation scheme that sorts customers into homogeneous groups according to the way they buy and use the product. Such a scheme provides the essential framework within which marketing strategies may be planned to focus don the needs of different market segments.

There are at least four ways of segmenting industrial markets. The first is *by product.* A steel manufacturer, for example, might group his customers in terms of the products they buy-tool steel, stainless-steel plate, structural steel. Market segmentation by product is especially helpful if products are highly differentiated technically, and where conveying product knowledge to customers is a critical dimension of selling.

The second is by *end-use application.* A computer manufacturer may segment his markets into such groupings as airlines, banks and insurance companies, retail distribution, process industries, and research laboratories. The way each of these uses computers, and the software (computer programs) each typically employs, very greatly from one customer grouping to another. The most critical aspect of selling is understanding the customer's business and the way computers serve his needs.

The third is by *geography*. This segmentation scheme recognizes the widely different character of market environments in different parts of the world. The marketing of chemicals for agricultural/veterinarian use in such different environments as India, Brazil, France, and the United States may be quite different ball games. The differences may be in terms of government controls, monetary conditions, and the wide variances in the marketing infrastructure (available distribution and promotional media). Under these circumstances, understanding and coping effectively with the local market environment may be the critical dimension of market success.

Finally, markets may be segmented *by the way customers buy*. Government agencies buy differently from commercial enterprises. The former typically require that suppliers submit bids, and, depending on the product, a number of different people may be involved in the buying decision. Large companies buy differently from small ones: Large customers use different and much more structured purchasing procedures than small ones and are characteristically more price sensitive.

What may be an appropriate scheme for classifying industrial customer-product, geography, end use, or buyer behavior-will vary from one industrial market to another. Moreover, the scheme that may be appropriate at one stage of market development may be outmoded at another. Generally speaking, segmenting the market by *product* is useful in the early stages when customers need product education, and the most essential factor in competitive effectiveness may be technical product knowledge and the ability to communicate it to customers. In the later stages of market development, a segmentation scheme by product tends to give way to segmentation by *end-use application,* when product uses have been identified and product knowledge has advanced to the point that much of it can be systematized by type of application. At this point competitive strength will be based on understanding technical aspects of the customer's business and of the use of the product in his production system. In the more mature stages of market development, when customer education in product and application knowledge is no longer a primary concern, when major competitors are approximately equal in the quality of the product and the service they provide, *buyer-behavior* segmentation schemes tend to take over. The critical element in marketing success at this stage is knowing customer buying processes and the relative emphasis they place on factors such as price, availability of supply, business entertaining, and trade relations.

Similarly, *geographic* schemes tend to be somewhat appropriate to earlier rather than later stages of market development. Markets in different parts of the world tend to become more alike as time goes on for any given product. Relatively common patterns of product use and of government influences on product forms, pricing, and promotion seem to emerge. Marketing infrastructures develop. Then suppliers tend to subordinate *geographic* distinctions in developing *strategy* and to employ a framework for strategy based on *end-use application* and *buyer behavior.*

The life of a geographic segmentation scheme tends to be prolonged, however, when the product or its manufacturing process is "culturally sensitive." Specifications for products such as tractors and harvesting equipment, for example, will vary from one country or region to another, depending on government regulations having to do, perhaps, with safety or pollution, and on the type of crop production that is characteristic of the area. Market environments may vary considerably from one part of the world to another for such products.

Products may be culturally sensitive, as well, when

there is strong national interest in whether they are manufactured locally or imported, and when export trade is considered important. Many smaller, developing countries require that local manufacturing facilities be constructed to make steel or trucks, for example. Trade barriers then prohibit imports, and strategically the country becomes a market segment unto itself for the large manufacturer who has committed production and selling resources to it.

The purpose in considering market segmentation schemes is primarily to understand the several possible dimensions along which market information may be gathered, customers classified, and strategies developed. Within a strategy formulated for a particular market segment, there should be strategies, as well, for individual customers. For that reason, it is useful to turn now to a consideration of how industrial customers buy.

BUYING MOTIVATIONS AND INFLUENCES

The factors that affect industrial-buying decision-making are *economic, behavioral,* and *organizational* in nature. *Economic* has to do with cost/profit considerations. *Behavioral* relates to the process of communicating with those responsible for making buying decisions and to the way selling messages are received. *Organizational* is concerned with how the buying decision-making process is structured in complex organizations and the effect of both structure and process on the ultimate procurement choice. The challenge in industrial marketing is to comprehend the "economics" of the purchasing decision as the prospective buyer sees it, to understand each "player" in the system, his relationship to the others (his "role"), the organizational framework within which he moves; and from these considerations, to determine what motivates him. Then it becomes possible to design account strategies that implement the overall marketing strategy but that are tailored to take cognizance of the factors that make every potential customer different from every other one.

Economic factors

Whatever the size or the nature of their operations, industrial customers, it is safe to assume, are in business to make a profit or, in the case of government units and nonprofit institutions, to operate within budgets. Consequently, the dominant buying motivations are economic. They relate to *price, availability of supply, and service.*

Price is relative. That is, the prospective buyer evaluates a price quoted to him by comparing it with other, competing offers. If the purchaser is considering some new material or component or some new piece of capital equipment, he will seek to relate its price to potential operating savings or to profits from the increased sales of his product that could result. For example, a buyer may be considering the purchase of a new piece of production equipment that operates faster and more efficiently than the old one he is now using, or requires less labor to operate, or takes less downtime for maintenance and repair. He is likely to calculate the potential savings (return) that could result from buying the new machine and relate this to its price (investment) in terms of a percentage return on investment (ROI). If the percentage return is favorable compared to the return that might be available from alternative uses for those same funds, the new-equipment purchase will be given a relatively high priority.

Similarly, the industrial buyer may be weighing the possibility of adopting an innovative packaging material for the products he makes. The new packaging may have more eye appear and may extend the shelf life of his product. If the new material costs more than the old, the prospective buyer will evaluate this added cost against the potential the new packaging offers for increased sales and profits on the products he makes and sells.

Availability of supply may be, and usually is, of critical concern to the industrial customer. This is especially true if the product in question is a material or component from which he makes the products he sells. Any interruption of supply might force him to shut down his production lines at some considerable loss in terms of production costs and possibly lost sales.

Actually, it is for this reason as much as price that

industrial buyers have a strong aversion to being dependent on a single source of supply. How strong depends on how important and critical the product is to their operations and what options they have in case of supply failure.

There is another side to availability of supply as a buying consideration. Industrial buyers, as a rule, seek to minimize investments in inventories in order to avoid tying up capital and to maximize ROI in the business. They tend to push the inventory-carrying function back onto their suppliers, the distributors and manufacturers. This means that the customers often want frequent deliveries in small amounts keyed to their usage schedules. When usage schedules. When usage schedules are unpredictable, then local stocking becomes important in order to minimize transportation delays between ordering the goods and receiving shipment.

Although price considerations are quite quantifiable, supply-availability considerations are not to easily reduced to numbers. Buyers might conceivably estimate the probabilities that suppliers could be hit with a strike or some catastrophe that might shut their plants down. But usually they don't. If there is any concern that the flow of purchased parts or materials could be interrupted and force a work stoppage, the buyer is likely to give this consideration primary emphasis-even above price-in making his decision as to the sources of supply he will use.

Sometimes, of course, the buyer is completely dependent on a single source and has no option, because there is no other supplier. For many years, for example, only du Pont manufactured and sold polyester fiber. Its Dacron was patented. Du Pont's customers, therefore, had to take the risk that supplies of this synthetic fiber could be cut off and could guard against that possibly by carrying ample inventories.

As for *service*, there is a variety of "fringe benefits" that may be important to industrial customers in selecting suppliers. Again, these benefits may be difficult, if not impossible, to quantify. For example, buyers exhibit a strong desire to do business with suppliers that hold position of technical leadership in their industries, thus giving buyers the early benefit of product improvements and perhaps technical help in developing their product lines.

Availability of spare parts and a supplier's program for maintaining and repairing his products in the field are especially important in the case of equipment and sometimes components like motors. Sales financing through extending credit or leasing is another dimension of service that can be highly important. In selling capital goods such as locomotives, aircraft, electrical generating equipment, and machine tools, the ability of the seller to arrange financing can be an important strategic advantage. This might be particularly true in markets abroad, where capital may be short and borrowing more difficult than in domestic markets.

Behavioural factors

Purchasing managers, engineers, and other who are involved in the buying process are exposed to a wide range to messages from a multiplicity of sources, both external and internal. They are likely to be exposed to influencing factors from advertising and from sales presentations and engineering conferences with suppliers' representatives. In addition, they cannot help but be affected by the opinions of others in their company and, indeed, in relevant trade and technical associations. According to recent research, the way in which the buying decision maker will receive and act upon these messages will depend on four sets of variables: the *sales message,* the *role of the decision maker,* the relative *degree of risk* (both corporate and personal) involved in making the buying decision, and, finally, the *buyer's personal and social needs* in an organizational context. It will be useful to comment briefly on each of these variables.

First, with regard to the *sales message,* Levitt in his study of industrial buying behavior describes two elements of sales-communication quality: *source effect* and presentation effect. Source effect generally refers to the company the field salesman represents. The extent to which it is known and highly regarded strongly influences the way in which prospective customers will react to sales messages. If the company has a prestigious reputation as opposed to being relatively unknown, buyers will be favorably inclined to do business with it. *Presentation effect* refers to the way in which the sales message is delivered: its clarity, its substance, and the perceived competence of the sales representative. According to Levitt, both source and presentation influences tend to deteriorate over time, although the latter tends to be more lasting than the former. Both then may need periodic reinforcement from repeated sales calls and from advertising, especially if the company has a source-effect advantage.

Industrial buying often involves technical personnel as well as purchasing managers. The *role* that each plays in the decision-making process and his particular expertise are themselves determinants of how each receives and acts upon sales messages. Technically qualified engineers are likely to react differently, to both source and presentation from purchasing managers with little technical training.

As for *risk*, a high-risk situation could be one involving a decision to buy a new product with possible implications for changing the quality of the buyer's products or disrupting his production process. Risk might also be incurred with regard to continuity of supply. Low-risk decisions, on the other hand, may be those involving routine reorders. Inevitably, risks are *personal* as well as *corporate*, in the respect that they involve the purchasing manager's relations with other managers, the prestige he enjoys both inside his company and out, the way his performance is measured, and, ultimately, his professional progress. If a purchasing manager elects, for example, to give a potential supplier's sales representative access to high-status production and engineering personnel in his company, he takes a risk. If these personnel perceive the call as a waste of time, they will be less willing in the future to entertain salesman sent by the purchasing manager.

Hence, the latter has risked his credibility and standing with men in the organization on whom he depends to get his work done effectively.

Personal and social needs as a factor in communicating with industrial buyers are best explained in Webster's words:

> Every prospective buyer has at least two kinds of needs: his *personal* needs which motivate his behavior and his *social* needs which define the kinds of need fulfillment activity which will be acceptable to relevant other persons in the social situation. While this is only a crude cut across the complex set of needs which determine behavior, it makes an important distinction. For example, the industrial buyer may be motivated by a personal need for recognition and advancement and by the social need to satisfy the using department. His need for the salesman's product will not exist unless he can see how a buying decision will allow him to satisfy both sets of needs. Those particular personal and social needs will determine: (1) whether the prospect grants an interview to the salesman, (2) which parts of the presentation he really listens to, (3) the information he will remember, and (4) the influence of the sales presentation on his decision to buy. In psychological terms, these are the process of *selective exposure,* selective attention, and *selective retention,* and the final step of *conviction or attitude change.*

One important finding in both the Webster and Levitt studies is that these four sets of variables (sales message, decision maker's role degree of risk, personal and social needs) are interactive. Thus, source effect becomes increasingly important relative to presentation effect as buying risk increases and becomes dominant. In any case, source seems to be more of an influence on technical personnel than on purchasing managers. On the other hand, presentation tends to register more strongly with purchasing managers than with technical personnel as buying risk increases. According to Levitt:

> The research found that the power of source

effect (company reputation for credibility) varies by the character and "competence" of the recipient of a sales message. Thus, there is some indication that, in the case of complex industrial materials, purchasing agents, who are usually highly competent as professional buyers, may be less influenced by a company's generalized reputation than are technical personnel, who are presumably less competent as buyers but more competent as judges of a complex product's merits. In first appraising complex new materials on the basis of sales presentations made directly to them, technically sophisticated personnel seem to be influenced by the seller's reputation to a point that is unexpectedly higher than the influence of that reputation on such technically less sophisticated personnel as purchasing agents. In short, technical personnel are probably influenced far more by company reputation than has been widely assumed, and certainly more than such technically less sophisticated people as purchasing agents.

While all audiences seem to be influenced by the quality of the sales presentation, important differences apparently exist between purchasing agents and technical personnel. In the lower-risk decision situation of whether to give a newly presented complex new product a further hearing, technical personnel are more powerfully influenced by the quality of a direct sales presentation than are purchasing agents. Put differently, on low-risk purchasing decisions, the technically less sophisticated purchasing agents seem to rely less heavily on the quality of the sales presentation than do the technically more sophisticated personnel in making their decisions. But on high-risk decision (whether actually to buy the product) the reverse is true: that is, the greater the risk, the more favorably purchasing agents are influenced by good sales presentations, and the less favorably technical personnel are influenced by such presentations. The greater the risk, the more likely technical personnel are to rely on their technical judgment about a new product's virtues rather than on the quality of the sales presentation in favor of the product. But purchasing agents, being technically less sophisticated, seem forced, in high-risk situations, to rely more heavily on the seller's presentation.

Organi-sational factors

Finally, to understand industrial buying behavior, one must understand buying decision-making processes in organizations. Depending on the relative size of the contractual commitment, purchase proposals may move up through several levels of approval, from the plant to the division, to corporate headquarters, to the board of directors. Procurements are typically governed by a series of rules stipulating the maximum amount of a single purchase that can be approved at any organizational level. The rules may require as well that bids be solicited from two or more suppliers if the purchase exceeds some stated dollars amount.

In addition to being screened at different organizational levels, a procurement action may involve managers in such different functions as engineering, production, control, and occasionally marketing. Engineering personnel may be called on to evaluate competing products. Manufacturing personnel may be needed to assess the way a supplier's materials or parts perform in production. The marketing people come in to appraise the effect on sales of any implied changes in product specifications and packaging that a change in suppliers and materials might portend.

Multilevel and multifunctional involvement in purchasing decision-making significantly affects the outcomes. The reason is that each buying influence point is likely to have a somewhat different perspective. At divisional or operating levels, product availability and the continuity of relationships with satisfactory suppliers may be most important. At the corporate level, price and ROI measures may be the major reference points.

As between the different function in a business, engineering and technical people are likely to favor technical excellence and consistently high product quality. Procurement managers have characteristically stressed price and product availability possibly at the sacrifice of some degree of technical superiority if the margin of difference does not have a perceived value in use. Typically, initial procurement decision to adopt some new product and new source of supply-say, a new grinding wheel-may have a high engineering involvement. Once the product specifications have been determined and the product has been tested in use, engineering's role in follow-on purchase decisions diminishes and procurement's increases. Typically, then, procurement managers will shop for equal quality at the lowest price. The original supplier may have a favored, but not a secure, position even though he may have provided considerable technical service during the initial testing of some new item.

It is important for industrial marketers of understand buying decision making in customer organizations. Then, selling communications with various managers in the customer company may be tailored to deal with those aspects of a transaction that are of direct interest to individuals in different functions and at different levels.

In planning selling strategies for individual accounts, the industrial marketer may usefully distinguish between situations involving routine reorders and those that imply change in some respect or another for the customer. He might will distinguish, in addition, between procurements that can be made at the operating-division level and those that call for approval at higher levels. Understanding the nature of the buying decision-making process from the customer's viewpoint is essential to determining who will be involved in making the decision and what their respective roles, interests, and internal relationships are. Not infrequently, the interests of managers at different levels in the organization and in different functional roles come into conflict in the buying process. *Goal incongruence* develops between division and headquarters management and among procurement managers, engineers, and plant managers. It is important that the industrial marketer be able to understand these differences in viewpoint and objective. His success can come only through seeking to resolve them in some optimizing manner, rather than in taking sides.

The development and use of bargaining power

Any treatment of buying behavior would be incomplete without considering the ways in which industrial buyers develop and use power in negotiating with suppliers. In any transaction, it is in the nature of things that each side seeks to develop a favorable bargaining position relative to the other. The literature on developing and using power and on bargaining strategy in military, political, legal, and economic matters is fairly copious. The same broad principles developed in these environments would be applicable in buying/selling situations, as well.

Engaged as he is in a continuing series of transactions, the industrial buyer seeks constantly to build a position of strength from which he can bargain effectively. He does this in the way he (1) develops and preserves his options, (2) gathers and uses information, (3) builds internal support, and (4) develops and practices negotiating skills.

Preserving options

The paramount concern of the industrial buyer is that he preserve multiple sources of supply, if at all possible. He is normally quite unwilling to become dependent upon a single source of supply for fear of becoming "locked in" on price and product availability. It is not enough that there may be more than one supplier competing for the buyer's business. It is important that this competition be *effective.* Alternative sources of supply must be perceived as being roughly comparable in quality of product, technical service, and availability of supply. The effectiveness of competition will be determined, as well, by how important the buyer's business is to prospective suppliers. Accordingly, buyers are inclined to work with a limited number of supplier, so that the business they give to each one represents a significant volume. That fact and the hope of getting substantial future orders are intended to motivate suppliers to quote low competitive prices and to provide good service.

Too limited a number of suppliers, however, may be self-defeating. If there are, for example, only two or three who serve as continuing sources, there may be a tendency for them to settle tacitly into the comfortable routine of sharing the buyer's business and to de-emphasize price competition. This typically oligopolistic behavior may apply as much to a limited number of firms competing for the business available from a single large account as it would to a few large competitors in a market. Hence, in preserving effective price competition, industrial buyers often try to strike a balance between having too few sources (say, one or two) and too many sources (say, five or more) on large and important purchases.

On maintenance items and small components, one way the industrial buyer makes his business important to potential suppliers is to lump his requirements for a full year and offer to enter into "annual buy" contracts. Rather than purchase individual items as needed, he groups his purchases into broad categories such as cutting tools, janitorial supplies, or semiconductors, and asks competing companies to bid on his anticipated annual requirements. By so doing, he considerably enhances his bargaining power.

Using information

The old adage, "Knowledge is power," succinctly expresses the idea that when one party in a negotiation has relevant information that the other party does not have, the latter's position is weakened. Purchasing managers typically, and appropriately, withhold information from supplier on what sources they have available and what prices these sources are quoting. In turn, they seek as much information as possible about supply conditions. How large are suppliers' backlogs? Do they have purchase commitments that will utilize their plant capacity for the coming year, or are they anxiously seeking orders? The supplier who needs orders to keep his factory running or to unload stocks in inventory, and who has no knowledge of what prices competitors are offering a prospective customer, may make much bigger price concessions than he has to.

Building internal support

In a real sense, the buyer's "Customers" are the people he serves inside his own organization. He has to satisfy the plant manager, technical personnel, and administrative staff by supplying them with goods and services with which they can perform their tasks efficiently. To a significant extend, the buyer's power in dealing with his outside sources is derived from having inside support. If the plant manager, for example, agrees to test some new material or supply them coming from a new supplier, the purchasing manager has increased his options and thereby gains bargaining strength. Alternatively, a purchasing manager at the corporate level may lose strength if contracts he has negotiated on supply items are circumvented at the division level and other vendors are used instead.

Internal conflict can significantly affect an organization's ability to deal with suppliers. In one case history of a military procurement, for example, a civilian contractor had successfully escalated what had started out to be an $8 an internal struggle between two units in the military procurement organization-one a new project management group seeking to gain jurisdiction over contract work, the second an established unit unwilling to yield its traditional control of the procurement function. Under the circumstances, decisions regarding critical work elements were being made by default at the lowest operating levels in the organization. There is reason to suspect in this case that internal conflict in the government agency was being fully exploited by the contractor.

Practicing the art of negotiation

In the process of creating effective competition for the business he can dispense, in gathering information about his suppliers and supply conditions, and in developing and nurturing internal support, the buyer builds his position of power. He uses this power in negotiating with his vendors. Accordingly, he develops, often intuitively, a sense of what power is and how it may be used with greatest effectiveness.

Karrass makes these observations:

> For practical purposes power may be defined as a ability of a negotiator to influence the behavior of an opponent. The eight principles listed below are applicable to most transactions.
>
> First, power is always relative. Rarely if ever does a buyer or seller enjoy complete power.
>
> Second, power may be real or apparent. The fact that a position is supported by logic, justice or force does not guarantee success. A seller may be in a preferred position, but if neither he nor the buyer perceives the advantage, he has none. Conversely, the seller may be in a weak position due to lack of business, but if the buyer does not perceive this, the buyer's power is not enhanced.
>
> Third, power may be exerted without action. If an opponent believes that action can and will be taken against him, it may not be necessary to act.
>
> Fourth, power is always limited. Its range depends upon the situation, government regulations, ethical standards and present or future competition.
>
> Fifth, power exists to the extent that it is accepted. A buyer who insists that he will not be exploited by a monopolistic seller is less likely to be victimized. Some people are simply less willing to be dominated than others and would rather do without than be exploited.
>
> Sixth, the ends of power cannot be separated from the means. One cannot hope to develop a loyal customer by using exploitative tactics.

> Seventh, the exercise of power always entails cost and risk.
>
> Eighth, power relationships change over time. The balance of power moves as the balance of benefits and contributions from the parties changes.

As essential of negotiating skill, therefore, is the ability to assess the strength and weakness of the opposing party and to understand fully what he has to stake. At the same time, it becomes important that the buyer not disclose what he has at stake in either a corporate or a personal sense. The negotiator must sometimes be willing to take calculated risks-to let his opponent believe that he (the buyer) is negotiating from a position of strength, a position that he may not in fact enjoy to the extent that he might imply. In this respect, negotiating is acting or role playing. There is room in the role for emotion, for being arbitrary, and for disregarding the apparent logic of the situation-up to a point. That point comes when the opponent himself may be forced to emotional responses and irrational behavior.

Bruce Henderson writes:

> The negotiator's skill lies in being as arbitrary as necessary to obtain the best possible compromise without actually destroying the basis for voluntary mutual cooperation to self-restraint. There are some commonsense rules for success in such an endeavor:

1. Be sure that your rival is fully aware of what he can gain if he cooperates and what it will cost him if he does not.

2. Avoid any action which will arouse his emotions, since it is essential that he behave in a logical, reasonable fashion.

3. Convince your opponent that you are emotionally dedicated to your position and are completely convinced that it is reasonable.

> It is worth emphasizing that your competitor is under the maximum handicap if he acts in a completely rational, objective, and logical fashion. For then he will cooperate as long as he thinks he benefits at all. In fact, if he is completely logical, he will not forego the profit of cooperation as long as there is any net benefit. If the acts in this manner, and you have followed the preceding rules, you can give him a token reward and keep the rest for yourself.

To perceive the buyer in his role as a bargainer is to understand that good buyers have certain personality traits. They have political skills and instincts. They are good in face-to-face confrontation. They are sensitive to people and are usually perceptive in judging the character of those with whom they deal. They get satisfaction from winning for the sake of winning and derive a sense of achievement from having made a good bargain.

And, to quote Karrass again:

> The ideal negotiator should have a high tolerance for ambiguity and uncertainty as well as the open-mindedness to test his own assumptions and the opponent's intentions. This requires courage. Finally, in every good negotiator there must be an inner desire to achieve, to aspire, to take that sensible but extra measure of risk that represents a commitment to one's strivings.

6

MANAGING THE PRODUCT OFFERING

Product Management is not strictly a marketing activity. It involves consideration of factors of production, finance, purchasing, labor relations, and general management as well as marketing. So most product decisions are made at the top management level.

But the growing realization in management thinking of the paramount importance of the customer to the success of the firm has caused the marketing manager to have much more voice in decisions about products than he once did. The core of product management lies in offering the products the customer wants the needs, in the quantities he wants, and when he wants them. Since the marketing manager has closer contacts with the customer than any other executive of the firm, he plays an increasingly important role in product management.

In our economy, very few concerns make and sell only one product. Some industrial goods houses confine their activities to a single *line of products,* by which we mean a group of articles that serve the same general purpose or are otherwise so closely associated that customers want to buy them together. Examples are abrasives, grinding machines, power transmission equipment, and materials handling equipment. Many firms spread their activities over a number of product lines. The entire product complex of a firm is called its *product mix.*

Some of the most difficult problems of product management cluster around the question: What should belong to our product mix? Closely allied to this is the range of items or varieties to be offered within each product line. There are important questions of price levels to be charged, quality standards, and guarantees to be offered. Quality as a consideration includes the whole range of product specifications and design. It also involves the question of whether the company wishes to be a leader in design or a follower of others who carry on the pioneering work.

The degree of custom manufacturing to meet the needs of individual buyers versus quantity production of a limited range of product types is a significant problem of product-planning policy. An important consideration is the type and amount of engineering and amount of engineering and other services to be offered prior to, during, and after sale. For some industrial goods, engineering service is vital to a successful selling program and to continued consumer goodwill, even though it requires large expenditures and is subject to abuse.

Determining how much of each product line to manufacture and when it should be made is an important part of the product-planning task. Related closely to this is the practice to be pursued in warehousing stock. These questions are affected by the ability of management to forecast sales. Mistakes in judgment resulting in overproduction are painfully apparent and may cause substantial loss. Those that result in underproduction and inability of a company to take advantage to market demands are much less apparent, but can be just as serious to the welfare of the firm.

Another type of product decision related to the dropping of items or even of entire product lines. This activity tends to be less will organized than many others connected with product planning. It is more satisfying to add items than it is to drop them, and many manufacturers have been shocked by the large number of slow-moving of unprofitable products that come to light in a critical review of their offerings.

Finally, there are questions about the procedure by which new articles are to be added to the product mix. The development of new products within the company itself through research and development activities is a very common method. Other methods are copying unpatented products of other firms, negotiating royalty arrangements, and purchase from outside sources, either of the product itself with manufacturing and sales rights or of an entire company with its product mix and its manufacturing and marketing organization.

PRODUCT PLANNING AS A COMPETITVE WEAPON

Industrial marketing is characterized by keen competition. Competitive behavior takes several main forms: the product-planning and development activity that shapes the product mix being offered, the price levels at which these products are sold, the services rendered the customer, and selling and advertising programs. Of these forms of competition, product planning is probably the most important. Furthermore, its stature as a competitive weapon seems to be increasing.

The economy of the United States is growing steadily and becoming increasingly dynamic and complex. More customers request special product variations to meet real or fancied needs. Buyers are increasingly critical as the purchasing function becomes more professional. Technical research is growing rapidly in importance and has resulted in vastly improved products, materials, and manufacturing processes. Many companies find that from one third to one half of their total sales are of products that were not being produced 10 years before. Another factor contributing to the increasing importance of product policy is the higher break-even point characteristic of modern industry, which results mainly from the widespread adoption of mechanization and automation. Unless the product mix is properly adjusted to market needs, sales may be too low to support the high fixed cost.

One difficulty in effective management of product planning and development is that the product mix of a company is shaped by a multitude of forces, many of which are not within the control of its executives. This means that a considerable amount of product management effort must consist of skillful adjustment of shifting market opportunities and to competitive action. Since the area of direct control is smaller than in many other types of management activity, it is vital to follow a purposeful policy rather than to drift with the tide.

Every manufacturing company is to some degree unique in that it has its own history behind it, particular personalities who have shaped its growth, its own inventory of skills and know-how, a certain assembly of production equipment and labor, a distinctive sales organization, set of market contacts, and fund of goodwill. These aspects of the enterprise represent both strength and weaknesses in relation to which decisions regarding the product mix must be made. It is management's responsibility to take them into account in looking ahead to determine the product policy most profitable during the foreseeable future.

These strengths and weakness of the firm are not immutable over time. Effective correction of company weakness and continued growth in corporate strength require forward planning. The formulation of a product-planning program for 5 years, perhaps 10 years, ahead can provide a significant guide to changes in the enterprise deemed desirable and feasible.

The fundamental forces affecting the product mix of a manufacturing company will be discussed in the first section of this chapter. Second, the appraisal of company strengths and weakness will be considered as a means of formulating a sound product-planning policy. The third section will briefly discuss the organization structures used in implementing product-planning and development policy. The fourth section deals with the process of developing new industrial products, and a final short section treats product deletion.

DETERMINANTS OF PRODUCT MIX

Product policy implies a course of action or set of principles thought through in advance so as to result in a consistent pattern of decision and action regarding the product mix. Careful attention by top management to the formulation of product-planning policy is by no means standard practice. In the absence of such a policy, decisions regarding the product mix of a company are likely to be based on the pressures of the moment. Although such decisions usually take account of the dominant characteristics of the company, they often do so an intuitive basis and incompletely.

Let us seek to identify the fundamental determinants of the product mix of company in order to understand a little better the problems of making product policy. Management's role consists of adjusting the resources of the enterprise to these forces as skillfully as possible, and of guiding the firm along product paths that will lead to future growth and profit. We will limit this discussion to the determinants that are fundamental, and will make no effort to treat in detail the various specific reasons or motivations underlying company product action.

Changes in the product mix of company involve changes in the design of individual products already in the mix, changes in the variety of present product lines, the addition of products new to be company, and the elimination of products formerly in the product mix. A new product is one new to the particular company, and usually involves significant tensions, difficulties, and adjustments during its assimilation by the manufacturing, sales, and other departments within the company. By this definition, a new product need not be new to the market, only to the company. It should be born in mind, though, that the problems of introducing a hitherto unknown product differ widely from those of adding one already known to the market but new to the company.

TECHNICAL RESEARCH AND DEVELOPMENT

The most potent factor tending to broaden and diversify the product mix both of industry as a whole and of the, typical firm is scientific research. Much of this is now done by business concerns or under their sponsorship. In certain areas, such as electronics and aviation, most research is sponsored and paid for by the government, although the actual work may be done by scientists in educational institutions, research foundations, and the laboratories of business concerns. In other areas, most research is done in the laboratories of individual firms, although some of it is carried on by academic scientists either on their own or on grants from industrial concerns.

Comparatively little industrial research is basic in the sense that it is directed to the discovery of new principles or knowledge. By far the greatest industrial use of research and development is in the application of existing knowledge to the development of new products and processes or the improvement of existing ones. The rare of technological change is accelerating, and technical research is unquestionably the most basic force affecting the product mix of the individual company. It underlines a number of the other determinants of product policy, which we will discuss.

CHANGES IN COMPETITORS PRODUCT MIXES

A second important determinant of a firm's product mix is found in the changes in competitors' products by companies not now considered to be competitors. This has happened increasingly in recent years, with the growing tendency of industrial firms to enlarge their product mixes and to include product lines in fields and markets not previously served. Changes in competitive products represent a direct challenge to a company, and if the change is a truly significant improvement, it may prove disastrous unless it can be matched or surpassed within a reasonable length of time. This matter of the time element explains why firms seemingly in a solid product position spend large sums on research to discover new products that render their present ones obsolete. When asked why his firm was doing this, one chief executive replied, "If we don't, some one else will."

In addition to changes in their product designs, competitors may make changes in their overall product mix and put a firm at a competitive disadvantage. As will be pointed out later, there are important forces favoring a product mix of considerable breadth. Broadening product lines may be a real advantage in distributor relation and in lowering selling costs. The number of competitors may change. An increase in numbers is likely to result in keener competition and lowered profit margins. Significant increases in numbers of competitors is especially likely in industries where the capital investment necessary for entry is modest. In such situations, a product that enjoys a rapid increase in sales is likely to attract many new entrants into the field, some of whom will not survive the period of consolidation, or shakeout, as it is sometimes called. In industries that require large investment, increases in the number of competitors are less dramatic. When they occur, the new competitors tend to reach for volume by cutting price, which reduces both the total sales and the gross profit rate of the original innovator. The result is that as soon as a firm introduces a new product on the market, it starts research to improve it and to find new products to replace it when competition develops.

CHANGES IN MARKET DEMAND FOR PRODUCT LINES

Although declines in demand are most disturbing to management and may result in an expansion of the product mix in an effort to replace lost business, upward changes are also of significance. Management's responsibility is to capitalize as fully as possible on expanding product fields just as much as to meet the challenge of declining markets. These changes in product demand are of various types.

Shift in Customer's product Mix. The industrial marketer, by definition, sells his product to other business either for incorporation in their products or for use in running their business. Materials that enter customer products are therefore vulnerable to changes in the product lines manufactured by customers. It the customer is himself an industrial goods producer selling to other industries, his shift may be triggered by changes *his* customers have found necessary. Such a chain reaction may have several links, all within the field of industrial marketing. In contrast, the immediate customer may be a manufacturer of customer goods, and a change in his product mix will have repercussions because of his efforts to satisfy ultimate consumers more precisely with his offerings. The widespread use of annual models in the consumer field introduces a regular periodicity to changes and intensifies the need for planning ahead. Many annual models are designed years before they appear, and the seller of components or equipment who fails to establish and maintain sales and other contacts through which to learn about such changes, and to provide materials or equipment to facilitate them may suddenly find his product obsolete.

In addition to the product demand shifts brought about the customer's changes in product line design to meet their own customer needs, some regular customers may engage in diversification programs that expand their product mix and offer opportunities for sale of additional quantities or for modification of the seller's product mix to capitalize on additional quantities or for modification of the seller's product mix to capitalize on additional business available from them. Since diversification programs often grow out of a decline in business or the fear of a future decline, there may well be concurrent drops in demand.

Some customers may pursue a policy of simplification of product mix. If this is confined to dropping low-volume items, the decline in their purchases will not be large. However, a drastic simplification of the total product mix, involving the elimination of some lines that are selling in substantial volume, will cause a significant shrinkage in purchasing requirements.

Changes in availability or cost of materials or components. A material or part used in making an end product may become scare or its price may go up so as to distort the competitive relationships in either the components or the end product market. This necessitates product modification or change by the firm that makes the components.

For example, during recent years the price of tin has been increasing, until in 1965, as reported in *Sales Management*, January 1, 1965, the cost of a tin needed to coat a tin can was about four times that of the aluminium required for the same purpose, and the price of the combined steel and tin sheet in a tin can was greater than that of a sheet composed entirely of aluminum. The United States Steel Company developed a vapor-coating process for coating light-gauge, flat-rolled steel sheets with aluminum. It thus sought to retain the steel tonnage that had formerly gone into tin cans, even at the expense of expanding the market for its competitor material, aluminium.

Changes in manufacturing processes. Changes in manufacturing methods by customer firms may affect the demand for the supplying company's product. This is most likely for manufacturers of major special-purpose machines, since a change in the manufacturing process may render them obsolate. A producer of raw or processed materials can also be affected because of the considerable freedom of choice that exists among the materials of which a product may be made. A change in a customer's manufacturing process may result in a larger yield from each unit of material, so that he needs to buy less of the material to produce the same output.

Shifts in location of customers. Transportation cost are important for many types of industrial goods. These costs limit the geographical extent of the market that can be profitably served by an industrial marketer, and any shift to customers out of this market area can result in major declines in sales and the necessity for replacing this lost business with other products. Sometimes, migration of customers or potential customers into the are economically served by a producer helps offset losses from outward migration. Some manufacturers, however have been so closely tied to particular industries-for example, textile-that large-scale migration becomes a death sentence unless the supplier also moves.

Changes in levels of business activity. The examples just given of changes in product demand are based upon market changes of various types. There may also be changes in demand because of seasonal fluctuations in the industries served. Nearly every producer facts some types of seasonal pattern of sales, and also is vulnerable in greater or less extent to major shifts in the level of general business. Some companies have extended their product mix by adding lines whose seasonal patterns offset those of their present lines, and thus have obtained a reasonably even rate of total production and sales activity throughout the year. This consideration also applies to distributors who may feel the need for a product mix that evens out seasonal fluctuations.

In somewhat similar fashion, some companies have sought to add product lines less sensitive to business-cycle fluctuation than are their existing ones. Many manufacturers of machinery, particularly in the major equipment groups, are concerned about their sensitivity to cyclical drops in demand and would like to meet this drop through diversification. Cyclical fluctuations are often to the rolling type in that demand does not decline in all industries at the same time. When this happens, a supplier who diversifies to sell to a number of industries may diminish the sharpness and extent of the decline in his sales volume.

In addition to changes in general business activity, there may be variations in local or regional markets or in individual industries.

Government controls. The last several decades have been a period of war and general tension in international relations. It seems certain that for many years in the future there will be a high level of government spending for national defense, coupled with the possibility of limited-scale military action. Under such conditions, certain materials are of great strategic importance, and the government may take steps to limit their usage for civilian purposes in order to manufacture military material or to build stockpiles. Such government controls have widespread ramifications through industry, and tend to cause major changes in sales volume for particular product lines. When there is no possibility of substituting materials, little product action can be taken. Frequently, however, such a tight material situation may encourage experimentation and research on substitute materials to perform the function. This leads to changes in product offerings.

Difficulties in predicting product demand changes. Although marketing research is of great assistance in measuring trends in demand for products and thus aids in predicting future demands, considerable uncertainty will always remain. This has led some managements to diversify product lines in order to spread to risk of unforeseen declines in demand for particular items.

Forces tending to broaden product mix

Several forces have the effect of tending to broaden the product mix of the industrial goods marketer. Let us briefly discuss the most important of them.

Industrial buyers prefer to buy several product lines from one source. The industrial buyer prefers to buy several products from one source of supply instead of a single item or line from each of several sources. This preference stems from the time saved in purchasing, from the benefits of reliance on a single source for technical service and for settling of complaints; from pooling shipments of several products at lower transportation cost, and from the possibility of price savings on quantity purchases. Furthermore, because the combined purchases of several lines represent a sum large enough to be quite important to the supplier and his salesman, the buyer may feel that he will get more service and attention than he would if he dealt with several suppliers.

Interestingly enough, while the industrial buyer's tendency to protect his continuity of supply of each important article from such risks as fire, strikes, and other disturbances by splitting his purchases among two or more suppliers might be expected to limit the effect of this factor on expansion of suppliers' product lines, it actually has precisely the opposite effect. If the split is made by simply dividing total purchases of each article among several suppliers, the effect is to reduce the total volume of sales each manufacturer of the article can hope to get. If his finances or facilities enable him to handle more than that, he must get it by making and marketing some other product. If the buyer seeks to achieve his purpose by the less intelligent method of placing a limit on his dollar purchases from any one supplier, he not only limits the supplying firm's potential volume but also makes it impossible for the supplier to increase his sales except by adding items that can be sold to some other industry. This usually involves adding a new line to the product mix.

Industrial salesmen can effectively sell several lines. Provided the product lines sold by an industrial salesman do not require a high degree of technical knowledge or a radically different type of knowledge for each line, it is feasible for him to sell several products. There is, of course, an inevitable dilution of his knowledge and selling skills and time as the number of product lines is increased, and the reaches a point where the addition of further lines will drop the level of his sales skill below the needs of the customer. It is important to be sure that the salesman is at least above this threshold of competence for most of the accounts he will be selling to. It is to be expected that some customers will require more technical help than he can supply, and usually an industrial producer provides for this by having a technical service department to back up the salesman.

Marketing costs reduced by several product lines. When a salesman is handling a number of product lines, the fixed cost involved in customer contacts is spread over the sales of the several products. With several product lines, there is more chance that his call will coincide with a buying cycle in one of the lines, and thus there is a higher probability of making sales than would be true if he handled a single product line. This increase in sales volume per call results in a lower percentage of direct sales expense. Marketing costs are also reduced by spreading the expense of company institutional advertising and marketing administration over several product lines.

Special put-ups incubate new products. Every manufacturing company has a particular structure, a particular product mix, particular behavior patterns, and other factors that distinguish it from other manufacturers. These differences affect it's need for purchased products. Thus, the buyer finds it necessary to make many compromises in product specifications between his ideal needs and what the market offers. If such compromises become too expensive or inconvenient, he may ask his supplier to produce special variations, which are often called special put-ups. A few of these may be found to serve a fairly general need among customer firms, and may be added to the supplier's line, thereby broadening it.

Several product more appealing to distributors. Many manufacturers market through industrial distributors. The manufacturer of a single product line may find that its sales represent such a small proportion of the total sales of his distributors that it receives little attention, so he has little bargaining power with the distributor in efforts to improve sales effectiveness. As the number of a manufacturer's product lines increases, assuming that they fit into the distributor's markets and capacities, the relationship improves, and he is able to get more help from distributors and finds them generally more receptive to suggestions regarding sales and inventory coverage as well as selling methods.

Unutilized capacity. Perhaps the most important single force driving manufacturers to broaden their product mix stems from unutilized capacity in some part of the business. This may be in production equipment, in the marketing organization, in the research department, in financial capacity or in management skills-in fact, in any aspect of the enterprise. The existence of unutilized capacity usually stems from changes of the types just discussed. In some instances, these changes can be foreseen with adequate analysis, while in others they are very difficult or impossible to predict.

Another source of unutilized capacity arises because increases in production or marketing capacity can rarely be made in small increments. This is particularly true of production facilities, which are usually made up of complexes of machines interrelated in function. When demand outruns existing facilities and a new equipment complex is bought, there may be a period in which it is not totally utilized in satisfying existing demand, and there is pressure on management to find new products to keep it busy. Similarly, when a marketing organization is set up to serve a particular market for a single product line, it often becomes apparent that the salesmen could handle other lines as well, and pressure is generated to find products they can sell profitably.

The management of a profitable firm may not find it necessary or desirable to pay out all profits in dividends to stockholders. Retained earnings become part of the capital the company and must be put to work instead of being allowed to languish in the cash account. The management of the average profitable company must constantly search for new product opportunities to put its earnings to work.

Utilization of by-products. Many industrial processes involve by-products as an inevitable concomitant of production of the main line. It is rare that some use cannot be found for what would otherwise be waste, and considerable effort and attention may be applied to the problem of getting the maximum possible return out of such by-products. If successful, this leads to expansion of the number of lines in the product mix.

The various forces just described are largely external to the business and tend to mold the product mix of a manufacturing company. The company, of course, does not assume a passive role in this, but may attempt to innovate in both products and marketing methods and thus have an impact on the environment. The task of management is that of skillful adjustment plus forward planning. The influence a company can bring to bear in shaping its product mix is greatly affected by its character and by the circumstances in which it operates. Let us examine some of them.

Appraisal of company strengths and weaknesses

In many respects, a business enterprise may be compared to a human being. Definite flows and rhythms of activity characterize it. A company has a physical structure of a certain size and shape, and a power to perform that reflects its strength and endurance. Intelligence of a certain level is brought to bear in the combined efforts of the people who constitute its management and work force. It has certain behavior patterns that are the product of past environment and policy and do not change rapidly. A company may display imagination in its activities, or may not; the degree of alertness and response to both internal and external challenge varies widely among firms. There is room for argument about whether the people in a firm create and maintain the corporate character or the corporation attracts people who fit into its character and personality. Perhaps the firm's chief difference from the human organism is that a corporate form of organization makes possible an indefinite life span, whereas the life span of human being is finite.

The variety of the forces that influence the particular product mix and industrial marketer offers to buyers makes it especially important that management develop product-planning policy with the greatest care. Not only will such a policy guide the addition of new products that mesh sell into the company's accustomed operations, but it will indicate the general directions in which management should move to correct practices, which, if unchecked, will cripple its earning power in future years.

A well-conceived product policy also charts the general course the company is to follow, and thus enables research personnel and others throughout the organization to move in directions that give promise of profitable returns. In the absence of such a chart, considerable manpower and funds are liable to be committed to projects later abandons when management really faces up to its decision to move the product into semiworks or full-scale manufacturing and sales. Such mistakes are not only costly to the enterprise, but also can have unfortunate effects on the morale of the organization. Finally, a product policy tends to assure that worthwhile opportunities will not be overlooked because middle managers do not know what top management wants.

A sound product policy must be thought through for several years in advance, because a substantial number of years may elapse between the decision to move ahead on a promising idea and the time when a resulting new product is actually earning profits for the company. In fact, there is no area of business management decision where so long a time leg exists between an initial green light to explore a new idea on a limited scale and the final goal of profitable operations. The situation is aggravated because financially during his time everything is going out and nothing is coming in.

The general policy guides for product planning, which result from the appraisal processes being discussed, find their application in defining the general areas of product search. In considering specific new product ideas, however, management does not always keep these general product policies in sufficiently sharp focus to aid in the screening process. For such applications, these guides should be translated into a series of questions, checklists, or formulas to make certain that all aspects of product suitability are taken into account in arriving at a decision.

The general method of appraising a company's capabilities is to take an inventory of its present position and to trace the route by which it has arrived there. An important part of this procedure is to make continuous comparisons with competitors. Such comparison is not limited to industrial marketers who make comparable product lines, but should be extended to those who make goods that can serve as satisfactory substitutes for the firm's products. Although the yardstick of competitive practice is reasonably adequate for most situations, in some cases competition may be so weak that other yardsticks must be found in order to make sound appraisals of company capabilities. Such yardsticks may have to be adapted from analogous situations and, while necessarily crude, are nonetheless useful.

A detailed appraisal of capabilities is beyond the scope of this discussion, because it would involve an extent and depth of coverage not necessary to illustrate the general idea and because many of the details are peculiar to the individual company and have no general application. It will suffice to consider the appraisal in terms of product mix, production facilities, processes, materials and labor, research and development, technical service, marketing organization and activities, financial resources, executive groups, and ownership groups.

Product mix audit. The first step here is to analyze sales, gross profits and net profits, if at all possible, or if net profits are not available by products, contribution of each product or product group to general overhead and net profit for the most recent annual accounting period available and for a period of several years prior to that time. A 10-year period is normally adequate, while anything less than a 5-year period will not present a very complete picture. The exact period chosen depends not only on the availability of records, but also on the timing of any major fluctuations in business levels of the industry in which the company operates, as well as major fluctuations in general business.

The amount of detail in which such an analysis should be made depends on the character of the product mix itself. Certainly, product lines should be studied separately and probably the most important items within each line. In addition to analyses by product lines and some items within each line, important additional information will be gained if the distribution of such product sales and profits can be shown by industry markets. Another dimension of experience that can be very useful in appraising the present product mix related to the end uses of different product lines. Thus, the sales volume of electric motors is spread among a wide range of considerably smaller listing.

The type of analysis just sketched is incomplete as a reflection of the adequacy of the product mix unless it can be compared with similar information about competitive companies. Although at times it may be possible to obtain detailed information about individual competitors, the more usually accessible information is limited to sales and often consists of estimates of total industry sales. This makes it possible to calculate share of market figures by various product lines and, in some cases, to analyze them by industry markets and, at times, by end uses. Such share-of-market figures are a measure of total company sales performance for particular product lines. This performance includes not only the product but also the price at which it is sold, the amount and quality of the marketing effort expanded, and similar factors. Because the influence of the product is so important in the total result, it becomes necessary to separate this from the total picture of sales results and to analyze product attributes in comparison to those of competitive product lines. Thus, it is possible to judge the skill of the company in keeping abreast of or ahead of competitive product offerings. In such comparisons, the effect of services offered should not be ignored.

Coupled with these analysis, a field survey measuring the attitudes of customers and prospects regarding the company and its product offerings can be very helpful.

Production facilities, processes, materials, and labour. There should be an analysis of the production activities of the company in terms of equipment and other facilities used, processes of manufacture, materials used, and labour force. This analysis would likewise be historical, for past behavior is often the most accurate basis on which to forecast future behavior. In addition to a detailed description of the plant and equipment devoted to various product lines, the study should include measurement of the degree of utilization and some indication of production efficiency.

The type of production know-how possessed by the company personnel is also important. For example, in the chemical business one company is highly skilled in applying many of the techniques of large-scale production to what is essentially a small-quantity operation, while another is equally skillful in wringing the last fraction of the penny out of cost through large-scale operation in making and marketing chemicals by the carload or trainload. A firm that makes speciality castings has developed skills in metallurgical manipulation and precision in making exactly the products its market needs. Comparisons with competitors practices in production should also be made. Much can be learned about the alertness of a company by studying the degree to which it has been an innovator of new methods of production or has been quick to adopt such improved methods.

Comparisons of production cost by product lines with competitive costs, when available, reveal both strengths and weaknesses. It is rare that a company is equally efficient in the production of its various products, and his pattern often suggests promising areas for new product expansion. This information about competitors is hard to come by, since cost information is usually carefully guarded and different methods of allocating costs make comparison difficult. Shrewd guesses can often be made on the basis of fragmentary facts.

Research and development. The size and types of activities carried on by the research and development staffs and the history of changes over a period of several years indicate the growth or lack of growth and the activities in which these groups have concentrated and presumably have special skills. Of even more importance, however, is the record the actual accomplishments of the research and development staffs over a period of time in terms of product improvement, development of new products, and assistance in uncovering new applications of old products. It is difficult to find yardsticks of measures the efficiency of research. One of the most useful comparisons is to study the research activities and accomplishments of competitive companies. Such comparisons will reveal the role management expects its research and development group to play in each of the companies covered.

It is also important to understand the areas of research within which people have special skills and know-how. For instance, a firm whose research group is especially skillful in inorganic chemical research will be handicapped in moving into a product area that requires organic research.

Technical service. Many industrial products require some degree of technical service in the selling program. This need arises primarily because customers do not know exactly how to use the product, or because particular customers want to use it to get special unusual effects in their end products or want to use it under unusual conditions.,

If the service needed is relatively simple, a properly trained salesman can handle it. If it is complex, a teamwork operation probably will be necessary. The salesman uncovers the need for service, gets a general picture of the problem, and calls on a technical service unit in the home office to do the work. A reputation for rendering good technical service is hard to get and not easy to keep. Not all firms have it hat think they do. This is a point in our appraisal where we may find a customer attitude survey worthwhile.

Marketing organization and activities. One prime function of the marketing division of an industrial goods company is to maintain adequate contact and communication with user customers and prospects, or with the various types of distributors who handle the company's product lines. It is important to know how the sales force is organized in terms of product lines handled and markets served, and whether the organization structure is flexible enough to absorb new products or new product lines without complete rebuilding. The quality of the distributor organization may be a source of major strength or weakness. There are never enough competent and aggressive distributors to satisfy all competing sellers, and some companies have been more successful than others in attracting and holding a strong distributor organization.

The skill of industrial advertising managers and industrial advertising agencies varies widely, and this potential resource justifies careful assessment. The present activities and the past contribution of the marketing research department to decision making will provide some indication of its value as a source of company strength. Finally, a very important marketing resource may be the goodwill the company has earned among customers in its markets. This is intangible and difficult to measure, but may be very important in facilitating the successful introduction of new products.

Throughout the evaluation of these various aspects of the company's marketing talents, comparisons with competitive facilities will make possible more meaningful judgments on strengths and weaknesses. Another factor of special importance is the degree to which the marketing organization and the distributor organization are currently working at capacity. As was pointed out earlier in this chapter, one of the important forces tending to broaden the product mix is that buyers prefer to purchase several product lines from one salesman and that a salesman can sell several product lines with reasonable effectiveness. One of the real strengths of a company may be found in excess capacity in some phase of its marketing activities and the opportunity this offers for the efficient marketing of new product lines.

Financial capabilities. The financial capabilities of a company and its financial history are relatively easy to measure, and they represent one of the most important controlling factors in planning for new products. The successful introduction of a new product may require a substantial investment in research and development work, in various types of technical and marketing studies, in a careful program of product evaluation, in the construction of a semiworks manufacturing plant, in the addition of new plant and equipment, and in outlays for market development work. Besides knowledge of the funds available for allocation to new products, it is vital to assess management's willingness to spend them for this purpose. This is particularly true in companies whose stock is closely held. The ownership interest may not wish to assume the risks to new ventures, even though substantially higher rates of return might be secured.

The investment necessary to add a new product of line of the established product mix varies widely. Production of one types of chemicals and of certain metals demands a large-scale investment and makes it impossible for a company with limited resources to consider entry into such fields. In contrast, entry is relatively easy in industries where capital requirements are low. Such industries tend to be characterized by keen competition and low rates of overhead expense. Companies accustomed to operating in high-investment industries are justifiably cautious about entering low-investment fields because experience has shown that they may have great difficulty in effectively competing on price.

As with the other aspects of an enterprise's resources, evaluation requires comparison with competitive financial resources. For example, if a manufacturing company is planning to embark on a particular new product program, the financial ability of competitors to follow suit is an important consideration.

Capabilities and attitude of the executive group. One of the most important factors in appraising a business is the judgment, skill, imagination, alterness, and physical vigor of the top executives and the middle management group. In part, this has already been revealed through the study of each aspect of the company's activities over the recent period. However, a certain amount of good fortune may have aided a mediocre team of executives, and it is desirable to be coldly objective in assessing the capacities of this group. One important characteristic is to be found in the age distribution of the executive personnel. If they are bunched at certain age levels, the company may face serious problems of retirement in a short span of time. Another factor to be investigated is the extent to which the company has a definite and well-thought-out program for uncovering and developing executive talent.

Two vital factors are the willingness of management to continue spending money on a promising new product until its potentialities are developed, and the courage and judgement to cut its losses and pull out when a product's early promise proves illusory. For example, consider a firm that has been operating in a field where the product development period is three or four years before pay-off begins. If it adds a product line that requires five or six or seven years to develop past the beak-even point, top management may get discouraged and pull out when the turning point is just over the next hill, unless the chief executives thoroughly understand the nature of the new venture and are emotionally committed to it.

Finally, there is the question of how nearly the executive group is working at capacity level. If the key executive are spread thinly over a vast range of problems and responsibilities, this may preclude additions of new products whose success depends on careful executive attention and follow-through. In order to secure the most realistic interpretation of executive strengths and weakness, some consideration should also be given to competitors' executives.

Organising for product planning and development

From our discussion so far it is evident that effective management of the product mix requires an unusually broad understanding of the company as it is and as it hopes to be, and of its competitive relationships, not only among its immediate group of rivals but also among producers of alternative or substitute materials, which often provide keen competition. However, the real core of the organization problem lies in the fact that product planning and product development cut across the entire operation of a company to a degree that exceeds any other function of comparable significance. The marketing department, the production department, the research department, the financial group, the legal counsel, and others are inevitably involved in the process of developing new products.

The scope of the product-planning and development task varies widely among companies in the same industry, depending on the method of operation that has evolved over a period of time. Some firms stress innovation of new products and have strong research groups. Others do not attempt to pioneer to the same degree, though they conduct a limited amount of research in the belief that this activity will pay for itself.

Still others pursue a follower policy and copy new products that have proved successful. Such a major differences in management philosophy obviously are reflected in the size and importance of the research function, and in the organization of the product-development process.

The essential product management jobs to be performed in an average company include:

1. A review of the product mix at regular intervals, and decision making on redesigning, adding, or dropping product lines or items.

2. A continuous radar-type monitoring of external forces, such as declines and growths in demand for particular products and in particular markets, product changes in competitive offerings, changes in technology, and so forth.

3. Carrying on technical research of the type appropriate to the particular company situation and dealing with both products and processes.

4. Providing for adequate technical service to customer in the application of present products, and assistance in evaluating any special requirements.

5. Securing adequate market-development effort, both during the process of evaluating or developing a new product and in introducing the product and expanding demand when it is ready for sale.

6. Carrying on a purposeful search for new-product ideas.

7. Achieving coordination and minimum-time requirements in the whole product development process from the initial idea through preliminary appraisal into technical research, semiworks, full-scale production, and market introduction.

Various organization arrangements of the development function are found in different companies. Although some of this variety reflects particular company situations, much of it stems from the fact that there is no clear-cut, obvious, or generally accepted way to organize for effective performance of a business function that is so inherently heterogeneous in its nature. Furthermore, management's appreciation of the need for a well-thought-out organization and procedure for the purpose varies among companies. This seems to be especially true of firms whose product lines are fairly stable and who do not create large numbers of new products. In such companies, the essentially sporadic nature of additions to the product mix tends to lead management to ignore the values of a well-worked-out procedure. Conversely, in companies where change in product mix is constant it is more likely that some define assignment of responsibility for procedure will be made.

Types of organisation

In one form of organization, the president or some other top executive take an interest in new product development and devotes time and attention to seeing that proper activities are undertaken. This has the advantage that the new product coordinator can speak with authority, and there is less danger of jealousy and friction between the departments that must participate. The danger, however, is that such major executive are usually so busy solving critical problems that they do not have adequate time for new product development, even though they recognize its vital importance. In an alternative arrangement, the top executive has a staff assistant who speaks for him and acts as coordinator and expediter.

A second plan of organization gives the research director and his staff substantial authority in making decisions regarding the product mix and in managing the development process. Many research directors feel that this is the most logical procedure, and point out that their job is to insure company profits in future years through development of salable products and through continuous reductions in production cost. With this arrangement, however, it is usually considered desirable to have one or more committees made up of key people from marketing, production, general management, finance, and sometimes the legal department. The function of such committees is to review the recommendations of the research director regarding projects he believes should be worked on, and also to evaluate project at various stages in their development. As the semiworks stage is approached, in which a substantial commitment of funds may be involved, there is usually an approval procedure that often involves a committee. The approval of keep personnel is also essential when the decision is made to move ahead with commercial-scale manufacture and market introduction. Despite the use of such committees, the essence of this arrangement is that the research department acts as the coordinator of the effort.

The third organization arrangement is to assign the responsibility of product planning and development to a special department. The functions of such a department and its relations to the other departments within a business are usually carefully delineated. This approach recognized that management of the product mix is a definite job, which will be done more effectively by fixing responsibility. There is substantial evidence that this approach to product planning and product development is on the increase.

A variation of the product-planning department is the new-product or commercial development department found in certain companies. Such a department is more likely to be used when the company has several main operating divisions, each with its own research and product-planning groups. It is assumed that these operating departments are capable of managing their particular product lines, but that they will not be interested in exploring or competent to explore lines substantially outside their present fields of activities and interests. Thus, new-product departments have evolved on the basis of providing for exploration of interesting new products and new applications that otherwise would not be developed. Such departments frequently are empowered to produce and sell small quantities of new products as one means of determining whether there is a real market need and what is the extent of that need. This type of organization unit is on the increase. A 1965 study made by Booz, Allen and Hamilton, which embraced 54 well-managed firms, showed that, in 1956, 12 of them had new-product departments; in 1960 the figure was 28; in 1965 it was 46. In 1965, these firms introduced 366 new products, 67 percent of which are successful-a figure well above the usual batting average.

Even in companies without new-product department, analogous situations may arise, usually as a by-product of a research program. A research director may have faith that the new product has a field, but he may be unable to persuade his management that it is worthwhile to spend money on it. Some companies definitely recognize that this situation may arise, and the research department is empowered to undertake small-scale production and sale. Sometimes, this is done with the active blessing and support of top level executives, sometimes with their tacit acquiescence, and now and then without their knowledge.

Another type of organization places responsibility for the product line on a product manager. In a number of industrial companies, several product lines may be sold by same sales force, but for each line there may be product managers who have a staff relationship to the sales force and who work through the manager of the sales force in their relations with the salesmen. If the other duties of the product manager leave him adequate time to carry on the product-planning responsibilities, this arrangement may work reasonably well.

It is necessary that an overall procedure be developed and well understood throughout the organization for development of new products. If this is not done, a product manager may meet much resistance from other departments. In particular, production department executives, who believe, with some justice, that they are being judged on their cost performance, tend to resist anything that might slow up production and thus raise costs. This type of resistance is encountered during the stage of transition of a new product form research and development into regular manufacturing operations. It must be recognized as a natural and inevitable situation, and steps must be taken to get around it. In one company, the research department had in its own budget a fund, which could be used to assist production groups in various plants in the experimental process of adapting new products to production procedures.

Some companies conduct their product management work largely through committees. This may work reasonably well, provided there is either one individual who takes the product-planning and development function as major responsibility or, less desirable, the procedure is so well spelled out that action cannot be avoided or unduly delayed. For such committee activity to be fruitful, however, a considerable amount of staff work must be carried on by someone in preparing material for committee consideration so that meeting time can be spent efficiently. Although committees are essential working tools in a product-planning and development program, they appear to be used most effectively as an adjunct to a staff group with responsibility for seeking the most profitable product mix.

An American Management Association study, reported in *Sales Management*, July 5, 1963, showed that 35 percent of the companies reporting had a vice president as head of their new-product planning and development work. In 50 percent of the firms, the man in charge of new product work, whatever his title, reported to the chief executive officer. In this year, 58 percent of the firms had product-planning committees, as against 33 percent in similar study in 1959. Of the total product planning committees, 69 percent were headed by members of top management, while in 1959 the figure was only 31 percent.

Despite the variety of organization forms in use, one central fact emerges: effective product planning and development require clear-cut recognition of the function and definite assignment of responsibility for it at a very high level. We will discuss typical sequences of activities in the development of new industrial products.

Managing new product development

The details of the process of new-product development vary from firm to firm. Certain types of activity must be carried on by every company, regardless of how the details may be arranged. We will direct our attention to these activity types.

Let us assume that the company has an adequate technical research department and various staff groups concerned with development engineering, technical service, marketing research, and market development. To further simplify our study, let us assume that top management has organized for the administration of product planning and product development by setting up a product planning department responsible for making decisions regarding the product mix, coordinating the activities of various company departments involved in product development, making up schedules of activities, and following through to see that the entire operation runs smoothly. Once a particular new-product development project is on the books, one man from this product planning department is likely to be appointed project supervisor. His responsibility will terminate only when the product is in full-scale production and is being marketed through the regular company organization or when it is dropped unsaleble or unprofitable.

Complicating factors

Several fundamental characteristics pervade the entire new-product development process and complicate its management. The first is that all functional units of the enterprise are involved at various points, and many of them throughout the entire process. They must be carefully mobilized and their natural resistance to cooperative action overcome. Second, many different types of activity must be carried on concurrently. Practically all of these are necessary prerequisites to later activities. Thus, there is an acute problem of skillful timing with the establishment of the target dates and follow up to determine progress. Failure to do a careful scheduling job, coupled with careful expediting, will not only result in confusion and frustration but will also stretch out the entire process longer than is necessary. For products that require a substantial amount of technical research and development work, the period from original concept of the idea until sales return a net income stream to the company is typically in the 5-10 year time span. Acceleration of this process without incurring excessive risk is obviously desirable.

A third fundamental element in new product development is the need for several stopping points at which the project is considered in all of its aspects and decisions are reached-whether it should be abandoned, put on the shelf, or continued at a given rate of work. There is no set number of such stopping points, although the most obvious occur at the point of preliminary screening of new product ideas, at the time substantial amounts of expenditures are authorized for research and development and market development programs, and at the time of decision regarding full-scale manufacture and marketing. The process of reviewing the project in its manifold technical and economic aspects at each of these stopping points becomes increasingly more detailed and thorough as larger and larger amounts of company resources must be committed by decisions to continue it.

Another basic characteristic is that new products that are quite similar to the present line in production and selling characteristics will not require a process of development to elaborate or so long as those that are more alien to the established knowledge and know-how of the company organization.

Stages in development process

These factors complicate selection of the most pertinent outline of activities or stages of activities for consideration. There is a temptation to make a detailed listing, which has the disadvantage of being confusing and also of implying time sequences among activities that may be concurrent. The other extreme is to present a very few stages in the process. This has the merit of overall simplicity but means that each stage requires substantial examination. The outline adopted here is in the midzone between these two extremes and consists of the following steps:

1. Finding new-product ideas.

2. Preliminary appraisal of new product ideas the selection of projects.

3. Research on products and markets.

4. Research on manufacturing process.

5. Semiworks operations in production and marketing.

6. Transition full-scale production and marketing.

With the exception of the second step, we have left out the appraisals that are likely to be made near the end of one stage and the beginning of the next.

Finding new-product ideas. An adequate flow of new-product ideas is essential to the most efficient management of new-product development. These ideas should be reasonably relevant to the capabilities of the enterprise, and they should be gathered in sufficient number to present a real choice of opportunities. Securing relevant ideas depends in large part on the formulation of a product-planning policy based upon careful appraisal of the enterprise and the communication of this policy throughout the organization so that each individual or group is aware of the kinds of new-product fields the company is most interested in. This procedure not only stimulates thinking in desired areas but also diminishes the number of ideas that must be discarded because of their inherent lack of suitability. Otherwise, people who submit ideas are often not aware of the yardsticks by which they are judged and become discouraged when they are consistently turned down.

Of course, the danger in utilizing a product-planning policy statement of this sort is that company personnel will develop blinders, which lead them to ignore new-product ideas with such large profit potentials that management might wisely disregard the limitations of the enterprise and set up an entirely new manufacturing and selling organization to exploit them. This danger is probably more fancied than real in most situation, although it must be accepted as a risk. It can be avoided in part in the process of communication the product-planning policy by stressing the willingness of the company to enter completely new fields, provided the growth and profit potentials appear sufficiently compelling. In fact, this can be made one of the planks in the policy platform.

Finding new-product ideas involves both the identification of the many sources from which may be derived and purposeful efforts to stimulates maximum flow from each source. Means of stimulating ideas flow consist primarily of gaining and holding the interest of individuals and groups within the organization. It is very important that adequate machinery be set up for acknowledgment, prompt review, and communication of the decision to the submitter as quickly as may be feasible. Delay is usually interpreted as lack of interest on the part of management and discourages originality more quickly than any other single factor. Financial rewards have their place in the picture, and here again prompt administration is highly important. Some companies have experimented with suggestion systems as a means of encouraging new-product ideas, and when properly managed they have been of some value. They appear to be less effective, however, in encouraging new-product ideas than in developing suggestions for other phases of company operations.

The major sources of product ideas include field surveys of users, prospects, and distributors, as well as surveys or related or different markets, the research and development staff, the technical service staff, salesmen, executive personnel of the company, analyses of competitive product mixed, analyses of company sales, the patent department, inventors, literature search, and various outside source such as a trade associations, professional societies, trade shows and exhibits, and so forth.

Field surveys represent a define effort to uncover industrial needs for product modifications and for new products. Although a technically trained salesman should always be alert to such needs, he is often too busy selling to devote adequate attention to searching out new product opportunities. Furthermore, a field survey may be directed as much to the research personnel of customers and prospects as it is to their buying and production personnel. The research groups are working on products the customer will have in production sometime in the future. Since the new-product development process often takes years takes years, an intelligent search for ideas must look to the period ahead, rather than strictly to the present product lines of customer. The same kind of forward thinking applies to new serve future manufacturing process.

In addition to the study of present customers and prospects, a new product field survey may will be directed at related markets or, in some cases, entirely new markets, provided there is a logical reason for considering entry into them. In one progressive manufacturing company, a new product was developed for the printing field because the company had unusual manufacturing know-how that could be applied to the product. Prior to that time, no sales had been made to the printing industry, and therefore it was necessary to recruit, train, and operate a new sales force. When this had been done, the company management realized that the sales force was capable of handling more than one product line for the printing trade, and so it undertook a study of printing to uncover new items that could be made efficiently with the company's know-how and manufacturing facilities. This study revealed that there was a real opportunity for an article that would appreciably increase labor productivity in one aspect of the printing operation.

The research and development departments represent unusually fruitful source of new-product ideas. Many of the men in research and development are highly imaginative and are accustomed to working with new concepts. Although they are not always fully aware of the commercial requirements of new products, this limitation can be met in part by communication of the product-planning policy and more largely through the efforts of the research director to create in his staff an understanding of cost and profit problems. One important characteristic of research workers as a source is that they are typically thinking ahead to future technology and are not too heavily influenced by current industrial practices.

In addition to ideas that may spring from research workers themselves, an active program of research in a company inevitably produces many by-products in terms of possible materials or equipment not among the primary objectives of the research effort. When a research project directed to a certain end turns up new-product ideas not contemplated in its original purpose, they are usually shelved in a "possible project" file or examination at a future time. Too often, they are forgotten. These by-products frequently represent promising opportunities, either for development by the company or for sale or license to other firms. One chemical company found it very worthwhile to review the new-product projects it had placed on the shelf (because they did not fit company needs closely enough), and, through license arrangements or sale, to exploit these properties and derive some income from them.

The technical service staff is in close contact with the problems of applying company products to customer needs. Such staffs frequently are specialized by customer industries and thus have an intimate knowledge of their changing needs. The technical service group usually handles customers' complaints about the technical characteristics or performance of the product. These complaints sometimes suggest new-product ideas. In general, though, the technical service group probably will suggest improvements of present products rather than new products.

The sales force as a source of product ideas suffers from a tendency to closely relate ideas to present product lines, and particularly to variations of those lines, in order to meet specific customer desires. However, the salesman is in an unusually good position to uncover opportunities for new products because of his day-to-day contact with customers and the necessity of thorough familiarity with competitive products and activities. If he is alert and has the right kind of contacts with his customers, he may be able to pick up some indications of the direction of their product planning and research, which may provide tip-offs about materials and equipment they are likely to need in the future.

The value of the industrial sales force as a source depends somewhat on the distribution policy followed by the company. If sales flow mainly through distributor channels, these provide a sort of insulation between user and company with regard to detailed knowledge of the user's needs and desires. However, even here an alert sales force will maintain close contact with some of the larger customers of distributors, and will attempt to learn all they can from the distributors and their salesmen about problems and conditions of product use. More new-product ideas will come from salesmen when a considerable portion of sales are made direct to user accounts.

Executives in sales, production, research, and general management have perspective on the needs and probably future course of the company. They represent a source of new-product ideas that should be well adjusted to company capabilities. Some of them are likely to possess an intuitive sense of profit opportunities and of the proper timing for maximum exploitation of such ideas. In addition, they are apt to have access to the high-level trade grapevines that often carry surprisingly accurate news about the product planning and research of customers and competitors, which is a raw material for new-product ideas.

An obvious, and often rewarding, source of product ideas can be found in an analysis of the product mixes of competitors. This is particularly important in determining questions about the breadth of the product line to be handled by the company sales force or by the distributing organization. The concept of full line is somewhat difficult of define. We have indicated that it is often desirable to sell more than one product line competitors appear to be selling successfully may serve as a crude yardstick in thinking through one's own product-mix policy. Analysis of company sales results by product lines and by items are useful in indicating the need for the redesign of existing products when sales decline and growth opportunities when sales increase. Such analyses should not be limited to product lines, and major items within each line be should include a breakdown by type of industry to which sales are made and, if possible, by end uses.

The company patent department is often a fruitful source of ideas because its members are trained to think in terms of new products. In the course of patent searches and in writing patent descriptions for company inventions, ideas may occur to them.

Free-lance inventors represent a source of ideas, although it appears they are not so important as they once were. This is partly a reflection of the complex technology of our day, which makes it more difficult for the individual working alone to create viable products. Nonetheless, companies still add worthwhile products brought to them by free-lance inventors. And they also turn them down, as was illustrated by Xerox, which was refused by at least two blue-chip firms before it was finally introduced.

An obvious source of ideas may be found in literature searches, both in United States publications and in foreign journals. In one instance, a both in United States publications and in foreign journals. In one instance, a piece of medical equipment was development in a foreign country and secured extensive adoption in hospitals there. It later appeared in the United States through import channels. The practice of following foreign technical literature enabled one company to have similar equipment on sale before the imports appeared.

A variety of other sources a new-product ideas may be found outside the company. These include professional society meetings, trade shows and exhibits, government research programs and publication, university research activities, consulting organizations, and other. The problem is to be sure that these sources are tapped without excessive expenditure of time and energy.

By an orderly and imaginative effort to stimulate the flow of product ideas, a satisfactory pool of them can be developed for consideration in the preliminary screening process. The mortality of new-product ideas is very high. Some years ago, the Commercial Chemical Development Association questioned 20 chemical firms about the mortality rate of new-product ideas in their experience. It was found that in order to obtain one successful new product an average of:

540 possibilities in the idea stage were considered at the research level.

448 were eliminated during screening conferences.

92 were selected for preliminary laboratory investigation.

8 were sufficiently promising to warrant further development.

7 were dropped as unsalable for unprofitable before or during the semiworks stage.

1 survived and was placed in regular production.

An average of six years and two months was required from the time an idea was originally investigated in the research department until full scale production was attained.

This study indicates the scale of shrinkage that takes place in the original fund of new-product ideas in the chemical industry as they are developed into products that eventually are marketed. Another study covering companies in a number of industries shows an overall ratio of 40 to 1 from the screening stage to successful introduction. A study by the National Industrial Conference Board, reported in the *New York Times*, October 25, 1964, showed that 1 out of every 3 products put on the market by the 87 reporting companies failed. Adding new products is a risky business, and they need to be picked carefully.

Preliminary appraisal of new-product ideas. This step has two major purposes. The first is to eliminate ideas that are clearly unworthy of further consideration and investigation. The second is to select from among the remainder those with enough promise to be set up as new-product projects for exploratory work by the technical research and development staffs. Two steps seem desirable in this process. First, the product-planning staff may measure each new-product idea against the general product-planning policy of the company. This permits a substantial reduction in the number, and the remainder will be those that merit more careful consideration. The product-planning staff may, as a second step, gather certain readily accessible date on each idea to provide the new-product committee with additional information on which to base judgment.

A new-product committee normally consists of executive from marketing, production, research, and general management, with others brought in as the occasion requires.

In this preliminary appraisal process, much reliance is properly placed on the experience and judgement of the executives present. Because of the multiplicity of factors that affect the desirability of pursuing any specific new-product idea, it is often useful to develop a checklist of questions to be answered. The checklist approach has the merit of preventing the omission of vital factors in the heat of a discussion session. If the company product mix is fairly homogeneous, one such checklist may serve the purpose; if not, it may be necessary to have more than the. Generalized types of checklists have been published by the United States Department of Commerce. One of these relates specifically to industrial products. Although it is essential that the entire range of factors be considered, it is not necessary that detailed information be available at this stage. The emphasis is, rather, on uncovering possible weak points that might lead to a decision to drop the idea.

Major factors for consideration usually include such things as expected profit potential of the new product, the competitive situation, the general adaptability of the company on the new product, and the scale of investment that would be necessary in relation to the funds the company has available. Marketing considerations include the approximate size of the market, the trends operating within it, marketing methods that would be necessary for successful scale, price structures, and so forth.

Many new-product ideas involve problems of technical design. Thus, it becomes necessary to judge the technical feasibility of the idea and estimate the likelihood of success in solving technical problems. Production consideration also enter in the form of the nature of production facilities required, approximate costs of production, availability of materials, and continuity of their supply. At times, legal considerations also enter, both as to the patent situation and as to hazards that may accompany customer use of the product.

Meetings of the new-product committee to conduct preliminary appraisals should be held at regular intervals. The committee will probably also consider projects that were approved at earlier meetings and have now reached a point requiring more detailed consideration.

Several firms have attempted to develop formulas to use as tools in making new-product decisions. Such a formula worked out for use by a fine chemical house is shown in figure 8-1, with some changes to protect confidential information. A critical total score was worked out by applying the formula in retrospect to a number of products the company had introduced and comparing scores with actual performance.

Such a formula assures that all the factors generally significant in a new-product decision are considered in a systematic, uniform manner. But its use has dangers. When men have a formula, they tend to quit thinking. Any new-product idea may have one feature that outweight all others and that is not general in the sense that few other ideas or none have it. A formula is apt to be disastrous if used by a committee or staff group composed entirely of conformists. It may work very well for a group that contains one or more highly vocal people who always look for the unusual situation.

Although the use of formulas in making new-product decisions is growing slightly, it is still confined to a relatively small number of companies.

Research on products and markets. This stage covers the technical, economic, and market research carried on after an idea has been selected as a new-product project in the preliminary appraisal. The amount of technical research necessary will vary greatly, depending on the difficulties involved in achieving a satisfactory product. The more nearly similar the new product is to those currently being manufactured, the less likely is the need for significant amount of technical work. During this stage, the physical properties of the new product are discovered, small quantities are prepared in the laboratory, research on possible uses is initiated, preliminary work on patents starts, and preliminary estimates of production costs are made. Some industrial products, especially materials and supplies, lend themselves to limited field distribution to sample quantities, and thus permit preliminary evaluation of their suitability to the needs of selected consumers. The market development staff should also prepare a study to the economic possibilities of the new product.

Research on manufacturing process. In point of time, this stage may overlap research on the product and market. The technical groups study the most feasible methods for producing the new product and development information needed for patent application. Quality control problems are investigated, and plans made for handling this problem in the semiworks and later stages. The market development staff continues the search for prospective users of the new product and carries on the limited field testing possible with laboratory quantities. This testing work is usually done by selected customers who agree to cooperate, often in return for assurance of early supply if the product proves satisfactory.

Market development groups and marketing research groups at this stage begin work on a suitable product name and package. Also, there should be careful review of the product design to make sure that all feasible suggestions gathered by the limited field evaluation have been incorporated. As a result of process-development research in this stage and product research in this and the earlier stages, together with marketing and economic data, it is possible to prepare a report containing recommendations for follow-up action in the new-product project. The project should then be reviewed by the new-product committee in the light of the study and action taken on moving into the semiworks stage, undertaking further work if information seems inadequate, conducting further research if testing has shown serious product defects, or perhaps abandoning the project.

Semiworks stage. This portion of the development process has as one of its major objectives testing of the proposed method of manufacture by actually building a limited-scale plant and producing the article in small quantities. Since larger amounts of the product are available, the market development group can conduct reasonably full-scale testing with a limited number of customers. Total production at this stage, of course, is quite small, and the quantity available must be allocated carefully in order to get the maximum amount of market information. The technical groups continue work on process development untill the operating problems at the semiworks level are solved. They also carry on use research and develop information needed for patent applications. At this point, it is also possible for a technical service group to become familiar with the use problems of the new product.

The market development group continues its program of field evaluation and sales, and with the larger quantities available it should be able to more nearly approach actual conditions of later marketing. The sales organization can start to become familiar with the new product and perhaps engage in actual sales training. During this period, also, promotional strategy for the new product should be worked out and decisions reached concerning selling methods to be used.

About this time, the brand name of the new product is chosen, and if it must be sold in a container, package design is determined. Perhaps at this point, we might be wise to briefly discuss these matters. Neither the brand nor the package plays in industrial marketing a part so important as in consumer goods. But they are significant enough to justify careful attention.

Industrial goods that are highly standardized and sold in bulk, chiefly materials, are usually not branded. The same usually is true of component parts made to specification for the buying firm or not interchangeable among the end products of competing customers. For example, tires, batteries, and spark plugs that are interchangeable among different makes of cars and command an active replacement market are branded. Most castings and machined parts are not.

Major machinery tends to be sold under the name of the maker, although subsidiary brands are sometimes used to distinguish different types of sizes of a machine. This may be true to tractors and construction equipment, for example. Auxiliary machines are usually sold under brand. Process materials are quite generally branded, as are operating supplies.

In marketing industrial goods, the brand function of identifying and distinguishing the maker's product is much more important than its job of exerting a positive persuasive force at a point of sale, as in consumer goods. As a result, there is much less need for brands to be catchy, to have euphony, to sing when pronounced. But there is some point in their having a technical or scientific flavor. Such brand names as Kazon, Zembide, Nicarb, and Glycamide illustrate this tendency. The trick seems to be to pick a name near the scientific or chemical designation of the material or article, but not so near that it is legally indefensible. In originating names, some firms seek to reinforce imagination with science by using computers to develop a large stock of pronounceable combinations of the letters in the alphabet. The result are sometimes weird.

When a firm makes and markets a family a industrial products, special problems of branding arise. In the consumer goods field each one of a family of products must stand on its own feet at the point of sale, and there is no compelling reason for a family brand, since ultimate consumers tend to rely more on what they know about the product than on what they know about its maker in choosing articles. The industrial buyer, on the other hand, is heavily influenced by what he knows about the manufacturer of a product. So a family brand or a family resemblance among brands is highly important. But as the number of products in the family grows and becomes diversified, such a family brand system may become highly complicated and bewildering.

One solution to this dilemma is to use one overriding brand, preferably the company name or the dominating element in the company name, the applies to all products, and a system of subsidiary brand names that apply to individual products. For example, the Irwin Equipment Company might make and sell the Irwin Earth Master of heavy excavation jobs, the Irwin Little Giant for finer earth-moving work, the Irwin Ditchdigger's Delight, and similar but perhaps less euphonious and more dignified brands for other construction implements. This is not the only solution, but simplicity and consistency are attributes to be earnestly sought.

The primary purposes of the industrial goods package are to protect the contents and to facilitate handling. Its use as a promotional device is definitely secondary, since the buyer usually does not have the package before him when he orders the product. But the package can contribute sales appeal if its size and shape facilitate handling by the user's material handling equipment and it fits snugly into the standard shelving or other storage facilities generally used in his warehouses, and if its color scheme is such that it can be readily located and recognized on his shelves or storage floor.

Certain materials that are corrosive, or must be delivered under pressure, or that deteriorate if exposed to air, or absorb moisture, or evaporate rapidly, to mention only a few of the may hazards, must be sold in packages that are fairly costly and often heavy. This adds to the cost of transportation and may create a package return problem that always contributes a high nuisance value and leads to disputes and misunderstandings. The manufacturer of such products can wisely afford considerable research to develop nonreturnable packages in which to deliver them.

The same is true with packages that are very heavy. For example, a firm that sells gases used in refrigeration and air-conditioning units packaged its product in two sizes of steel containers, the larger weighing 72 pounds with contents, and the smaller 40 pounds. The distributors' service men had to lug them over roofs and down into basements and other awkward places. Aluminium containers with overall weights of 64 and 35 pounds, respectively, cost more but won the hearts of service men, and so the business of the distributors who employed them.

The makers of certain kinds of industrial materials and equipment face legal hurdles in introducing new products. For example, before the producers of a chemical used in medicines can market it, he must gain approval of the Food and Drug Administration by supplying evidence that it will do what he says it will do, and will have no more than allowable toxic side effects. In order to gain clearance, he must submit the results of approved independent clinical tests to satisfy the Administration.

This requirement has both good and bad effects on the manufacturer's marketing activities.

1. It delays the introduction of the product. Not only

does it take a long time to complete clinical tests, but after they are submitted the manufacturer must await completion of any supplementary tests the Administration decides to make and the slow unwinding of its bureaucratic red tape, which is further delayed by chronic undermanning due to the niggardly policy to Congress in dealing with its budget.

2. The conduct of such clinical tests and presentation of their results in a form that suits the needs of the Administration is an art in itself.

3. The timing of the Administration's release may bear no relation to the ebb and flow of demand. Many disease are seasonal, and the release of a product at the end of the season may lose the maker a whole year in its introduction to the market. Nor can the time of release be forecast with any accuracy. So marketing plans must be prepared in detail and then held in abeyance, often to become outdated before they can be put into effect.

4. On the otherhand, once the Administration issues a release, this in itself goes far to assure users that the product will do what is claimed for it, and thus materially eases the marketing task.

The maker of a food additive must have a release from the Administration, showing that its use will have no dangerous toxic effects on the people who consume the end products containing it. The manufacturer of a plant protective material or one designed to cure or prevent diseases of animal, poultry, or plants must obtain such a release, assuring that no toxic residue remains in the meat, milk, eggs, fruits, or vegetables when prepared for human consumption. This requirement add all the handicaps mentioned above in connection with medicinal materials, but does not establish that the product will do what it is designed to do. It constitutes merely a manufacturer's hunting license to try to capture sales, and affords no particular help in doing so.

Aside from the benefits of the Administration's work in protecting the public health, most manufacturers of such materials welcome these restriction because they tend to preclude irresponsible producers from plaguing them with a type of competition very difficult to combat.

The makers of many kinds of building materials and equipment must see to it that the safety and fire-resisting properties of their products meet the requirements of the Board of Fire Underwriters and the local building codes. Since the codes differ from city to city, meeting their standards may be very cumbersome, time-consuming, and expensive.

As a result of the semiworks stage, information is usually at hand concerning production methods for full-scale operation and estimates of production costs. Likewise, the product should have proved itself in market-evaluation tests, and information about probably uses should be available. Prices will have been set during the semiworks stage, and the expected price on full-scale production will be known. With this information, it is possible to reexamine the size of the market. With all of this information, profit return on the new product can be estimated. The report is presented to the new-product committee, and if the project is approved for full-scale manufacturing and marketing it may be sent to top management for final action. This is a point at which the company commits large funds.

Full-scale manufacturing and marketing. New-product projects approved for movement into full-scale manufacturing and marketing are in the final stage of assimilation by the company organization. During the period required to get into full-scale production, various activities started earlier during the development process, such as providing packaging, shipping containers, advertising, technical literature, and the like, can be completed so that the new product will be ready for introduction to market wider than could be served with the limited quantity available in the semiworks stage.

The final step in product development is making plans and programs for introducing the new product on the market, and merging it into the product mix. In the course of doing this, a number of question must be answered. Some of the most important are the following.

1. What channels of distribution shall be used in marketing the new product? The situation is ideal, of course, when a firm can effectively sell its new product through the same channels used for its other products. This is not always possible, for the new product may serve different groups of buyers or require different marketing treatment from the items already in the line. Sometimes, plans for adding a new product must be abandoned because it cannot be marketed effectively through existing channels and cannot be sold in sufficient volume through its natural outlets to support the cost of cultivating them. Difficulties such as this should be faced long before a new product reaches the full-scale manufacturing stage, but often they are not.

2. What should be the relation of the new product to those already in the line? The new product may be a complete addition to the product mix and simply make the whole mix more attractive to prospective buyers. Or it may be complete replacement of an old product, since it will perform all the functions of the old, and perform them more effectively. Again, the new product may perform some functions more effectively than the old one, but may serve other uses no better or even less efficiently. For example, a firm whose product was a preparation that when mixed with the feed of animals cured a certain disease developed a new preparation, which was a good preventive but no better cure. The management was faced with the problem of deciding the better policy: *(a)* to discontinue production and sale of the old product, for which it had built up a considerable demand and which was widely known to the trade; or *(b)* to product the two side-by-side, thereby sacrificing some of the savings of large-scale production, and promote the one as a

cure and the other as a preventive. Sometimes, a new machine replaces an old one used in conjunction with another machine that must be replaced or scrapped when the new one is put into operation. For example, a dictating machine company brought out a new machine, which recorded on nonreusable, foldable, fileable belts instead of on wax cylinders that could be shaved and reused. Buyers of the new machine had no use for the shaving machines (also sold by the company) they had in operation. The dictating machine company had the alternative of *(a)* continuing to produce the old machines until all customers gradually shifted to the new, or *(b)* discontinuing manufacture of the old machine and putting all its eggs in the new basket.

3. At what price should the new product be sold, and what pricing policies should be adopted with respect to it? When the new article is entirely new and replaces no item previously in the line, this problem is highly complex. Complexity becomes even more confusing when it replaces an old product already in the line, for which there are established prices and pricing policies. If the new product is highly attractive and there is obviously a ready demand for it, should its price be fixed at a very high figure that will enable the firm to amortize all its development costs and the cost of special equipment needed in its production within the six-month to two-year period that usually elapses before serious competition develops? Or is it better policy to fix the price at about the level where it may be expected to settle under competitive conditions and thus perhaps discourage the development of competition? These and other matters affecting the pricing of new products will be discussed in a later chapter.

4. What should be the policy with respect to inventories of the new product? Enough will be needed to service an unknown and uncertain demand, but the amount stocked must be kept small enough so that the possible failure of the new

product to capture demand will not result in an overly serious commitment of the firm's funds in inventory.

5. What appeals will be most effective in promoting the sale of the new product? It is task of no small difficulty to find out why people buy or refuse to buy a product that is well known and has been long on the market. It is infinitely harder to discover what motivations will determine customer behavior toward a new unknown product. These difficulties are somewhat less with industrial goods than with consumer goods, since the former tend to be bought largely on the basis of a dollars-and-cents analysis, while sales of the latter occur to a great extent in response to consumer taste, whim, and emotion. Marketing research through the use of various product and market-testing devices can be of considerable aid in determining what buying motives are apt to be the most influential in effecting sales of new product; but often a true appraisal of the power of its several sales appeals must await the application of the trial and error method in the market.

Importance of timing

Timing is usually the essence of good performance in introducing new products into the market. If the operations of the buying industries are subject to seasonal ebb and flow, a decision must be made on whether the new product shall be brought out during the slack season, when buyers can give more time to examining it and learning about it, or at the beginning of the busy season, when they may be expected to be more in the buying mood. There are strong arguments for both sides of this issue. In many cases, the matter may be settled by the incidence of the widely attended trade shows or expositions that operate in most industries. Such an event offers a highly effective platform from which to introduce a new product-so effective, in fact, that many firms as a matter of course utilize the show for this purpose. Of course, the developmental activities of competitors may supply the decisive factor in timing the introduction of the new product. It two competing firms are at work on the development of about the same kind of product-a situation that prevails more often than is commonly thought-the one that breaks the new product first enjoys a definite advantage.

Once the release date for a new product fixed, plans must be made to synchronize a whole program of activities, each of which is vital to its successful and profitable launching. In some cases, new or additional production equipment must be procured, installed, and put into operation so that its output will be available in time to supply the expected demand when the new product is launched. Adequate inventory must be built up to service the demand that may be reasonably expected; if sales are to be made through distributors, a supply must be placed in the stocks of each according to his probable needs. If the new product supplants an old one, the stocks of the old product, both in the hands of distributors and of the industrial marketer, must be depleted to the minimum consistent with continuing service to customers. One machine maker uses an option plan whereby it announces new models a long time ahead of their introduction, and accords customers the option to buying old models during the interim to be exchanged for new models when they appear, less a $25-a-month use charge.

The sales of the manufacturer and of his distributors must be trained to handle the new product. The start of active selling work must be synchronized with the availability of the product in the stocks of the marketer or his distributors. The advertising must be timed to stimulate demand when the new product is released and to take advantage of the publicity value of its newness; but it must not effect this result too early, because orders that cannot be filled have a corroding influence on customer goodwill.

In the introduction of certain types of new industrial products, the timing of all these activities is complicated by the necessity or desirability of obtaining releases from governmental bodies, such as the Food and Drug Administration, or the approval of public or semipublic bodies, such as a American Medical Association or the National Board of Fire Underwriters.

Produt delettion

One more problem management remains to be discussed-deletion. Products die, just as they are born. Like people, many of them take a long time to die, and in the process they become decrepit so that their bills must be paid by others. A declining product usually yields little profit, or none at all; it uses capital, labor, and facilities for which it makes no adequate return; it demands an exorbitant amount of executive time and attention.

Unlike homicide, to kill aging products is no crime. Unless a firm in a dynamic industry has a procedure for doing so, and unless its management sees to it that the process of deletion is carried on consistently, its product mix is almost bound to be cluttered with items that do not pull their weight. Such a procedure includes several steps.

Selecting candidates for deletion

This involves examining the product mix to discover items that should be studied with the understanding that one of the possible outcome of the study may be a decision to delete. Some factors that suggest a product as a subject of such a study are:

A declining volume of sales.

A falling rate of profit.

A declining share of the market.

The appearance of a substitute that represents an improvement.

An increasing cost of production.

A declining market.

The need for constant executive attention to prevent loss.

No one of these things is cause of deletion. The occurrence of any one or a combination of them does suggest the need for a careful examination of why it is happening and what can be done about it. Deletion is one of the things that may be done.

Gathering and analysing information for decision

Usually, the organization unit that has the job of Selecting candidates for deletion should also be charged with the task of gathering facts about products that are suspect, analyzing them, and making recommendations for decision. Probably the first objective of such a study should be to discover why the product is going sour, and how far and in what direction the process of deterioration has gone. In the process of finding these facts, the group will probably uncover numerous suggestion on what to do about the matter and facts that indicate the feasibility of each alternative.,

In the course of this study, the decision makers should seek the answers to several questions.

1. Is there any way in which we can salvage the product and restore its profitability? We may try earnestly, but not too optimistically, to cut costs. We may market it in a less costly or more effective way. We may change its design to increase its customer benefits or to reduce its costs. We may cut price, hoping to get enough increase in sales volume to make cost reduction possible.

2. If we delete the product, how much of the capital how used in making and marketing it can we salvage? The working capital-that invested in accounts receivable and inventories of materials, goods in process, and finished goods-will drain back into the cash account as final production runs of the product are made, sold, and paid for if the deletion process is done properly and before it becomes a crisis action.

The capital invested in equipment is another matter. The machines may be flexible so that they can be used to make some other product if one is available. Or we may be able to sell them for their unamortized value. Or we may face the choice of scrapping them and writing off the loss or continuing to make and sell the product as long as its price yields something more than the direct costs, or until the entire investment has been amortized.

3. If we delete the product, have we in sight for the

capital and human resources released some use that promises to met the company more than the product now does? This matter of opportunity cost is one often overlooked.

4. What will deletion do to our labor relations and to our moral obligations to our employees? Theoretically, if we can make our peace with the union we should worry no further about the effect of a deletion on the lives of our employees. But if the demise of a product will take the jobs of a group of long-time pipe-bending shop workers who know nothing but pipe-bending and are too old to learn other skills, management may show a pronounced reluctance to dispense with its pipebending operations.

5. How will the deletion of this product affect our marketing operations? It may be that the resulting decline in sales will force a reduction in either the number of quality of our salesmen. A much more general danger, though, lies in the possibility that the product to be deleted is needed by customers who buy from us sizable volumes of profitable products and who will switch their entire patronage if they must go elsewhere to get their supply of the product. This matter needs careful, cold-blooded analysis without the semihysterical assumptions a volume-conscious sales force is likely to harbor.

6. What will deletion do to operating costs? It is often assumed that dropping a product relieves a firm of all its so-called direct costs, mainly labor and materials. This is usually true of materials but not always of labor. The same people often work on several products. When one of these products is dropped, most of the people are still needed to handle the remaining ones. Dropping a product often causes a decline in direct costs that is less than proportional to the decrease in sales volume it brings about.

Very rarely will the decision of a product enable a

firm to make any reduction in its overhead costs. They remain about the same and must be respread over the surviving products.

7. What effect will a product's deletion have on total net profits? In answering this question, the decision maker must take into account its effect on costs, on volume of sales not only to the dropped product but of others as well, the effect of the shift of salvaged resources to the most promising alternative uses, the volume of gross profit, and other factors. If the volume involved is large, perhaps it will be worthwhile to compare an estimated budget after all foreseeable adjustments are made with the budget to be expected if the product is retained in the mix.

Once à deletion decision is made, its details must be planned. It should be timed so as to cause the least distruption of the firm's operations and of those of distributors and customers. If the article is mechanical, a supply of spare parts must be provided for the soon-to-be orphan product. Customers should be informed far enough ahead to make new arrangement for their needs, but not far enough to prevent the cleaning out company stocks and those of distributors.

7

IMR AND ITS ROLE IN MARKETING

In considering the role of marketing in the firm it has become common practice to start with an explanation of the 'marketing concept'. So let us stay with tradition and consider a classical statement of its meaning. Felton offers the following basic definition.

> 'a corporate state of mind that insists on the integration and coordination of all marketing functions which in turn are melded with all other corporate functions for the basic objective of producing maximum long range profits.'

This statement immediately raises some problems if we look at the mixed economy of the United Kingdom in the middle of the 1970s: there is considerable argument today about whether or not the objective of an organization should be to produce maximum long range profits. This argument rages particularly strongly in connection with the nationalized industries, for governments often choose to use these industries as a means of promoting their natural economic objectives with the result that profitability may often not be the most important objective in the hierarchy of alternatives.

The marketing concept has also been interpreted to stress the focus on the customer For example, in Kotler there is an interpretation of the marketing concept defined in terms of customer orientation, integrated marketing, and customer satisfaction.

When we come to industrial marketing we have not just a customer, but a processes by which a large number of individuals collectively behave in such a way that ultimately our products are purchased. This in turn means that although there may be some firms who are only concerned with the immediate customer most firms find their business ultimately in the hand of a much wider group, wither as final consumers or as individuals who influence the state of our economy and therefore the total demand for all raw materials, goods, and services.

THE MARKETING PLAN

Central to the operation of the company is the marketing plan: from it flows the estimate of demands on production, needs fro raw materials, estimates of revenue and costs, and capital requirements. The marketing plan commonly consists of a detailed statement for the next year or two together with more sketchy figure stretching on to the next five years or perhaps to the next decade (depending on the nature of the business of the company concerned).

The evolution of such a plan is clearly defined pattern of events is, of course, an oversimplification. Making a plan is like deriving in some unknown busy city where the signposting is slightly eccentric: sometimes you find hold-ups, delays, one-ways, detours, cul-de-sacs, and perhaps the need to retrace your tracks to some previous point in order to locate where you are and to check the suitability of your planned route.

The marketing plan starts with some understanding as to the general area of you business: the nature of your products, the generic needs you seek to meet in the markets you naturally serve, and the key technologies which you employ. How far these factors are likely to be open to variation is a function of circumstances: the longer you look ahead the more are you able to modify the set of assets and competence which characterize you organization. But in the one-year plan many factors are already pre-set.

So, your corporate strategy is more or less given, and this input acts as an over-riding guideline to the planning process. There are two other inputs; external, the changing characteristics of the market, and perhaps an audit of the appropriateness of your existing marketing instruments.

Given, then, the inputs of facts, forecasts, and realistic assumptions, the planning process goes on to examine alternative feasible strategies. Sometimes alternatives are few and the strategy is clear; at other times the contrary is the case. There may be a number of segments at home and overseas and, with limited resources, a choice has to be made: what products, through what channels, to what markets, with what promotions?

In principle the procedure should be to identify alternative strategies and assess their economies; cost, revenue, probability of success. The strategy to be adopted is selected, and so on to develop the detail of the plan: budgets of capital, revenue and current expenditure, and of cash flow, setting of target dates and identifying of personal responsibilities.

Certainly the plan as the central feature of the company's forward look requires full, careful, and detailed consideration. Yet we can never really foretell the future and most plans have been shaken to the heart by the national and international lurches of the early 1970s. So we have to monitor the environment and be prepared to adapt the plan when changes in raw material availability, patterns of demand, and the discountinuities of politics and like problems reveal the need. The idea that a plan is set unchangedly is not valid.

When preparing the plan, keep careful note of the why and wherefores. This can help adjustment if need be. The value of the process of planning and linked budgeting has often been cited as a worthwhile spin-off: it really does leave us with an understanding of the total operation of our company as a system.

Then follows the stage of measuring results at many points in the company and checking the accuracy: of forecasts of sales by company and industry, of the state of the world economy, of raw material prices, etc. But feedback is the key to keeping the company on course, and revising that course as necessary.

A firm undertaking company planning sets out to answer the questions:

1. Where are we now?
2. Where are we likely to be in five year time?
3. Where should we be trying to get to in five years time?
4. How should we try to get there?

Five years is a common planning horizon for firms serving industrial markets. Individual circumstance may require a shorter or longer period. The role of IMR is to provide information on those matters external to the company that determine its present situation and condition its future prospects. This is crucial to the whole process.

In practice, a company plan consists almost entirely of numbers. The criteria on which performance is judged are financial. The apex of the planning pyramid is a time series of financial accounts that describe the past and present performance of the company and project the performance that has been set as a target over the planning period. Detailed quantitative analyses, covering all relevant aspects of the company's activity, are carried out to 'explain' the past and present performance and are used as sources from which the target projection evolve. IMR is primarily concerned with the analyses that 'explain' income from sales net of marketing costs and set the targets for this element of the forward plan.

The analysis of income from sales is best tackled by breaking down the total value into a set of product-market matrices. The number of Product rows and Market columns in a matrix is governed by individual circumstances. General guidelines are that a 'Product' should be defined as the single article or collection of articles offered by the company to satisfy a definable need. A 'Market' should be defined as a group of users and potential users who have a common need and who are likely to be subject to the same general set of external influences on their own businesses. Having distributed net sales income over the product-market matrix we then are faced with explaining the value in each cell. This is done by constructing a profile of each cell. The profile covers the following information:

Total demand.

Our share of demand.

Main competitors with their shares.

Our relative standing on
    product properties;
    price-levels and structure;
    delivery-quotation and reliability;
    service-before and after sales.

Our marketing activities compared with competitors'

promotion-amount and quality;

selling-methods and intensity;

distribution-channels and mix;

technical service-amount and quality.

This process, when completed, answers the question. 'Where are we now?' As it relates to our standing and performance in the markets currently being served.

It also provides the basis of an answer, to. 'Where are we likely to find ourselves?. The first step in this is to estimate the forward movement in total demand, in quantity and value, in each product-market cell. Armed with the detailed analysis of our strengths and weaknesses provided by the cell profiles we can then form judgments of the likely movement in our share of demand and hence in net sales income. These judgments will take account, where relevant, of any increases or decreases in the strength of competition that can be anticipated from trends to date.

More positively, the information generated by the

analytical processes is used, together with internal information on product profitability, in formulating businesses target and in developing action programmes to achieve them. Preferred directions of change in the amount and type of marketing activity undertaken in various markets and for various products are worked out. The general objective is to maximize the advantage extracted from opportunities and minimize the effect of threats highlighted by the forward projections.

This process is common to all forms of planning. The aspect that distinguishes Company planning is the extended time horizon involved and consequently the increased freedom to consider changes in things that are of necessity fixed in short-run plans. We can legitimately ask ourselves. 'What products supplied to what markets using what marketing resources offer the greatest expectation of profitable growth to the company?' This offers a substantial challenge to the marketing researcher. It involves the need to see the company clearly as an organic system within its industrial and commercial environment, to conceive sometimes radical ideas for change, and to demonstrate the validity of such propositions on the basis of solid information and sound reasoning.

The product-market matrix is a useful tool for generating ideas for development of the company's activities. The questions to ask are:

'What other markets, not currently served by us, have a demand for our products?

'What other products, not currently supplied by us, are required by the customers making up the markets we serve?

This leads to an extended matrix that can be examined for opportunities to exploit potential synergy. If any such opportunities are identified, the question of how best to purpose them calls for further research. The basic options are:

(i) Extending existing products into new markets

(a) Invest in new marketing resources.

(b) Acquire a company with suitable marketing expertise.

(c) Appoint suitable agents.

(d) Find suitable licensees for the products.

(ii) Additional products for markets in which the Company is established

(a) Invest in resources to develop new products.

(b) Acquire a company with suitable products.

(c) Take on marketing agencies for suitable products

(d) Obtain licences to manufacture suitable products.

Only through desk and field research will enable an appropriate choice to be made.

All planning is a team effort. It is difficult, and dangerous, to draw demarcation lines round the responsibilities of individual members of the team. The contribution of the marketing researcher is two-fold. As a specialist, he is responsible for ensuring that the planning team is provided with the best possible information based on the external market environment. As a member of the team his unique contribution should be a facility to place himself in the customer's shoes and interpret the reaction and response of the market to proposed strategies and actions as the company plan evolves.

8

INTERMEDIATE CUSTOMERS

This chapter will discuss these intermediate consumers: who they are, where they are, and how they buy. We will emphasize the buying behavior of manufacturers. But other intermediate customers seem to buy in much the same way. In fact, buyers for all kinds of organizations are often loosely referred to as "industrial buyers." To keep the discussion specific, we will focus on the United States, but most of the ideas apply to international markets as well.

There are great marketing opportunities in serving intermediate customers and a student heading toward a business career has a good chance a working in this area.

Intermediate customers are different

There are about 15 million intermediate customers in the United States. These customers do many different jobs- and many different market dimensions are needed to describe all the different intermediate customer markets.

Intermediate customers buy for a purpose

Intermediate buyers purchase goods and services to met needs- just as final consumers do. But here the needs are usually easier to define because the buyers are trying to satisfy their customers. A business firm wants to make a profit by producing or reselling products. A town government wants to meet its legal and social obligations to citizens. A country club wants to help its members enjoy their leisure time. Such organizations buy goods and services that will help them meet the demand for the goods and services that they in turn supply to their markets.

Even small differences are important

Understanding how and why intermediate customers buy is important because competition is often rugged in intermediate markets. Even "trivial' differences may affect the success of a marketing mix.

Since sellers usually approach each intermediate customer directly-through a sales representative- they have more chance to adjust the marketing mix for each individual customer. Sellers may even have a special marketing strategy for each individual customer. This is carrying target marketing to its extreme. But when the customer's size and sales volume make this possible, it may be not only desirable but necessary in order to compete.

In such situations, the individuals sales rep has to carry more responsibility for strategy planning. This face is relevant to your career planning since these jobs are very challenging- and they pay well, too.

Manufacturers are important customers

There are not many big ones

One of the most striking facts about manufacturers is how few there are compared to final consumers. In the industrial market, there are about 350,000 factories. The majority of these are quite small-half have less than 10 workers. But these small firms account for only about 3 percent of manufacturing activity. In small plants, the owners often do the buying. And they buy less formally than buyers in the relatively few large manufacturing plants- which employ most of the workers and produce a large share of the "value added" by manufacturing. For example, plants with 250 or more employees make up only about 4 percent of the total-yet they employ nearly 60 percent of the production employees and produce about two thirds of the "value added" by manufacturers. Because these large plants are so important, it may be desirable to segment industrial markets on the basis of size.

Customers cluster in geographic areas

In addition to concentration by size, industrial markets are concentrated in big metropolitan areas-especially in the Middle Atlantic states, and California.

The buyers for some of these larger manufacturers are even further concentrated in home offices- often in large metropolitan areas. U.S. Gypsum, one of the largest building materials manufacturers, does most of the buying for over 50 plants from its Chicago offices. In such a case, a sales rep may be able to sell to plants all over the country without leaving a base city. This makes selling easier for competitors, too, so the market may be extremely competitive. The importance of such big buyers has led some companies to set up "national account" sales forces- specially trained to cater to these needs. A geographically bound salesperson can be at a real disadvantage against such competitors.

Concentration by industry

In addition to concentration by size of firm and geographic location, there is also concentration by industry. Manufacturers of advanced electronics systems are concentrated in California's famous Silicon Valley near San Francisco and along Boston's Route 128. The steel industry is heavily concentrated in the Pittsburgh, Birmingham, and Chicago areas.

Much data is available on industrial markets by SIC codes

In industrial markets, marketing mangers can focus their attention on a relatively few clearly defined markets and reach the majority of the business. The availability of very detailed information can aid their efforts. The federal government regularly collects and publishes data by Standards Industrial Classification codes—groups of firms in similar lines of business. The number of establishments, sales volumes, and number of employees- broken down by geographic areas- are given for each SIC code. These codes are a real help in market research- for companies that can relate their own sales to their customers' type of business. SIC code breakdowns start with such broad industry categories as food and related products tobacco product, textile mill products, apparel, and so on.

Within each tow-digit industry breakdown, much more detailed data may be available for three-digit and four-digit industries. Four-digit detail isn't available for all industries in every geographic areas because the government does not provide data when only one or two plants are located in an area.

SIC codes are not perfect. Some companies have sales in several categories but are listed in only one-the code with the largest sales. In addition, some newer businesses don't fit any of the categories very well. So, although a lot of good information is available, the codes must be used carefully.

Many firms find their current customers' SIC codes and then look at SIC-coded lists for similar companies that may need the same goods and services.

Other companies look at which SIC categories are growing or declining- to discover new opportunities. If companies aiming at industrial target markets know exactly who they are aiming at, readily available data organized by SIC codes can be valuable. Most trade associations and private organizations that gather industrial market data also use SIC codes.

Buyers are problem solvers

Some people think of industrial buying as entirely different from consumer buying- but there are many similarities.

Three kinds of buying processes are useful

We discussed problem solving by consumers and how it might vary from extended problem solving to routine buying. In industrial markets, we can adapt these concepts slightly and work with three similar buying processes: a new- task buying process, a modified rebuy process, or a straight rebuy.

New-task buying occurs when a firm has a new need and the buyer wants a great deal of information. New-task buying can involve setting product specifications, sources of supply, and an order routine that can be followed in the future- if results are satisfactory.

A *straight rebuy* is a routine repurchase that may have been made many times before, Buyers probably don't bother looking for new information or new sources of supply. Most of a company's small or recurring purchases are of this type- but they take only a small part of an organized buyer's time.

The modified rebuy is the in-between process where some review of the buying situation is done-though not as much as in new-task buying. sometimes a competitor will get lazy enjoying a straight rebuy situation. An alert marketer can turn these situations into opportunities by providing more information.

Note that a particular product may be bought in any of the three ways. Careful market analysis is needed to determine how the firm's products are bought- and by whom. A new-task buy takes much longer than a straight rebuy and the seller's promotion has much more chance to have an impact.

Purchasing agents are buying specialists

Some producers are so large that they need buying specialists. Purchasing agents are buying specialists for their employers. Salespeople usually have to see the purchasing agent first- before they contract any other employee.

These buyers hold important positions and take dim view of sales reps who try to go around them. In large companies, purchasing agents usually specialize by product area and are real experts.

Rather than being "sold", these buyers expect accurate information that will help them buy wisely. They like information on new goods and services- and tips of potential price changes, strikes, and other changes in business conditions. Most industrial buyers are serious and educated- and sales representatives should treat them accordingly"

Basic purchasing needs are economic

Industrial buyers are usually less emotional in their buying than final consumers. Buyers look for certain product characteristics-including economy both in original cost and in use, productivity, uniformity, purity, and ability to make the buyer's final product better.

In addition to product characteristics, buyers consider the seller's reliability and general cooperativeness; is ability to provide speedy maintenance and repair, steady supply under all conditions, and reliable and fast delivery; and any past and present relationships.

Many buyers use vendor analysis- formal rating of suppliers on all relevant areas of performance. Evaluating suppliers and how they are working out results in better buying decisions.

Emotional needs are relevant, too

Vendor analysis tries to focus economic factors, but industrial purchasing does have emotional overtones. Modern buyers are human-and want friendly relationships with suppliers. some buyers seem eager to imitate progressive competitors-or even to be the first to try new products. Such "innovators" might deserve special attention when new products are being introduced.

Buyers are also human with respect to protecting their own interests- and their own position in the company. "Looking good" is serious matter for some purchasing agents. They have to buy a wide variety of products from many sources and make decisions involving many factors beyond their control. If a new source delivers low-quality materials, you can guess who will be blamed. Poor services or late delivery also reflect on the buyer's ability. Therefore, anyone or anything that helps the buyer look good has a definite appeal. In fact, this one factor may make the difference between a successful and unsuccessful marketing mix.

Supply sources must be dependable

This matter of dependability deserves further emphasis. There is nothing worse to a purchasing agent and a production manger than shutting sown a production line because sellers haven't delivered the goods. Product quality is important, too. The cost of a small item may have little to do with its importance. If it causes a larger unit to break down, it may result in a large loss completely out o proportion to its own cost.

A seller's marketing mix should satisfy both the needs of the buyer's company as well as the buyer's individual needs. Therefore, sellers need to find and overlapping area where both can be satisfied.

Multiple buying influences in buying center

Much of the work of the typical purchasing agent consists of straight rebuys. When a purchase requisition comes in, the purchasing agent places an order without consulting anyone else. But, in many cases- especially new-task buying-multiple buying influence may be important. Multiple buying influence means the buyer shares the purchasing decision with several people-perhaps even top management. Possible buying influences include;

1. *Users*—perhaps production line workers or their supervisors.

2. *Influences*—perhaps engineering or R&D people who help write specifications or supply information for evaluating alternatives.
3. *Buyers*—the purchasing agents who have the responsibility for selecting suppliers and arranging the terms of the sale.
4. *Deciders*—the people in the organization who have the power to select or approve the supplier-usually the purchasing agent for small items, but perhaps top management for larger purchases.
5. *Gatekeepers*-people who control the flow of information within the organization- perhaps purchasing agents who shield users or other deciders.

Gatekeepers can also include receptionists, secretaries, research assistants, and others who influence the flow of information about potential purchases.

An examples shows how the different buying influences work. Suppose Adidas wants to buy a machine to attach running shoes soles to the tops. Different vendor are eager for the business. Several people help to evaluate the choices. A finance manger worries about the high cost and suggests leasing the machine. The quality control people want a machine that will do a more accurate job- although it's more expensive. The production manager is interested in speed of operation. The production line workers and their supervisors want the machine that is easiest to use- so workers can continue to rotate jobs.

The company president asks the purchasing department to assemble all the information but retain the power to select and approve the supplier. The purchasing manager's administrative assistant has been deciding what information to pass on to higher-ups as well as scheduling visits for salespeople. After all these buying influences are considered, one of the purchasing agents for the firm will be the buyer. He will be responsible for making recommendations and arranging the terms of the sale.

It is helpful to think of a buying center as all the

people who participate in or influence a purchase. Different people may make up a buying center from one decision to the next. This makes the marketing job difficult.

The salesperson must study each case carefully. Just learning who to talk with may be hard- but thinking about the various roles in the buying center can help.

The salesperson may have to talk to every member of the buying center-stressing different topics for each. This not only complicates the promotion job but also lengthens it. Approval of a routine order may take anywhere from a week to several months. On very important purchases- a new computer system, a new plant, or major equipment-the selling period may stretch out to a year or more.

Basic methods and practices in industrial buying

Should you inspect, sample, describe, or negotiate?

Industrial buyers (really, buyers of all types, including final consumers) use four basic approaches to evaluating and buying projects: Inspection, sampling, description, and negotiated contracts. Understanding the differences in these buying methods is important in strategy planning-so let's look at each approach.

Inspection buying means looking at every item. It's used for products that are not standardized and require examination. Here each product is different-as in the case of livestock or used equipment. Such products are often sold inspect the goods and either "higgle" with the seller- or bid against competitors.

Sampling looks at some

Sampling buying means looking at only part of a potential purchase. As products become more standardized perhaps because of careful grading or quality control-buying by sample becomes possible. For example, a power company might buy miles of heavy electric cable. A sample section might be heated to the melting point to be certain the cable is safe.

Prices may be based on a sample. Although demand and supply forces may set the general price level, the actual price may vary depending on the quality of a specific sample. For example, this kind of buying is used in grain markets where the actual price is based on a sample that has been withdrawn from a carload of grain and analyzed.

People in less-developed economies do a lot of buying by inspection or sampling- regardless of the product. The reason is skepticism about quality-or lack of faith in the seller.

Description just describes accurately

Description buying means buying from a written description of the product. Most manufactured items and many agricultural commodities are bought this way-often without inspection. When quality can almost be guaranteed, buying by description-grade, brand, or specification- may be satisfactory, especially when there is mutual trust between buyers and sellers. This methods, of course, reduces the cost of buying and is used by buyers whenever practical.

Services are usually purchased by description. Since a service is usually not performed until it is purchased, buyers have nothing to inspect ahead of time.

Negotiated contracts explain how to handle relationships.

Negotiated contract buying means agreeing to a contract that allows for changes in the purchase arrangements.

Sometimes, the buyer knows roughly what the company needs- but can't fix all the details in advance. The specifications or total requirements may change as the job progress. This situation is common, for example, in research and development work and in the building of special purpose machinery or buildings. In such cases, the general project is described, and a basic price may be agreed on-with provision for changes and price adjustments up or down. Or a supplier may be willing to accept a contract that provides some type of incentive-such as full coverage of costs plus a fixed fee or full costs plus a profit percentage tied to costs. The whole contract may even be subject to renegotiation as the work proceeds.

Buyers may favor loyal, helpful suppliers

To be sure of dependable quality, a buyer may develop loyalty to certain suppliers. This is especially important when buying non-standardized products. When a supplier and buyer develop a friendly relationship over the years, the supplier practically becomes a part of the buyer's organization.

When a seller proposes a new idea that saves the buyer's company money the buyer usually rewards the seller with orders, and this encourages future suggestions. In contrast, buyers who use a bid system exclusively-either by choice or necessity, as in some government and institutional purchasing-may not be offered much beyond basic goods and services. They are interested primarily in price.

Until recently, Ford, Chrysler, and GM relied heavily in bid-convinced this would result in lower prices from competing suppliers. But Japanese competition made them rethink this approach. Japanese producers and their suppliers often work together very closely. They view the effort as a partnership.

Suppliers are consulted before design changes are made, to make certain that a planned change won't create problems. Now the Detroit automakers are also using this approach, often giving a single supplier a long-term contract to supply a needed part. In return, they are expecting-and getting-more help from the supplier. In fact, Ford credits suggestions from its suppliers for the improved quality of its new cars.

But most buyers seek several sources to spread their risk

Even if a firm has developed the best marketing mix possible, it probably won't get all its industrial customer's business. Buyers often look for several dependable sources of supply- to protect themselves from unpredictable events, such as strikes, fires, or floods in one of their supplier's plants. Still, a good marketing mix is likely to win a larger share of the total business.

Most buyers try too routinize buying

Most firms use a buying procedure that tries to routinize the process. When some person or unit wants to buy something, a requisition-a request to buy something-is filled out. After approval by some operating supervisor, the requisition is forwarded to the buyer for placement with the "best" seller.

Approved requisitions are converted to purchase orders as quickly s possible. Straight rebuys are usually made the day the requisition is received, while new-task and modified rebuys take longer. If time is important, the buyer may place the order by telephone-and then a confirming purchases order is typed and sent out.

It pays to know the buyer

Notice the importance of being one of the regular source of supply. For straight rebuys, the buyer may place an order without even calling other potential sources. Sellers' sales reps regularly call on these buyers- but not to sell a particular item. Rather, they want to maintain relations, become a source, and/or point out new developments that might cause the buyer to reevaluate his present "straight rebuy" procedure and give some business to the sales rep's company.

Having a favorable image can be profitable for a seller. Unless a buyer has to allocate a definite share of the business to each of several sources, a favored source will probably get a larger share. Moving from a 20 percent to a 30 percent share may not seem like much from a buyer's point of view, but for the seller it's a 50 percent increase in sales.

Some buyers delegate a large part of their routine order-placing to computers. They program decision rules that tell the computer how to order and leave the details of following through to the machine. When economic conditions change, buyers modify the computer instructions. When nothing unusual happens, however, the computer system continues to routinely rebuy as needs develop-printing out new purchase orders to the regular suppliers.

Obviously, it's a big "sale" to be selected as a major supplier and routinely called- up in the buyer's computer program. It's also obvious that such a buyer will be more impressed by an attractive marketing mix for a whole line of products than just a lower price for a particular order. It may be too expensive and too much trouble to change the whole buying system just because somebody is offering a low price on a particular day.

Inventory policy may determine purchases

Industrial firms generally try to maintain an adequate inventory-certainly enough to keep production lines moving. There is no greater disaster in a factory than to have a production line close down.

No buyer wants to run out of needed products, but keeping too much inventory is expensive. Firms are now paying more attention to inventory costs-and looking to their suppliers for help in controlling them. This often means that a supplier must be able to provide "just-in-time" delivery-reliably getting products there just before the customer needs them.

Adequate inventory is often expressed in terms of number of days' supply for example. 10-or 30-days' supply. But what constitutes a 10-or 30-days' supply depends on the level of demand for the company's own products. If demand rises sharply- say, by 10 percent-then total purchases will expand by more than 10 percent to maintain safe inventory levels and meet the new needs. On he other hand, if sales decrease by 10 percent, actual needs and inventory requirements decreases, and total purchases may decrease drastically while inventory is being "worked off." During such a cutback, a seller probably couldn't stimulate sales- even by reducing price or offering more favorable credit terms. The buyer is just not in the market at that time.

Demand at the manufacturer level may fluctuate much more than demand at the final consumer level. Manufacturers try to predict the behavior of middlemen and other producers. If manufacturers believe prices are going to drop further, they may postpone all purchases. If they prices are at their lowest point, they may buy in large quantities in anticipation of their future needs.

Producers also try to predict changes in demand by final consumers. For example, if Black and Decker sees that consumer purchases of small appliances are slowing down-perhaps because of a bad economy—it may stop buying electric motors. It doesn't want a big inventory of motors or finished appliances.

Reciprocity means trading sales fro sales- that is, "if you buy from me, I'll buy from you." If a company's customers also can supply products that the firm buys, then the dales departments of both buyer and seller try to "trade" sales for sales. Purchasing agents generally resist reciprocity but often face pressure from their sales department.

When prices and quality are otherwise competitive, an outside supplier seldom can break a reciprocity relationship. The supplier can only hop to become an alternate source of supply and wait for the competitor to let its quality slip or prices rise.

The ustice Department frowns on reciprocity. It has tried to block reciprocal buying on the grounds that it is an attempt to monopolize-that is, to restrict the normal operation of the free market. some firms that relied heavily on reciprocity have been forced to reevaluate their marketing strategies.

9

TOTAL MARKETING COMMUNICATION

INDUSTRIAL ADVERTISING

Industrial advertising and selling has always been considered a Cinderella in comparison with its more glamorous consumer counterpart. The amount of money which spent on consumer advertising is widely publicized and a figure of £494 million a year was quoted by the Advertising Association 1968. It is true that this only represents 1.4 per cent of the gross national product of the UK. Nevertheless it seems an astronomical sum, and about this proportion of the gross national product is being spent on advertising in all the highly developed nations of the world. Industrial advertising appears to be quite small fry in comparison.

The Advertising Association estimates that some £44 million was spent in 1968 on trade and technical media advertising-a small sum compared with the $494 million total: However, these figure are not strictly comparable.

More and more press-advertising budget for industrial advertiser are finding their way into the national press. The classified pages of some of the big national newspapers are full of advertisements to technocrats in industry. The financial pages of the national newspapers have advertisements addressed to stockholders, many of whom are industrial people.

Industrial advertisers spend very considerable sums of money on catalogues, brochures, leaflets, exhibitions, conferences and seminars, industrial films and public and press relations.

When you add to this the costs of advertising departments in industry it can be conservatively estimated that the budgets of the advertising departments of British industry collectively total £200 million per year. But advertising is only part of the communication story.

The cost of industrial salesman

Salesman are an integral and important part of industrial marketing communication. It is estimated that there are some 150,000 salesman in the UK selling to industry. When you consider not only their salary and their cars, but also their travelling and subsistence expenditure, each salesman costs his company an average of £4,250 a year.

On top of this must be added the cost of sales management and sales office staffs which comes to over £1,500 per salesman, giving a cost per salesman of £6,000 a year. A total cost of 900 million to British industry.

Total communication costs

Combine those two sums of money (the total cost of advertising plus the total cost of the sales operation) and we have a grand total of £1,100 million which is being spent on industrial marketing communication efforts in the UK. That is well over 3½ per cent of the G.N.P.

All are agreed that much of this money is wasted every year by industry, not only in Britain but throughout the world, on advertising and selling to industry-money which could be used for more productive purposes.

Of course, no one deliberately wastes money. Profit margins are too closely pruned to have a surplus to waste. No manager goes out of his way to waste the money he spends on sales promotion. Indeed, sales management, advertising management, marketing management, advertising agencies, all these experts spend their lives trying to make the money spent in sales promotion more effective.

Yet, deliberately or not, the waste goes on everywhere in the world where one company sells its goods and services to another company.

It is the purpose of this book to point the way to

making more effective use of the money spent by presenting as much data as is available to the experienced seeker. The sources of this information are, in the main, the USA and the UK. But the experience which is the basis for the argument of this work is based on contact with industry throughout Western Europe.

This information cannot possibly supply all the answers for every company. What this book sets out to do is to highlight the available facts, and so give the lead to individual companies to fill the gaps in their own communication activities. And there are gaps—one point which is brought home by considering these facts is the poverty of much inter-company communication.

But the gap in knowledge *can* be filled by individual management. By spending relatively modest sums of money on marketing research and investigating the links between the company and its customers, a programme for more effective expenditure can be devised. The waste will be gradually cut as managers get to know more about the total marketing communication effort their company is making.

The complicated allocation of the sales promotion budget, the decision to spend certain proportions on salesman, certain proportions on press advertising, certain proportions on new product development and other proportions on all other forms of media communication are exceedingly complex and it would appear obvious that the computer can help management in getting the right balance

But the computer, to which management is turning more and more to help in solving this kind of difficult problem, is an electronic moron. It has to be fed with precise and accurate information. It cannot work it out for itself. The computer cannot decide whether a salesman is a more effective method of communication than a full page in a national paper or a one-minute spot on television. Neither can it decide to spend more money on Research and Development. Management will have to make these decision and have the computer programmed accordingly.

Marketing begins with the customer

Empathy: putting yourself in the other man's position. This is what all good salesman are trained to do. Most industrial salesmen are well enough trained to take the customer through all the stages of the sale until they come to the close and placing of the order. But do they think of the customer and his needs and desires or are they thinking more about themselves and the targets which their sales management have set them?

Sophisticated sales training recognizes that the best salesman is the man who helps the customer to come to a better buying decision. The best salesman does not think 'What can I sell this man?" but 'What does he need to buy? How can I help him to come to a better buying decision?"

If we are to consider total communication in all its aspects we must start by recognizing that it is with the customer that we are communicating, that he will only listen to what interest him and that every time we issue a message either verbally or visually we must always consider its effect on the customer. After all, a listener is essential to communication.

The marketing concept

Mark Vardy of the Ashridge Management College has set out his views of the marketing concept as follows:

1. The marketing concept suggests that a business should look for profit rather than volume.

2. A business should be consumer orientated and not be merely a goods-producing unit.

3. Change is to be expected but the business should contribute to change through its own research and development.

4. Long-range planning is a vital element of success.

5. Organization-activities that a business engages in which relate directly to the customer should be operated under one executive or department.

Probably the most important of his five headings is the second one: a business should be consumer orientated and not be merely a goods-producing unit. The snag is that current shows that people mouth the words 'consumer orientated' but the reality does not come up to expectations. In other words, people will claim wholeheartedly that theirs is a marketing-orientated organization though in practice few achieve this happy state.

This is the crux of everything to do with total communication. Unless it is firmly established that the consumer is the key to the whole communication exercise, very little further can be achieved. Marketing begins with the customer.

Public relations

It is impossible to have a commentary on total marketing communication without referring to the part played by public relations, because there is no effective marketing communication without public relations.

In arriving at a PR policy we believe that a company should interpret the term in its widest sense-the overall, conscious projection of its image of its various 'publics'. Thus PR must concern itself with advertising, the design and production of sales literature, press relations, exhibitions, seminars and conferences-all pointing towards the world outside; and, internally, the interpretation of management to employees. No company has a single public-and it may have different publics at different times. Some of those that the company way wish to influence include:

1. Shareholders and potential shareholders of the company, City editors, financial writers and stockbrokers.
2. Employees and potential employees, their families, appropriate trade unions, employment officers, appointment boards, schools, etc.
3. Suppliers and potential suppliers of raw materials and other goods and services.
4. Customers and potential customers-who may be industrial wholesale, retail or consumer groups such as housewives or motorists.

5. Local communities in which the company operates.

The influencing of these varying groups appropriately, efficiently and economically, is the task of the PR expert in conjunction with the executives normally involved in these areas of the firm's activity.

Frank Jefkins takes the definition of the Institute of Public Relations and analyses it. It is a very good analysis and here it is.

'The official definition of the Institute of PR says "Public relations practice is the deliberate, planned and sustained effort to established and maintain mutual understanding between an organization and its public". Let us take it apart analytically:

'*Public relations*- quite literally, relations with the public and not just cocktail parties in penthouse suites.

'*Deliberate*-according to a definite purpose.

'*Planned*-nothing haphazard but organized, usually on a long term basis.

'*Sustained Effort*-PR activity must be continuous and persistent effort. Not stunts or gimmicks but painstaking work.

'*Establish*-the creation of faith, which is not easy and requires a good product or service in the first place.

Maintain-it is not enough to create good will; it has to be nourished and kept healthy. Continuity is implied here, too and it is not always easy to maintain a good opinion in the face of competition, and sometimes when things go wrong.

'*Mutual Understanding*-PR is a two-way affair, making possible the passage of ideas, thoughts and desires. Communication is like a conversation, and one has to be a good listener as well as a good speaker!'

Let us emphasize once more you cannot have effective marketing communications without establishing and maintaining mutual understanding between your own company and your customers. This process must be deliberately planned and sustained as an integral part of the marketing communication strategy.

Corporate identity

Corporate Identity is a term used to describe the total identity and personality expressed and conveyed any an organization, but externally to the outside world and internally to the staff and executives of that organization. Ideally the corporate identity should reflect the inner truth about the organization; what it stands for in terms of integrity and purpose, the sector of business in which it deals and the true value of its products and services. This image can be improved by expert knowledge; and the importance of corporate identity to an organization's future development has brought about specialization in this area, as one of the basic techniques of the modern marketing man.

Difference between selling and marketing

Theodore Levitt of the Harvard Business School puts the difference between marketing and selling very clearly:

'Mass-production industries are impelled by a great drive to produce all they can. The prospect of steeply declining unit costs as output rises is more than most companies can usually resist. The profit possibilities look spectacular. All effort focuses on production. The result is that marketing gets neglected.

'Mass-production does indeed generate great pressure to "move" the product. But what usually gets emphasized is selling, not marketing. Marketing, being a more sophisticated and complex process, gets ignored.

'The difference between marketing and selling is more than semantic. Selling focuses on the needs of the seller, marketing on the needs of the buyer. Selling is preoccupied with the seller's need to convert his product into cash; marketing with the idea of satisfying the needs of the customer by means of the product and the whole cluster of things associated with creating, delivering and finally consuming it.'

Probably the foregoing quote from Theodore Levitt

has had as much to do with companies becoming, in theory, marketing orientated as any other quote. As we have noted, it has become fashionable for salesman to call themselves marketing men, because marketing is whizz-kid stuff, whereas selling is old hat. The salesman is a soft-hearted sort of guy trying to build up his ego in order to impress the customer and make a sale. At least that seems to be the popular image of the salesman-and it is all wrong.

Selling is the most difficult job that anyone in the company has to do. There is no practical production problem that cannot be solved. We can make anything-we are limited only by our imagination. Financial problems are understandable and can be programmed into computers. But selling is much more complex and much more difficult.

We can solve the technological problems of getting to the moon. We have not solved the problems of communication. In fact, we have the strange paradox that as communication techniques improve with the vast circulations of newspapers, with television beamed to every high population-density area in the world, with radio transmitted to every village in the Congo, yet nations still fail dismally in talking to each other, and so do people.

Selling has recently been overshadowed by marketing, but selling has got to be recognized again in its own right. This does not mean to say that more salesman have to go on the road. On the contrary, every company could cut back its sales force and yet increase its overall effectiveness in selling.

If the customer is all-important, if selling is difficult, then no one in the company should pass the responsibility for selling on to someone else.

Everything that the company does should be thinking not only about getting more output from the plant but about the customer who is at the receiving end of the production line. The accountant should not only be looking for more profit but finding out whether the pricing policy of the company is right for the customer. In fact, every single person in a company selling to industry should be constantly reminded that without the customer they would be out of a job.

Persuasion may be brought to bear on the individual, or on a group, in many different contexts. It is important in this book, therefore, to define persuasion as it applies to selling. This may well be done by contrast with other attempts at persuasion such as political persuasion in all its shades, or religious and moral persuasion. The contemporary world can provide many examples of the use of persuasion in these areas.

If we look at persuasion in its widest context, it is interesting to evaluate the different kinds of persuasion in three important areas of life today: (1) persuasion by a dictatorship, either communist or fascist; (2) persuasion offered by the Church; (3) persuasion as it applied to selling.

In his book, *Techniques of Persuasion,* J.A.C. Brown takes a look at the methods used by the Chinese in attempting to change attitudes in prisoner-of-war camps in Korea. In many respects the Chinese had ideal conditions for persuasion. They controlled all methods of communication, they engendered attitudes of fear, they encouraged self-criticism, and by cutting off all communication with the outside world they established the almost ideal situation for changing attitudes.

What was remarkable was the fact that these men who had been subjected to probably the most exacting form of persuasion so far practised in the history of the world were not permanently mentally disfigured by this monstrous treatment. In fact, as soon as they were restored to normal methods of communication the only people who were still persuaded were those few who were communists before they went to prisoner-of-war camps.

Persuasion in countries under dictatorship has the great advantage that, by censorship and restriction of free communication, and almost ideal persuasion technique can be applied. The recipient of the communication only hears what it is felt right for him to hear. He very rarely gets the opportunity of hearing another point of view.

The Church has been spreading the doctrine of Christianity throughout the world for nearly 2,000 years. Using the techniques of confession, submission and faith on evidence of things unseen, the Church has done a remarkable job of persuasion.

In most Christian countries the Church is in the centre of every community. Countries call themselves 'Christian countries' and the moral codes of such countries are broadly based on Christian principles. People who criticize the Church are often treated with some suspicion.

In fact, in many countries it is a social requirement to be seen at church. Yet the Church itself is going through a traumatic experience. Even the Pope confesses that he makes mistakes and says, 'After all I am human".

So, with almost everything in its favor, with very few voices in Christian countries speaking against Christianity, there is apathy and dissension in the Christian Church throughout the world, and the implications of this for the moral conduct of previously Christian communities are now being worked out in the agony of the new generations.

Compared with these major influences persuasion in the context of selling is surely the most difficult of all. No censorship helps the salesman. He cannot build an iron curtain around his customer to stop him from hearing the other point of view. The salesman is in active competition with his contemporaries.

In the course of a single day a buyer might be subjected to as many as ten, or even more, sales pitches delivered by salesman promoting products of identical function and price. In fact, very rarely indeed is a salesman in the fortunate position of selling a unique product at an exceptionally favourable price. Almost without exception the salesman is offering a product which can either replace something else or is precisely comparable with what is already being used. He is offering this product in the face of intense-competition. Truly the most difficult climate of all for persuasion.

How, then, can the salesman really become more effective? Or, more precisely, how can a company increase its selling effectiveness?

Management with its wide experience must look at the total communication between itself and its customers and improve the whole marketing communication structure. The task must not be left to the salesman or the sales manager.

How does management improve communication? At the moment, it is relying on the salesman to do this vital task because, in the main, industrial advertising is pretty poor stuff.

Some research conducted by the present author on behalf of the Institute of Practitioners in Advertising at the time of its fiftieth anniversary in 1967 was published in the IPA *Forum* in July 1967.

A selection was made of trade and technical journals which were still publishing after fifty years: *Engineering, Colliery Guardian, Foundry Trade Journal, Gas World and Municipal Engineering.* To make an exact comparison, advertisements appearing in June 1917 were studied and then the comparable advertisements in January 1967.

The observations were staggering. In fifty years of industrial advertising the changes have been very slight. Believe it or not there was one advertisement which has not been changed in fifty years. The same illustration, the same heading, the same typography. What was more remarkable was that almost any idea that was being used today was being used fifty years ago in industrial advertising. An advertisement asking for the recipient to fill in a coupon-there was an offer fifty years ago. The British Reinforced Concrete Company was illustrating one of its latest buildings in 1967; the same company was illustrating one of its buildings fifty years ago. Advertisers were emphasizing the efficiency of their service by making use of maps fifty years ago. The map of England with its points of service looked identical in 1967. Broom and Wade, the manufacturers of air compressors, had a picture of a compressor in their advertisement for 1967. Not quite the identical compressor, but one looking very similar was illustrated fifty years ago. And so on, and so on.

Almost every idea that was being used in 1967 was being used fifty years ago. Is it any wonder that industrial management does not look to advertising for help? It is any wonder that it continues to rely upon the individual salesman to act as its main method of communication?

Yet if management were to consider just how difficult selling is today, and how increasingly more difficult it is becoming, it would realize that it cannot afford to delegate the vital task of selling to the salesman alone. Every manager in a company should involve himself in this job of persuasion and communication.

It is an encouraging fact that managers who have been involved all their lives with machinery and production or with accounting find that putting their great skill into the art of communication and persuasion can be extremely satisfying. It is a difficult task and, as we have suggested, it is the most difficult job in the firm, but it can be mastered.

In September 1966 an article was printed in the publication *Case Conference*, a professional journal for the social worker and social administrator. The article was based on a talk given to a conference of agriculture salesman in West Virginia, USA. The author was Alan Keith-Lucas, Professor at the University of North Carolina. The point he made in his article was that social workers and teachers of social workers, ministers, welfare workers, probation officers, doctors, have something in common with salesmen in that in some way or another they are going to advise or counsel or instruct.

All good sales training programmes highlight the fact that a salesman is a problem-solver, but it is very interesting to see a university professor recognizing the similarity between the salesman and social workers.

As Alan Keith-Lucas points out, all these people-social workers, teachers and salesmen-are saying, 'Let me help you change your attitude-let me help you to do something different-let me help you begin to cope with whatever is making it hard for you to succeed.'

The surprising thing is that there has not been a great deal of study, nor is there a body of knowledge about helping people. We all think we know how to help our fellow man or woman; we do not seem to think it needs any training. We think we can do it intuitively; we can go about helping people casually, confident that, if we done all that we can do and it is up to the other person to accept or reject the advice.

Such is the case with most salesman, and particularly with technical salesmen. These men are skilled, they have product knowledge, they proffer advice. The customer can either accept or reject it.

The social worker has realized that it is not enough merely to offer advice. This is because social workers deal with people who may be weaker than the norm. They might even be stupid or idle or obstinate. Often the only recourse the social worker has is to turn to the law or some other authority to make a person accept help.

The salesman cannot do this. He is operating in a free, competitive society, dealing with people in many cases more skilled than himself. Certainly they know their own business better than the salesman. So how can the salesman help to solve a customer's problem?

The social worker has found that all real helping, that is the sort that really encourages change, takes place within a two-way relationship. This is why it is necessary for the salesman to have empathy to generate a rapport with his customer.

So far so good, but Alan Keith-Lucas then goes on to say that people seldom really want to be helped. They may sound eager and appear desirous to change. They may profess a need or even demand help, but what they really want is help on their own terms. Help that will not force them to change in any way, but will allow them to carry on just as they did in the past.

Let us look at this kind of problem-solving more closely in order to define what are the essential ingredients of change. Firstly, there has to be a recognition that something is wrong and that we cannot do anything about it on our own. Secondly, there must be a willingness to confess this weakness to another person. Thirdly, there must be a willingness to let him advise and, in fact, to have some power over our life. Fourthly, the greatest risk of all, there must be a willingness to risk the unknown-to give up our present situation, however intolerable this may be, for some unknown state that may look better, but may actually turn out to be worse.

This situation described by a social worker is identical to that faced by the salesman and the customer. The salesman in trying to sell some new product based on new technology must get the customer to take those four steps:

1. To recognize that the old product is not good enough and that something can be improved.
2. To admit that the old product is not good enough.
3. To accept advice willingly.
4. To risk the unknown; to buy the new product in place of the older tried and tested product which may well have been inefficient, but at least was something the customer understood.

These simple points help one to the realization that what prevents people asking for help in changing their attitudes is fear-the fear of change-the unwillingness to take a risk. It is not that people do not know what to do.

In the customer/salesman situation, customers are not fools. They are generally intelligent, well-read people who are possibly as aware of the technological changes as the salesman himself. It is not a lack of knowledge on their part that makes them hesitate. It is the fear of putting that knowledge of work for change.

The customer is very rarely content. He is anxious to increase his productivity, to improve his profitability, to achieve all the things that the salesman is offering, but deep down there is a very real fear. A fear of failure-*his* failure.

In the main, however, in the salesman/customer relationship this fear is unrealistic. Generally speaking, products offered by salesmen of companies of good quality and standing are tried, tested and proved, even though they may be new technology. It is very foolish firm indeed that would put an untested product on the market. Therefore, the main task of the salesman is to establish a relationship that can overcome the customer's reluctance to change.

Now overcoming a fear is not something that can be done for anyone. Help cannot be given. It can only be offered. This is the crunch. You hear so many people saying, 'Oh, I have given all the help I can', whereas what they should be saying is, 'I offered all the help I could'.

This consideration brings us to a principle that help depends upon choice. Help freely offered must be chosen freely. The option must remain for the person to do exactly the opposite if he feels like it. There must be no force involved where persuasion is the object.

The social worker accepts that in order to create this attitude for change the following conditions must apply:

1. The relationship must be centered entirely on the interests of the person served.

2. The help offered must deal with real things, however unpleasant they may be.

3. The person who is giving help needs not only courage, not only knowledge, not only self-understanding, but an entirely different virtue which Christians call humility.

So far as the salesman/customer relationship is concerned, this surely means that the salesman should:

1. Offer help entirely with the customer in mind. Think of solving the customer's problem and not the salesman's problem.
2. Help the customer to see that there is a real problem. Help him to understand the size and nature of the problem.
3. Support him through the difficult task of overcoming his fear of change, because he needs all the encouragement that the salesman can give to carry through his decision.

It is no good at all the salesman offering advice and then thinking to himself that the customer must be a fool for not accepting the advice. The customer needs courage to solve his problems and courage is only built on confidence. The salesman must be tolerant, understanding and sympathetic in such a way that will inspire this confidence. No wonder selling is so difficult. No wonder it is so much easier to concentrate on machinery which does not answer back, to concentrate on the financial side of the business which at least seems logical. No wonder the crucial selling role is handed over to happy extroverts who do not mind talking to other people, even though, in fact, they may be utterly the wrong people, even though, in fact, they may be utterly the wrong people to offer genuine help to the other man on his own terms.

The real task of selling to industry must begin with a realization of the complexity of the task.

Later on we shall look more closely at the many levels of influence it is necessary to reach in selling, but it is relevant in this chapter on total communication to appreciate that the point at which customer and salesman are face to face is a very small link in the total communication chain between company and customer.

In industrial selling, particularly of highly technological products where the risk is high, one man is very rarely given the authority to make the purchasing decision. So our communication task is made a great deal more complex.

When we talk of the salesman/customer relationship, or of the salesman helping the customer to solve his problems, we should not consider only one men. 'The customer's is often a team of men, each one seeing the problem from a different angle, each one with different knowledge and skills, seeking reassurance. They may well dislike each other.

This is why industrial management must get to grips with the problem and not leave it to people further down the line. This is why management makes use of other techniques of communication like advertisement in all its manifest media, from the press and television through direct mail, posters, and industrial films to exhibitions, seminars and conferences.

All these methods of communication must be used together with the sales force, in the right 'mix' for each company, in order that this company/customer communication chain is complete, and so that the huge sums spent on communication are used more effectively.

10

SAMPLE SURVEYES IN INDUSTRIAL MARKETS

Most people have an intuitive grasp of the principles of sampling, based on their everyday experience. 'Shake the mixture before use,' for instance, is good advice to ensure that the sediment is evenly distributed, and that the tablespoonful when taken is in the same proportions as the prescription made up by the chemist. In statistical language, the sample should be truly representative of the population. Another example is the drawing of numbers from a hat to decide a winner. The hat is given a good shake to ensure that each number had the same chance of being drawn. Each entrant, therefore, has an equal probability of winning the prize. Also, to eliminate bias, the person making the draw is blindfolded so that he cannot see his own number and thus take an unfair advantage.

In these few sentences, then, we have already stated some of the basic principles of sampling. What we need is to discuss the subject in a logical and quantified manner so that it may be used in marketing research. If we do not do this, we may draw the wrong inferences from our procedure. If, for instance, from a list of 100 companies we select one and find that it uses ceramic tool tips, we are not entitled to assume that they all use ceramic tool tips. But if we select 10 companies at random (shaking the hat) and find that 5 us ceramic tool tips, we are entitled to assume that 50% of the 100 companies do use them, give or take a few. It is that last phrase that causes the difficulty, 'give or take a few'. We need to quantify our procedure.

We should sample for the same reason that we do anything else in life, either because we have to or because we expect some benefit.

If we send out a questionnaire and we get an x% response then, whether intended or not, we have taken a sample of x% from the people to whom we sent the questionnaire. Since few questionnaire give a 100% response (at least by mail) we can generalizing by saying that questionnaires usually involve us in unavoidable sampling. We shall see later what kinds of error thus arise.

As for the advantages of sampling, it is rather obvious that it saves time and money. In some cases it can give a more accurate answer, in other cases it can give a quicker answer, and in even more cases a cheaper answer. The technique of sampling, then, should be familiar to marketing researchers, even though they may not in practice master the technique or use it.

It is a fact that many industrial surveys (perhaps the majority) do not use a formalized sampling technique. Marketing researchers often use the '80-20' rule which is a generalization that in many markets 20% of the firms produce or consume 80% of the product. The researcher uses his judgment to select the vital 20%, which may be no more than a dozen firms, and concentrates his survey on those only, reasoning that he can thus cover 80% of the market more thoroughly than if he attempted to survey all the firms in the market. This is a judgment, or selective sample, and in the right hands can give results equally as satisfactory as random sampling, in which each firm has a known chance of being selected. However, only the latter method is amendable to statistical analysis.

Principal steps in a sample survey

This list of steps in designing and executing a sample survey is drawn primarily from Cochran. Most of the steps are also applicable to a complete enumeration or to a judgment survey. Some of the terms used in sampling theory will be defined.

Objective of the survey

A survey should begin with a lucid statement of the objective, such as, 'How many firms use ceramic tool tips?'. This will involve discussions with informed and interested parties, a review of the relevant literature, of existing statistics, and the requirements of the sponsor.

This may need much re-formulation of the objective, such as, 'How many firms in the U.K. use ceramic tool tips?' or 'How many firms in the U.K. use disposable ceramic tool tips?'. Mastery of the technology of the subject is imperative at the earliest stage lest important factors are overlooked.

Population to be sampled

Statisticians are usually precise in their use of words as well as numbers. However, the literature does not seem to be agreed on the meanings of the terms 'Universe' and 'Population'. Some authors think they are synonymous, others think that Universe is an obsolete term for Population, while still others drop the term Universe and use instead Physical Population and Statistical Population. However, marketing researchers could well adopt the definitions given by Ostle because they emphasize a very important concept. In these definitions, the Universe is a specified group of 'objects', such as people, households, or firms, from which a Population of numbers can be extracted. For instance, a Universe of 6000 selected firms in the U.K. (which is not the total number of firms in the U.K.) can give many different populations of numbers, such as the number of employees in each firm, the annual turnover, the capital employed, etc. When a sample is drawn, it may be drawn either from the Universe or from the population of numbers which has already been derived from the Universe. Whether the sample is drawn from the Universe or the population, there will be no difference in the results. The drawing of the sample from the one or the other is merely dependent on whether the elements comprising the Universe have been 'measured' before of after the sample is drawn.

A simple illustration makes this clear. If we compile a list of addresses of all the elements in the Universe (this defines 'list') which in this case will be 6000 companies, and we then sample 100 of them, we can then question the 100 firms to obtain the sample data. Alternatively, if the data pertaining to the 6000 companies are already available on file, we can sample the population of numbers by selecting 100 pieces of data from the file. Obviously, one would adopt that procedure which minimizes effort. In the one case we do not need to compile a list of 6000 companies because the 6000 pieces of data are already on file, and in the other case we do not extract 5900 pieces of data which will never be used. If this point is agreed, we can henceforth use the phrase 'sampling the population' to cover both methods, it being understood that either method can be used as a matter of practical convenience. It also simplifies matters as all textbooks commonly use this phrase. The statistician thinks of a population as a population of numbers (attributes will be discussed later), from which a sample of numbers will be drawn, in a similar manner to our previous illustration of drawing numbers from a hat. Given the population of numbers, the sample, and the method by which it was drawn, the statistician can use highly elegant theories to arrive at probabilistic conclusions, but if there is an imperfect correspondent between the Universe and the population, the results will be unrealistic. As an example, there has been endless trouble in trying to assess national R&D expenditures. The Universe of firms is known, but the population of numbers is extremely difficult to define because each firm seems to have its own idea of what constitutes R&D, and what expenditure should properly be attributed to it.

If there were to be a division of labour, it would be the marketing researcher's job to define the Universe, compile the list, and extract a homogeneous population of numbers which correspond exactly to what he wants to know about the Universe. The statistician would then be concerned with devising a method of sampling which gave the required precision for the minimum cost, and for analysing the result, drawing the conclusions, and testing them.

Data to be collected

Care is needed to verify that all the relevant data are included and no essential data omitted. One may, for instance, wish to specify 'all ceramic tool tips costing less than 10', or 'all ceramic tool tips purchased directly from the manufacturer'.

Degree of precision required

The degree of precision obtainable in a survey is a combination of the statistical error and the systematic error. Systematic error is also called bias. Many authorities believe that the error due to bias is larger than the statistical error due to sampling, but this will be treated in greater detail later. The last word on the degree of precision required must rest with the sponsor of the survey, and the issue must be placed squarely before him at the planning stage.

Methods of measurement By this we mean 'how do we extract the data required from the sample drawn from the list?'. We may for instance sample 500 addresses from the list of 6000 and then get the data from those 500 firms. The primary measuring instrument is the question, although other indirect methods may be used. The marketing researcher can be expected to be familiar with mail questionnaires, telephone interviews, and visits.

The list This has already been defined. The term 'Frame' is sometimes used rather than 'List' as having a slightly less restricted connotation-for example, maps can be used as sampling frames. The compilation of a list is work that is frankly dull, exacting, and frustrating, but nevertheless of cardinal importance since the list is the foundation on which the whole survey stands.

Method of selecting the sample This is the only area which is almost exclusively the province of the statistician. Various methods will be described later. It is this topic which often appears most baffling to the beginner, but it must be remembered that this is a branch of applied mathematics which has been developed by long and frequent usage in scientific disciplines such as agriculture and medicine. If it is any consolation to the marketing researcher only an elementary understanding of these principles is required. Anything deeper should be left to the statistician.

The pre-test This may be necessary in order to get some information for the statistician if nothing whatever is known about the population beforehand. It may also be a pilot run for the main survey, designed to show up ambiguities in questions, and test the methods of coding and analysis.

Organization of the fieldwork These problems are mainly administrative, but competent organization of the fieldwork can give useful reductions in cost.

Summary and analysis of the data

The completed questionnaire must be edited both to amend obvious recording errors by the respondent and if possible to detect erroneous data resulting from misunderstandings. It will sometimes be necessary to refer to the respondent and ask questions such as, 'Are you sure these were your annual sales and not your monthly sales?' The disadvantage of an anonymous questionnaire is immediately apparent. It is imperative to check the input data.

Precision of the survey

The precision of the survey is made up of the sampling error (statistical) and the systematic error (bias). A typical survey, shows that as the accuracy increase the cost also increases. The total error is the sum of the systematic error and the sample error. The systematic error is shown as larger than the sample error because many authorities believe that systematic error is always the larger of the two.

Bias in sampling

Twelve factors are listed which could affect the ultimate usefulness of a survey.

(i) Variability in response: There are two kinds of variability in response: (a) that which is given by the same person at two different times; and (b) that given by different persons. Both kinds of error are often much greater than is ordinarily supposed. An example of the second kind of variability in response is the discrepancy between duplicate reports of the occupations of workers, one report coming from the worker himself and the other coming from the worker's employer. Edwards-Deming points out that this type of error is one of the reasons why even 100% coverage cannot give absolute accuracy. This latter term is, infact, non-definable. If one were to make two surveys, both of them having 100% coverage, the variability of response would make the results of one survey differ from its identical succeeding one.

(ii) Differences between different kinds and degrees of canvass: Differences are obtained between postal, telephone, and interview canvasses. The problem is not whether differences exist but how great are the differences and why they do exist.

(iii) Bias and variation arising from the interviewer: Variation

attributable to the interviewer arises from many factors; the political religious, and social beliefs of the interviewer; his economic status, environment, and education. Another source of bias arises in the interviewer having a lack of understanding of the subject under investigation and its purpose, without which the interviewer cannot evaluate a situation or properly record the respondent's statements.

(iv) Bias caused by the sponsor's 'image' : It is also well recognized that both government and private organizations sometimes attempt to hide their identities by subcontracting the collection of data, so that the respondents will be unaware of the sponsoring agency.

(v) Imperfections in the design of the questionnaire and tabulation plans: Faulty design of the questions, which can be a considerable cause of bias, often arises from lack of knowledge of the subject matter and the possible different replies from the respondent. Many jokes are based on deliberately ambiguous questions. Ambiguity often arises from misguided attempts at brevity.

(vi) Changes that take place in the Universe before tabulations are available: One may be assessing the market-share for product X, but if during the survey another competitive product Y reaches the market, the assessment will be in error.

(vii) Bias arising from non-response: It is curious how many fail to see that non-response can cause a very large bias. Why do people not return questionnaires? One cause has already been discussed under. Another cause of non-response is the failure to address the questionnaire to the appropriate source of data in the firm. This may cause a bias due to a late return. It is not sufficiently appreciated that a 70% response on a complete coverage may be unusable, whereas a 95% response on a 10% sample can be quite useful.

(viii) Bias arising from late returns: This form of non-response is not strictly speaking attributable to the non-respondent but to the inability to process delayed reports because of the necessity for a 'cut-off'.

(ix) Bias arising from an unrepresentative selection of data for the survey, or for the period covered: The problem here is one of seasonal variation in purchasing, such as for airline tickets which peak during the holiday season. It is probably of most relevance to researchers estimating derived demand where the derived demand is seasonal in nature.

(x) Bias arising from an unrepresentative selection of respondents: This can arise from the inability to complete a satisfactory list of the Universe. Another possibility is an unrepresentative choice of respondents which often arises as a matter of convenience to the interviewer, or his inability to cover the whole list, e.g. those at home and abroad. If often arises also in the 'invitation questionnaire' where a patron of the goods or service is supplied with a questionnaire asking for comments. The returns show only the extremes in satisfaction or vexation and that only from the articulate.

(xi) Processing errors: These may range from a simple error in recording to a major difference of opinion between the respondent and the coder. Two coders working on the same set of schedules will give different sets of results.

(xii) Errors in interpretation: Errors and difference in interpretation often arise from a misunderstanding of the question, either on the part of the interviewer or the respondent.

Statistics of sampling and sample size

We turn now to the other source of error, statistical error due to sampling, and also the determination of the optimum sample size. Before going any further it should be pointed out that the use of analytical methods of determining the optimum sample size may not be possible because they require: (a) some foreknowledge of the population; and (b) the sponsor to state the degree of accuracy required and to justify his requirement for that accuracy. Also, it is necessary to distinguish carefully between the different methods of sampling, because the statistical treatment varies between one method and another.

All methods of sampling can be classified into either

'random' or 'non-random'. Only random methods are amenable to statistical analysis. Non-random methods are called judgment, or selective samples, because, unlike the drawing of numbers from a hat, the sample is selected with a purpose in mind. This does not imply that there is no rationality in selective sampling, or that it is not done in a highly organized way. In quota sampling, for instance, each interviewer is given a quota of firms to interview, e.g. so many engineering firms, so many textile firms, so many chemical firms, etc. The choice of which particular firm to interview is then left to the interviewer. This method is usually more economical than other sampling methods, firstly because it is easier to administer, secondly because each interviewing expert can deal with his own particular industry, and thirdly because there are fewer follow-ups. It will however give biased samples and it is impossible to apply statistics to calculate sampling errors. It is a method, however, which may have to be used if one is doing an international survey.

Random sampling

Random sampling does not mean haphazard sampling. It is a term used by the statistician to mean that each member of the population has a calculable and nonzero probability of selection. We need to distinguish between three different methods of random sampling.

(i) Sampling without replacement from an infinite population: The term 'infinite population' refers to one which is inexhaustible. If for instance we were to sample a uniformly distributed population of the single digit numbers from 0 to 9, taking as a sample one digit at a time, it is clear that the population is inexhaustible, and therefore, as a concept, infinite. As another example, the population may be so large that it can be regarded for the purposes of the survey as being infinite, although in fact it is not so.

(ii) Sampling with replacement from c finite population: As an example, let us consider the sampling of a pack of playing cards, one card being drawn at a time as a sample, its denomination noted, and the card then returned to the pack before the next card is drawn. It is clear that the population being sampled is always 52

playing cards, and for no matter how long the sampling is continued the population remains constant, or inexhaustible. The population is therefore, as a concept, infinite, and the same statistical treatment can be applied as in case (i) above. However, it may be thought that the sample will not be representative of the population, because the same card, e.g. the Queen of Hearts, could be drawn more than once, yet the cards in the pack each have a unique identity. It must be remembered that although we are physically sampling from a finite population of 52 cards, we are effectively sampling from an infinitely large pack of cards which contains an infinite number of Queens of Hearts. There is really no difference here from the previous example of selecting single digits from 0 to 9, where each digit is written on a card, and the card after sampling is returned to the population.

The term 'representative' can cause a great deal of philosophical argument, and yet most people have an intuitive grasp of what it means. It is that the sample shall be a microcosm, or miniature, of the population, in which each part of the population is present, or 'represented', but not 'over-represented'. As applied to parliamentary democracy, the term is quite clear. Each electron constituency has one, and only one, representative in Parliament.

Because of this difficulty to representativeness, the marketing researcher is not recommended to use the method of random sampling with replacement, although, as a method, it is based on impeccable statistical theory. It is better to retain the intuitive concept of representativeness but use the modified theory of sampling without replacement.

(iii) Sampling without replacement from a finite population: In using this method, we select a sample from the population and retain it so that it cannot be selected again. If for instance we have a long list of firms and we randomly select one firm from the list, we then delete that firm from the list before taking the next sample.

However, it can be argued that once again we may

not get a representative sample because a complete sector of the population may be omitted, purely by chance. This is undoubtedly correct, and is one of the reasons for adopting stratified random sampling. This is a variant in which the population is stratified before sampling, e.g. into SIC (or NACE) classification, and each stratum, or classification, is then sampled independently. In this way we ensure that all sectors in the population are represented in the sample. A further refinement is that the statistician can sometimes arrange the procedure so that stratification can increase the precision.

Simple random sampling is a technical term used for any random sampling method in which each member of the population has an equal chance of being selected. 'Simple' is not used as an adjective in the ordinary sense of the word, i.e. the opposite of complex.

Clearly, sampling methods (i) and (ii) above are simple random methods, whereas (iii) is not, and, therefore, the latter is properly referred to as 'random sampling'. However, method (iii) is no more complex in practice than the other two methods.

Random sampling from the list, using random numbers

Let us assume we have defined the Universe and that we have complied a satisfactory list. Let this list of firms be numbered serially from O to N, where (N + 1) is the number of firms on the list. The firms on the list may be arranged in any order. e.g. alphabetically or geographically, etc. We need to sample the numbers, each of which represents a particular firm.

Physically, there are many different ways of sampling a population of numbers from O to N. All of them have disadvantages. We may for instance write each number on a slip of paper, each slip of paper of the same size, weight, colour, and texture, and we may put all of these slips of paper into a rotating drum to mix them thoroughly before drawing one at random. Or we could perhaps use a 10-sided die, or a roulette wheel, or a spinning pointer. Each method depends for its freedom from bias on the exactitude of mechanical construction, which is never perfect. Each method, before use, should be thoroughly tested to ensure the sample is strictly random. Such methods are lengthy and time-consuming.

It is for these reasons that we choose to select the sample by selecting, or generating, random numbers from O to N. When a random number in the specified range is selected, the firm on the list which has that number is selected for the sample (if more than one in the sample) and the same firm is then deleted from the list. We can use random numbers from tables such as A Million Random Digits, in which case tests for randomness will have been made on the tables, and they are therefore termed 'true random numbers'. Alternatively, random number can be generated using mathematical functions, in which case, although believed to be random, they have not been tested for randomness, and hence are termed 'pseudo-random numbers'. In practice there is no perceptible difference between the two, although the statistician would naturally prefer to use only tested methods.

Two procedures for obtaining integer random numbers in the range O to N

(i) True random numbers can be obtained from tables. To obtain an integer random number in the range O to N, select a series of digits from the table to make a number which has the same number of digits as N itself. Express this random number as a decimal fraction. Multiply the decimal fraction by N + 1 and take the integer part of the result. The number so obtained will be that which is required.

Example: To find an integer random number in the range 0 to 1700.

(a) Select 4 digits to form a 4 digit number. Say 3824.

(b) Express this as a decimal fraction, 0.3824.

(c) Multiply 0.3824 by 1701.

(d) The result is 650.4624.

(e) The integer of this number is 650, which is the number required.

(f) Repeat for as many random numbers as required. They will all lie within the range 0-1700.

(ii) Alternatively, with an electronic calculator generate the uniformly distributed pseudo-random number using the previously generated number X using.

$$\text{decimal portion} \quad \left(X_i + \frac{11}{87} \right) \times 87$$

a pseudo-random seed between 0 is 1 needed to initialize the procedure. A typical seed is 1/p. The seed should contain as many digits as in *R* (the random number) itself, although as a precaution it is best to take a seed with (*R* + 1) digits and discard the last digit of the random number in case there is any tendency for it to be cyclic. Then, as above, to obtain an integer random number in the range *O* to *N*, multiply the decimal portion by (*N* + 1) and take the integer part of the result. This will be an integer pseudo-random number in the range *O*—*N*. The whole calculation can be set up in less than 200 steps on a programmable calculator. It is available on a cartridge for the Tektronix 31 programmable calculator.

Where sampling error is important

The foregoing discussion has emphasized the importance of systematic error over sampling error. Systematic error is not only important but also insidious because it often remains undetected. In the laboratory, systematic error is investigated by measuring the variable to be assessed in many different ways and comparing the results, but this procedure is rarely available to the marketing researcher, who must do the best he can by intuition and experience.

However, in UMR sampling error would be important where we are doing repeated surveys, month after month or year after year, in order to monitor some parameter of the market, such as the rate of penetration with time. Obviously, in order to draw valid conclusions between one sample and the next, the sampling error must be less than the change of the parameter with time. otherwise we would not be able to detect the trend because of random variation. This is where the theory outlined above can be used, because the survey previous to the one being conducted can be used as the pilot survey, and sample size can be adjusted as the series of surveys proceeds. There is another type of survey when sampling error is important, and that is in election polls, where the result is critically dependent on the accuracy of the 'yes' or 'no' answers. If there are 50.1% 'yes' and 49.9% 'no', the forecast can be 100% wrong if the total error exceeds 0.1%. Fortunately, however, this is not IMR.

Sample surveys and forecasting

It is instructive to classify sample surveys into those which are retrospective and those which are prospective, the latter being the ones which will be involved with forecasting. The two kinds of error, statistical and systematic, occur in both types of survey, but the magnitude of the total error in forecast sample surveys can be so enormous that the sampling statistical error becomes trivial, provided of course that the sample size is not itself ridiculously small.

As an example, there is a case which is known, but not published, of an industrial marketing survey undertaken by consultants of international repute who estimated the market demand 5 years ahead at 50m. As the product was of a highly sophisticated technological nature, a second survey was commissioned from different but equally distinguished consultants who reached substantially the same conclusion. The forecast market demand proved to be in error by a factor of 50, involving the manufacturing firm in an eventual loss of 10m. The difference in scale between errors of this magnitude and those in the examples discussed earlier makes one wonder whether a difference of principle is involved, but this is not so. The error was due to systematic bias in the assessment.

One can easily see how such a situation can arise by considering the difference between the two questions 'Did you purchase product A last year?', and 'Will you purchase product A when it reaches the market 5 years hence?' Future demand is not of course assessed in such a simplistic way. Extrapolation methods, for instance, are used, except where a new product with no historic data is to be marketed. Now, it can be argued that all forecasts are to some extent conditional, being based for instance on relative price changes, or changes in real net disposable income, etc. When these conditions are not fulfilled, the forecast is in error. These errors are systematic because, unlike the sampling error, they do not decrease in magnitude as the sample size increases. The marketing researcher would do well to bear this point constantly in mind, because, as has been stated earlier, the sample error could well be the least of his worries.

11

INDUSTRIAL MARKETING RESEARCH

INTRODUCTION

The comparative reluctance of companies making industrial products to research their markets systematically. Now that markets in general have grown more competitive, industrial companies have began to take a greater interest in what marketing research might be able to do for them, and in many cases they have discovered for the first time that it can, in fact, give them highly relevant and pragmatic help. Consumer marketing research has tended to attract attention because of its immediate impact on many members of the public, and industrialists may have been led to believe that the role of marketing research is confined to fast-moving 'supermarket products.' But, marketing research has applications over virtually *all* products and services, including the public sector industries and services.

Before considering in some detail the techniques of industrial marketing research, a brief look at some of the fundamental influences in industrial buying behaviour should help in further discussion of this specialized sector of research. It would also be useful to note that the term industrial is used in a wider sense than, for example, industrial capital equipment or technical products; it should be viewed as covering not only those kinds of products, but also technical services, and the many other activities which now characterize industrial production and markets.

A firm seeks its objectives through the medium of profit, and more specifically, through conversion of its resources into goods and/or services and then obtaining a return on these by selling them to customers.

Organizations are interested in survival and development, which the earning of profit allows, and it can reasonably be assumed that all organizations are similarly motivated. In seeking to achieve these organizational goals, buyers will also be influenced by their personal goals-their wish for survival, growth and personal profit.

It has been commonly assumed that knowledge is widespread and that expert decisions in organizational buying are based firmly on rational and functional grounds. Consumer buying on the other hand, has been considered to be far less 'scientific' and subject to irrational behaviour impulse buying and lack of market knowledge. But these sweeping generalizations overstate the case; the organizational buyer cannot live in a rational vacuum. Feelings can, and open do intrude into his or her buying behaviour.

Apart from the mixed motivations which influence buyers of industrial products, it is also important to study *how* buying decisions are taken. *Who,* in fact, is the key figure in deciding to buy a particular product and what is the contribution made by other members of the firm? Research has indicated the in many cases quite important decisions are influenced by an *ad hoc* committee which meets once a day at lunchtime in the management dinning-room.

Most business executives have had some experience of this type of influence, and some organizations go so far as to construct lunchtime agendas for discussion among senior members of staff.

Complex decision making

Industrial buying processes are generally more complex than consumers 'buying' decisions often several executives, from different departments, are involved in buying the many goods and services used by companies in the production of their manufacturers. In 1958, for instance, a Dun and Bradstreet study showed that no fewer than nine people influenced the average firm's buying decisions.

Alexander *et al.* reported that a study of 106

industrial firms revealed that three or more persons influenced the buying processes in over 75 per cent of the companies examined.

McGraw-hill, in a special investigation of British engineering firms, reported that in companies with between 400 and 1000 employees, there were more than five buying influences and in companies of over 1000 employees, more than six persons influenced the buying decision.

Almost always, industrial buying negotiations are relatively sophisticated, and often highly complex in the case of very large capital investment or entry into new areas of manufacturing activity necessitating considerable long-term commitments in production and marketing strategies.

Roles in industrial buying Five roles have been described as typical of the industrial buying processes: gatekeeper, user, influencer, buyer, and decider, which make up the 'Buying Centre'. There are times when the same person fulfils all of these functions but, more frequently, different people are active in their various roles in particular buying situations.

The degree to which individuals may affect buying decisions is obviously related to their specialist knowledge and to their status in the management hierarchy.

Functional specialists influence the choice of supplier far more than the buyer, who is frequently little more than an approved signature on the order form.

Products of a highly technical nature, e.g., electronic equipment, tend to have buying procedures quite different from those customary in firms having a range of fairly simple, standard items. In the latter case, ordering is largely a matter of routine involving a fairly narrow range of components for which standards of quality, price, and service have been well established. The buyer, in these circumstances, has more real authority, as his decisions a fairly straightforward and based on ascertainable commercial facts. With highly technical products in dynamic market conditions the buyer is at a disadvantage; he cannot possibly be a specialists in such areas, though there is a tendency to appoint specialists buyers in large organizations who have the opportunity to develop expert knowledge over a narrower field of purchasing activities.

George Stratus, Professor of Business Administration, made a detailed study of buying agents in 142 firms, biased strongly towards large engineering companies; since agents in these firms face the most complex problems. Suggesting alternatives is specifications quantities, substitute materials, etc., helps the buyer to keep the initiative; he no longer feels that he is at the end of the line. He experiences conflict with other departmental chiefs but he can skillfully reduce this by using formal and informal techniques to influence the buying requisitions. This requires an appreciation of the needs of engineering production and other functional specialists.

Strauss found that most buyers used a variety of techniques, depending on the problem, to keep their status in the organization. 'Expansionists' favoured informal tactics and were markedly flexible in their approach: They had long-run strategies and sought to influence decisions before they were made'.

As a professional the industrial buyers regards the limitation of his authority with some disfavourable and as a person he feels that he has suffered some loss of status in the organization. His personal feelings may well become more evident in those buying situations where his power as a buyer is unchallenged. In this way, he can assert his authority in the competitive structure of the managerial system.

Leonard Sayles, Professor of Business Administration, states that: 'Most managers have stretched or shrunk their jobs to suit their own personalities and the expediencies of the situation. Buyers must inevitably take an active part in the decision-making processes of the organizations to which they belong, and their success will largely be determined by the way in which they can 'work the organization.

When the organization is viewed as a complex series of interlocking patterns of human relationships, work-flow patterns and control patterns, the opportunity for the individual to innovate and shape his own environment becomes apparent.

That this view of the buyer is no illusion can be seen in a survey of 47 firms undertaken by PEP and completed in 1964 under the patronage of the Nuffield Foundation. Among a wealth of information, the report states:

> Within the management hierarchy it often appeared that the buyer was a relatively unimportant member of the firm and sometimes he was no more than a senior clerk with direct responsibility to a senior member of management, who might be the accountant, the works director or the commercial manager.

The buyer's status may be further affected by contracts for some strategic supplies being decided at board level. He may, therefore, experience professional dissatisfaction at having large and vital areas of decision making taken from him, apart from those involving highly technical matters. In more progressive organizations, the buyer is encouraged to from close working arrangements with other executives which result in a ready flow of information between the various departmental heads. The buyer refers sellers representatives to individual technical specialists for appraisal of their particular products. In turn, the technicians provide the buyer with accurate data so that the he can obtain competitive quotations and also, from time to time, discuss with them possible alternative specifications which may affect economics. Strauss's study, already noted, underlines this approach towards 'value analysis. It was further high-lighted in a report, published in 1964, by the British Productivity Council of

16 case studies which showed clearly that significant advantages were obtained from discussing problems jointly with suppliers' representatives, company technicians, and the buyers.

This type of cooperation will obviously grow with the development of more complex methods of production. The acceptance of risk is inevitable in business, the buyer wishes to minimize the risks while achieving maximum efficiency. It is to his or her professional advantage to bring together all those who are interested in a particular transaction so that the final decision is made with the agreement of all parties involved in the transaction.

Concentrated buying power

Marketing transactions for individual products tend to be more specialized than for consumer products. There are greater differences between buyers, and the actual number of buyers for specific products is smaller than in consumer markets. Buying power is concentrated in far fewer centres, and industries tend to concentration in certain geographic areas, e.g., pottery in Stoke-on-Trent, printing and hosiery in Leicester, cutlery in Sheffield, etc. Apart from geographical concentration, industries are frequently dominated by a small number of firms whose aggregate output covers the majority of the markets in which they operate. For example, over 80 per cent of the capital products turnover owned electronics companies is accounted for by the indigenous manufactures. Buyers for such companies are in a position to place large orders, frequently on a long-term basis for which competitive terms have to be negotiated. Such orders may in fact, represent a high proportion of the total output of a supplier, and this may well be distributed over a small number of customers. Risks inherent in this type of restricted selling need to be carefully assessed, and a marketing policy drawn up which allows the company to retain flexibility in its operations.

Inter-dependence of buyers and sellers

Industrial transactions are often involved and may take many months to complete. The average industrial order is likely to be much greater value than those booked in consumer markets, and so the capital risks involved are higher. In addition, there may be widespread repercussions in manufacturing processes if industrial goods fail to satisfy standards of quality, or if the delivery promises are not fulfilled. Heavy financial loss may be incurred through the closure (or part working) of a busy production line, owing to the lack of vital raw materials or components. For industrial suppliers which are vital to the production process, risk and uncertainty are considerable factors in influencing the buying decision. The buyer seeks to reduce those elements by satisfactory long-term contracts. He or she is reluctant to change suppliers once they have proved reliable and satisfactory in other respects. Price must take its place among the many factors to be considered when placing business.

Price by itself is always a hazardous way of holding business, so suppliers should aim to provide non-product advantage—to build round their products a constellation of buying motives in order to attract interest in their products. There is generally a range of prices for specific products, and the industrial buyer will not necessarily buy the lowest-priced product. With many products, made to BSI or some other standard specification, there is virtually intrinsic difference manufacturing products. Price is considered but buying decisions are also strongly affected by reliability and service. Sometimes, buyers make these assessments subjectively preferring to deal with the well-known firms, even though their prices may be marginally higher.

Between industrial buyer and salesman confidence is important and this may take many months, even years, to establish: it will not be lightly set side Industrial buyers become heavily dependent upon their suppliers and choose them with care. Some specialist products require an efficient maintenance service which suppliers contract to give. Other industrial products of a standards of quality, e.g., the stainless steel used in aircraft engines.

Industrial buyers recognize that the true value of products is made up of many parts all of which require careful investigation. It is the responsibility of industrial buyers to obtain agreement on what values are necessary in specific products, the relative importance of intrinsic qualities and the various 'added values'—the services—which surround them. Included in this with particular will be the non-rational factors, the pleasantness (or otherwise) of doing business with particular firms, for buyers tend to be persuaded by a salesman whose personality is acceptable to them provided his product meet their needs.

The building-in of values in industrial products extends to the selling of complete systems e.g., computers, where companies offer a package deal covering the training to staff, design of the system installation of the machine, and supply of software. Industrial security firms offer comprehensive services for the protection of factory premises, screening of personal, and the transaction of cash funds.

DEFINITION Various definitions of the general function of marketing research were given including that of the Industrial Marketing Research Association (IMRA), viz....The systematic objective and exhaustive for and study of facts relevant to any problem in the filed of industrial marketing. The term industrial marketing has been defined by IMRA as follows: 'All business and activities involving or influencing the movement of industrial products from the manufacturer to the industrial or commercial user.

Industrial products and services are of many kinds, and many attempts have been made to define them. Some of these definitions overlap; the uses to which products are put will bias classifications; 'original equipment' sales although involving the same product, will probably be placed in a different category from replacement sales.

The Industrial Marketing Research Association has given the following definition: 'Materials, machinery and capital equipment used by services provided for industrial and institutional establishments. On which basis industrial products were classified as:

1. *Capital goods*: 'sold as an inherent whole to. further production in machines,, accessories or components.

2. *Primary products*: basic materials lie steel, chemical, or aluminium bars sold to manufacturer's.

3. *Intermediate products*: such as tubes, castings or building materials, which have undergone some major change of form.

CHARACTERISTICS OF INDUSTRIAL MARKETING RESEARCH

Five sequential stages of marketing research were identified and discussed principally with reference to consumer product markets. The same general approach is applicable to researching opportunities for industrial products and services. Although the application of certain techniques may be modified the essential process of developing an objective and effective research design remains unchanged.

As in consumer marketing research, the first step is obtain agreement on the nature of the problem to be investigated. This initial stage may take up considerable time and it requires the patience and stamina of both clients and researchers to arrive at a workable brief. But this process of clarification and definition should not be shirked; unless the matters on which the research will focus are fully understood and agreed, little productive research is likely later on.

For a client to say: 'We want you to look at our market', is a totally inadequate research brief. Many firms operate in several markets which share, perhaps, general characteristics but which also tend to have distinct features. Also, there are usually particular features of a market which may affect the likehood of success and investigation may be needed in some depth in these areas. There may be times when a client is so unwilling to give adequate insight into her problem that no worthwhile marketing research would be feasible. Usually, however, experienced researchers are able to generate an atmosphere of trust and confidence which attracts even hesitant clients to cooperate in delineating their business problems.

Desk research As with consumer research, data collection, should at the secondary level, and full advantage should be taken of available information, both within companies and that published externally, to give a sound base to the whole research program. There are many sources of published data to which researchers instinctively turn, but, usually, there are valuable data to be gathered also from production, accounting and sales records. Marketing research data may be could from theses internal sources at very low cost and, with a little ingenuity, a regular flow of specific information from the various areas of functional management could be great value to developing and guiding marketing strategies.

The Census of Production covers production, which is defined as 'industrial production, including construction, gas, electricity and water supply and mines and quarries'. It covers production by private firms, nationalized industries, and central and local government. Information, under the authority of the Statistics of Trade Act is collected by postal census of 'establishments;, classified according to their main products on the basis of the Standard Industrial Classification.

While this classification is valuable, it may result in the total production of some important firms being included under one classification, whereas they may, in fact, produce considerable quantities of some other products which are important in these particular markets, but represent only a relatively small proportion of total output.

The Census was originally planned on a quinquennial basis: It has now been replaced by an annual one, the first of which took place in 1970. Quarterly enquiries are supplemented by monthly enquiries, in addition, detailed enquiries may also be extended into purchase of materials at there-year intervals.

In compliance with the requirements of the Statistical Office of the European Communities certain changes were made in the Census from 1973. Previously, census returns had to be submitted by establishments employing 25 or more people, except that in 13 industries where small firms made an important contribution to total output, the coverage was extended to establishments with 11 or more employees.

New questions covered payments for outworkers and the cost of goods bought for merchanting questions on transport were generally discontinued. Establishments with 100 or more employees were also asked these new questions, and also questions related to value-added tax and the cost of non-industrial services.

OFFICIAL INDUSTRY CLASSIFI-CATION

In Britain, the basic framework for measuring industrial production is known as the *Standard Industrial Classification* (SIC). This originated in 1948 to encourage uniformity in UK official statistics for industrial aware made in 1958, 1968, and 1980. These revisions have tended to make study of trends in certain industrial sectors rather difficult. The SIC has been described by the chief statistician of the Central Statistical office as an empirical classification which tries to reflect the existing structure of economic activities in the UK.

The unit of classification in the SIC is the 'establishment', i.e., the whole of the production at a particular address of a farm, mine factory of shop, classified according to main products on the basis of the SIC. However, care should be exercised when interpreting data from SIC sources.

While the official classification and sub-headings of industrial activities often provide valuable data for marketing research purposes, specific products tend to be subsumed under fairly broad headings. In some cases, it may be possible, on application to the Business Statistics Office, to obtain more relevant information.

Trade Associations and Chambers of Commerce, should be contacted in the rigorous search for market data. In general, however, the search will not be very fruitful, for apart from a handful of such organizations they are limited to giving an overall view of particular industries or trades, and economic data are unlikely to be available.

It would be as well to bear in mind that membership is voluntary and one firms, for reasons of policy, may not be members. The collection of information within associations depends largely on goodwill. The complete reliability of the data supplied is a factor to be carefully considered.

Trade directors are of variable quality; it is useful to check accuracy and reliability by scrutinizing entries relating to companies which are well known personally. In addition to these publications covering the market under survey.

Entries in exhibition catalogues can be use to build up a good general knowledge of particular industries, though it should not be assumed that these necessarily include all companies. Some may have individual methods of promotion which exclude trade exhibitions in some areas.

Some industries have research associations which publish market data; for example, the furniture Industry Association (FIRA). From this brief review of possible sources of extremely published information, it will readily be appreciated that an effective market researcher, particularly when industrial marketing problems are being surveyed, need to have some of the talents of the sleuth in tracking down relevant and useful data.

PROBLEMS OF PRIMARY RESEARCH

Samples frames

One of the salient problems of industrial marketing research is the availability of suitable lists of firms on which a survey could be based. Desk research enquiries, as just outlined, could be instrumental in developing sampling frames, in particular, the Statistics Office published *directories of Business Establishments* which, under SIC headings listed names and addresses of the majority of firms whose production figures were recorded anonymously in the Census of Production.

The Classified List of Manufacturing business originates

from the Business Statistics Office (BSO) of UK manufacturing businesses and is a result of the cooperation of firms which, from 1970, contributed to the Census of Production. The resultant list gives information about each manufacturing local unit, separate entries are made. Non-manufacturing units, in particular units which are offices, are not included, so the head office of a firm may not be listed. These valuable lists contain about 27000 business addresses and cover about two-thirds of the employment in the UK manufacturing sector.

Sampling frames may also be constructed from telephone enquiries. For example, it may be possible to check the suitability of companies as respondents or services. Further classification can be done by dividing users into some agreed definitions of heavy, medium, and light, so that specified research can be undertaken in these areas. Stratification of the sample, can then be designed and final figures can be suitably weighted. During telephone discussions it may be possible to obtain the names of other significant users and by this personal method to achieve a valid sampling frame, economically and quickly.

Expert informants

In most industries there are usually people known to be well-informed and to possess sound knowledge of the organization and movements within particular sphere of interest. Researchers should attempt to identify and contact experts, who may be recommended to them by trade associations and other helpful sources, group was reported to subdivided the market into homogenous sectors, and commence enquiries in each sector with the best-informed sources known. The sample size is not predetermined; successive firms are interviewed until a stable answer pattern emerges.

'Sounding' of expert trade opinion is valuable in forming hypotheses about certain market situations. It is responsibility of the researcher to evaluate these opinions objectively and to relate them to data obtained by other methods of enquiry.

The editors and professional journalists attached to the trade and industrial press may also be willing to discuss the market being surveyed, and about which they may have specially relevant knowledge.

SAMPLING Industrial markets differ considerably from mass consumer product markets in many ways, and so some aspects of the sampling methodologies already covered not be directly applicable, although, of course, the underlying concepts of representativeness and objectivity remain unchanged. Sometimes, industrial markets, for example, are very limited and it may be possible to measure consumption, etc., through a complete census. In other cases, the market is widespread, with many different structures and patterns of consumption behaviour, and sampling has to be devised which is both feasible and of course, valid.

Industrial products are often used in a variety of industries, and where a general survey is required it may be necessary to undertake a series of sample surveys into individual user industries. Alternatively, it may be possible to apply some method of weighting to the data of a general survey. The problem for the researcher is obtaining reliable information about a well defined area of investigation. Enquiries should therefore, be directed specifically to those industries (complete or segmented) which are significant for this purpose.

Constructing a sample for industrial marketing research demands some general knowledge of the particular industry concerned. The more perfect this knowledge, the better the researcher will be able to form a sample which adequately represents the population under survey. The total universe to be studied is usually small, from a mere handful of companies to a few hundred and, occasionally, a few thousand. Industrial marketing research typically requires far fewer interviews compared consumer enquiries.

Industries are often dominated by a small number of companies, whose total output represents a significant share of the market, perhaps as high as 90 per cent. This residual output may be contributed by mány comparatively small firms, whose individual market share is relatively unimportant although, of course, they may have a strong position in a specific market sector or niche. Some companies deal with a very restricted number of customers and, sometimes, two or three of these take almost the entire production.

In case like these, it would obviously be incorrect to use a random sampling technique, as the survey findings would be unreliable if one of the major companies were not included in the sample taken. To avoid errors of this nature, the whole population would have to be surveyed, i.e., a census would be necessary. In some instances, it may be possible to avoid taking a complete census by carefully weighting a sample.

A leading industrial marketing researcher has commented that when some establishments are very much mire important than others, the problem is to identify them, wither in advance or by means of a sample design which increases the probability of reaching these important firms without incurring heavy expenses in non-productive interviews.

A survey of the UK market for fork-lift trucks well illiterates some of the problems (and solutions) attached to industrial marketing research. It was known from previous surveys that fork-lift trucks had many industrial applicants and from various official statistics, a matrix of 13 business sectors (groupings of SIC codes) and seven size (employees) classifications was formed. Additional inputs were derived from dun and Bradstreet, Market Location (a commercial firm specializing in listing and mapping industrial and commercial firms in the UK), and the survey organization's (industrial Market Research Ltd.) own file.

It was known that the truck ownership was comparatively low generally and varied widely across and within market sectors, and so some type of disproportionate sampling design was considered necessary.

From earlier proprietary studies of this market, it was possible to compute an estimated penetration percentage for each cell in the matrix, and by applying these figures to the number of establishments, an estimate was made of the number of 'truck equipped establishment's. Sample quotas were then allocated to each cell in proportion to its relative importance in the total truck-owning market.

In order to safeguard the efficiency of the quota sampling scheme, lists of contacts were pre-selected and issued to interviewers on a controlled basis. As a further check, replacement addresses were issued only when the initial set had been fully accounted for. In addition, a sample of addresses from the data base for each business sector size cell was drawn related to 'believed non-users of trucks', and interviews were conducted to identify establishments which had recently acquired trucks. Further amendments to cell penetration levels were also made following enquiries which were largely centered on non-manufacturing firms not covered adequately by the Market Location data.

This relatively complex sampling procedure was followed by structured interviews by a team of 21 mostly home-based telephone interviewers. However, in cases of very large establishments with many trucks, personal interviews were made in order to collect detailed information including qualitative evaluation.

To build up a satisfactory sampling frame for industrial marketing research, considerable patience and ingenuity are necessary as the example just quoted illustrates. Comprehensive combing and integration of published data will help in filling gaps which are usually to be found in any one source of knowledge.

INTERVIEWING AND QUESTIONNARIRES

It will be recognized that interviewing is a critical function of marketing research which, unfortunately, is subject to bias of many kinds. Good research practice aims it eradicate sources of error, and to control, as far as possible, the conditions under which the enquiries are made. Industrial research interviewing should not be regarded as an alternative occupation for members of the sales force; they may be able to produce some information which at a superficial level appears satisfactory. There remains however, the risk of subjectivity, but despite this some organizations to rely on their sales staff to provide market information. It is argued that surveys are better undertaken by people who have an intimate knowledge of the product and the industry. But the fact remains, as a PER Report indicated 'that the man whose job is to sell is often unable to be objective about the reasons for his success or failure, about his competitors, and about many of the factors that contribute to a proper assessment of the firm's prospects in the market.

Interviewing in industrial marketing research tends to be largely unstructured, i.e., a formal questionnaires is not used and is sometimes replaced by an 'interviewing guide', which lists the main areas of research to be covered by the interviewer. It is more a guide to conversation. Since good 'timing' may sometimes attract the right response, the interview is left free to use discretion in the sequence of questing.

Where questionnaire are used, it is important to ensure that technical terms are correctly handled and that the area of scientific or technical enquiry is clearly understood by both parties. This calls for considerable skill in the drafting questions covering specialized fields of knowledge. It also demands interviewers capable of obtaining information, often of a highly technical nature from management over a representative range of companies. Such interviews need to have expert knowledge of the industries which are being covered by the survey, or they should have the intellectual ability to acquire sufficient information in a short period of intensive training. They should also possess the type of personality which will help them to be accepted by senior management with whom they must necessarily confidence if the interviews are to be successful.

The considerable debate about whether or not industrial marketing research interviewers need to be highly qualified technically in the specific industries they are surveying is not easily determined. Even in technical markets, factors other than those directly related to product design and manufacture may frequently be involved : for example delivery time, prices, credit policy, attitudes, or advertising effectiveness. To restrict interviewing to those who are highly trained specialists in engineering and so on, may well affect the findings of specific research surveys because they lack vital business orientation and experience.

Of course researchers including interviewers, need to be adequately briefed this may entail intensive study before field research starts. In a comparatively short time, intelligent field researchers can assimilate a surprising amount of background knowledge about particular industrial techniques and applications. Professional interviewing skills are necessarily the most important factor-technical competence alone does not ensure effective interviewing.

It is clearly important to interview whoever is able to provide relevant and accurate information about the subject of the survey, in many industrial buying decisions several executives from different management functions are likely to influence the source of supply. The buyer may not be able to give detailed answers to certain technical enquiries and it may well be necessary to interview executive in both technical and commercial spheres.

The survey may, therefore, be divided into several parts. Interviewers may have to exercise considerable diplomacy to ensure that the buyer, for instance, gives them the opportunity of meeting other key executives whose opinions on technical matters may be valuable.

On the whole, industrial research is more difficult than consumer research. Fewer calls can be made during the day, and it is advisable to book appointments, as it would be unreasonable to expect executives to lay aside their duties without reasonable advance notification. They may also wish to have a little time in which to obtain specific data. In some cases., a call-back ensures that the information given is reliable.

Frequently, research organizations offer to provide respondent firms with some of the general findings of the survey. This attracts cooperation and helps to ensure that valid and reliable answers are given. With some survey problems, it may be advantageous to institute continuous research at a certain agreed depth, and this could be done by forming a user panel.

OBSERVATIONAL TECHNIQUES

Industrial marketing research can also adopt observational techniques which can provide very useful information. This may involve checking types of equipment in use, or a study of the way in which certain tools are handled. Patterns of typical behaviour may be established which could prove valuable in the design of workshop equipment.

Observation may also be helpful in checking the validity of data supplied for instance, about certain characteristics of production. This technique of acquiring knowledge is prone to basis so observers should be specially trained to maintain as far as possible, objectively. Recording of observed behaviour should be systematic, and to encourage this it would be advisable to have standardized report sheets.

TELEPHONE SURVEYS

Telephone techniques were seen to be growing in popularity in consumer enquiries and new computer-based technologies have resulted in almost 'instant information. Industrial marketing research has also made increasing use of telephone surveys, although this approach has obvious restrictions. It cannot be used, for example, for very lengthy enquiries involving considerable detail, or where some research would be needed before answers could be given, although it may well be useful where the information sought is of a fairly rudimentary nature. In addition, as already noted, it is often used in forming sampling frames.

In a survey of the market potential for a new, small vending machine suitable only for serving between 6 and 30 employees, telephone interviewing was a readership survey undertaken by Mass Observation on behalf of Morgan Grampian's controlled circulation monthly Business Administration. Two hundred and fifty managing directors were interviewed in five weeks, and the response rate was over 50 per cent.

Before telephoning prospective respondents, some planning should be done.; for example, researchers should either prepare a well-structured questionnaire so that time is used productively, or write down the main topics of investigation in a logical progression. In addition, make sure that answers can be recorded adequately, perhaps by marking off appropriate codes or entering the information given on relevant data sheets.

It is particularly important to introduce quickly and clearly the nature of the survey and its objectives, to ensure that the person answering the telephone (or those to whom the call is transferred) is knowledge and bale to give valid information.

Telephone calls may be used to ask for support for a planned mail survey; it was found that a pre-notification telephone call to senior purchasing managers of manufacturing firms in the St. Paul. Minneapolis area to introduce a mail survey containing 40 scale responses related to various buying practices, resulted in 64 out of 66 potential respondents completing and returning the questionnaire. The researchers indicated that the pre-notification request must be brief and to the point..... we aimed for businesslike interaction...... The request by purchasing managers for information about the survey's topic resulted in extremes: some wanted almost no information while others asked very detailed questions that required specific answers. Another insight was the influence of the survey sponsors: the Twin City Purchasing Management Association: this established credibility with the executives contacted.

MAIL SURVEYS

Mail surveys are frequently chosen for research in industrial markets. They are particularly valuable where the population is large and perhaps, widely dispersed. Superficially, this method of enquiry is attractive in terms of economy simplicity, and speed. But closer examination of the real costs involved should be made; apart from printing and postage charges, which will be relatively modest, proportionate charges for overheads and salaries should be added. These latter costs should cover the preparatory work, such a drafting the questionnaire, and the subsequent task of analysis interpretation. Postal questionnaires are not easy to write. Since no interviewer is present to interpret the questions, they must be free from ambiguity. Several pilotings may be necessary; these obviously involve time and cost.

Another aspect to be carefully considered is the real cost of mail surveys, namely, the total cost of the operation spread over the number of effective replies received. The valid replay rate may often result in doubling or trebling the original 'crude' estimate distributed over the total number of questionnaire posted.

In addition, some should be made to compare the values of different methods of survey. This entails studying not merely comparative costs, but also considering the quality of the findings of alternative methods, such as postal surveys and personal interviews. Research had indicated that open-ended questions in postal surveys tended to attract answers maintaining dislike more frequently than when personal interviewing tool place. Admittedly, the initial overall costs of a postal a questionnaire may be only half of those involved in a personal interview covering domestic products, and they very substantially less than personal interviewing in an industrial survey. But the true costs depend on effective response rates and these vary significantly.

A seminar organized by IMRA reported that response rates varied widely, and that it was not also commented that low response rates may not necessarily invalidate the findings, provided that sufficient control data are available with which to weight the answers. With simple dichotomous (YES/NO) questions, one large motor manufacturer found that replies tended to stabilize their relationship after a 39 to 47 per cent response rat was achieved. IMRA remarks that 'if this were generally true then high response rates would be less important to the practical industrial researcher'.

Some ways in which mail surveys might be made more productive were examined detailed attention to the wording of questions is of paramount importance, since they have to be unambiguous and capable of being answered without too much trouble. Experiments have been conducted to see whether coloured questionnaire forms, attractively drafted accompanying letter alternative methods of reply-paid facilities, etc., are effective in raising responses. One about their marketing strategies in a two-page questionnaire.

Four 'treatments' were randomly applied to a sub-sample of 32 large companies: prior letter/white questionnaire prior letter/ blue questionnaire, no prior letter/white questionnaire, and no prior letter, blue questionnaire. The remaining 768 smaller companies which was white and hand-addressed. The questionnaire was accompanied by a covering letter explaining the purpose of the survey, stressing confidentiality, and offering a free copy of the report; a business reply envelope was included in the outward involve which was white and hand-addressed.

The prior letter had indicated briefly the nature of the survey, a questionnaire would shortly be sent, and offered a free copy of the resultant report.

The use of prior letter with this particular commercial population appeared to depress the response rate, and the researchers admit that the result in unique and contrary to previous studies of general population studies,. Blue questionnaire paper did not increase response over white paper.

While the findings related to the influence of a prior letter are surprising, the overall response rate at 57.2 per cent was 'quite high'. Experience has down that many factors influence the success of surveys, including sponsorship, which could be more important than the colour of the paper, and these particular survey findings may well not be universally applicable to industrial, mail surveys.

In an experimental mail survey of personal computer owners, computer retailers and computer manufacturers in California, subjects were randomly assigned to receive either a standard cover letter that offered results to respondents revealed that offering results to respondents did not increase the rate or speed of response, and had 'only a minor effect' on reducing the number of item omissions. It was reported that offering survey results 'increased the cost of the survey while providing minimal benefit's.

It was suggested that the reasons why offerings results failed to have a positive effect were (i) it represented a biased incentive that appealed only to those who had interest in the survey topic; and (ii) the respondent was not given anything tangible before cooperating in the survey. The study did not reveal any differences among the three sectors involved in their reaction to the offer of survey results, although it was found that manufacturers and retailers were much less likely to be responsive to a survey than PC owners.

How far this particular sectoral survey can be generalized is pen to debate.

Non-response is a serious limitation of postal surveys. The greater the response the more widely costs can be spread and although this economic aspect is relatively important, the principal concern of researchers is the likehood that non-respondents are significantly different from respondents in their attitudes towards the products under survey. The reasons for non-response are not known, and these may in fact, be directly relative to the problem surveyed. It is advisable to make some sort of check on non-respondents, either by telephone or personal interviewing in order to establish reasons for non-response. Data thus obtained can be compared with those secured from respondents.

Study of response factors in postal surveys covering social investigations has indicated that response is correlated with interest in the subject. This view was shared 'very strongly 'by IMRA seminar members, who felt 'lack of identification with the purpose of the survey... to be the most important single reason for non-response.

Non-response may also be attributable to ambiguous questions which confuse would be respondents who eventually discard the questionnaire. Some questionnaires may be unreasonable in the amount of information demanded, either being too lengthy or capable of being answered only after considerable reference to records. Another influencing factor may be the physical presentation of the survey; social survey studies have shown that the letter which accompanies a mail questionnaire can affect the response quite significantly. In general, it would be wise to ensure that the recipient forms a favourable attitude to the survey, and attention to the choice of paper, style of printing layout, reply-paid facility, and envelope, helps to win his cooperation.

As far as possible, survey questionnaire (with covering letters) should be addressed to these people able to deal with hem effectively. This may involve patient in the course of building sampling frames, so that key personal are identified. With some complex investigations, it may be helpful to subdivide the questionnaire into specific managerial areas of interest, so that the complete survey can be dealt with more conveniently. Direct posting of questionnaire sections can be done, or it may be possible to distribute these through the chief executive's office.

Some method of following up non-respondents should be devised. Inevitably, this extends the time taken to complete the survey, and of course, adds to the cost. Two remainder letters are customary, often at 14-day intervals. Replies received as the early respondents. Dealing with social surveys, Moser has commented that it would appear to be very reasonable to regard respondents to follow-up appeals as representative of all non-respondents rather than of initial respondents. This observation may well be borne in mind in industrial marketing research.

There is some evidence which suggests that the inclusion of a small premium gift, e.g., a pocket knife, with the questionnaire form, encourages response.

The popularity of postal surveys with researchers should be balanced by a clear understanding of the problems involved in using them. This appreciation will encourage better research design leading, in turn, to more reliable research findings.

GROUP DISCUSSIONS

The technique of group discussions was referred and it was seen to have usefulness in generating freer responses to enquiries about particular problems, often connected with household products. This qualitative research technique also has useful applications in industrial marketing investigation.

An example of the value of group discussions in industrial research related to a high-quality food manufacturer, subsidiary of a large international group, who wanted to extend his business in the catering market. A specialist research firm conducted four group discussions among caterers of various sizes and distributed over segments of the catering industry.

Discussants vigorously dealt with the usage of convenience foods, and general problems of catering, and strong views were expressed about the methods used by market leaders to launch new products.

The researchers felt that, through the interaction of knowledgeable respondents exchanging divergent views, more 'usable results' were obtained than through traditional interviewing techniques.

Brainstorming which Sampson qualifies as a special example of group interviewing was used as part of a research programme conducted for Post Office Telecommunications during 1979 to generate ideas for the possible uses of a range of visual services that would ultimately result in a full view-phone network, by means of which subscribers would be able both to speak to add see the person at the other end of line. A sample was generated from the 'Times' Top 1000' companies supplemented by other organizations, such as advertising agencies, energy boards and government departments which it was though might be interested in this new video phone service, which could be attractive for holding meetings between two or three people per terminal, or for transmitting soft-copy of graphics, documents, etc.

Before the main survey started, two brainstorming sessions were held and resulted in over 200 suggested uses, 'many of which were not business related; but of those that were, very few were new or original'. Following this rather disappointing phase, the research then focused on a survey of 240 organizations; the results indicated that there was a potential market for this novel service.

CONTINUOUS RESEARCH

There is some evidence of panel research in industrial markets. Some truck firms, for example, operate 'user panels' but this technique is by no means as widely used as in consumer product marketing research. There are opportunities, it would appear, for drawing systematically on the experience of customers, although the generic problems of ensuring representativeness and active participation are likely to discourage experiments.

BMRB operates a monthly telephone omnibus survey of 1000 department heads over various industries. Audience Selection organize a 'Key Directors Omnibus' survey based on a sample of 400 telephone enquiries each quarter.

The nature of demand for industrial products is characteristically derived, i.e., it is significantly affected by end-use and department on the rate of usage which may be several stages from the initial buyer. Capital goods suppliers, for example, are ultimately dependent on the demand for the products which their plant is capable of making. Likewise, the demand for raw materials and components will be heavily influenced by

the rate of sales in user industries, and eventually the general behaviour of the national economy and also, perhaps overseas markets. If car sales fall off because of lower consumer demand, the effects will reverberate, through many industries; for example steel, tyres electrical and electronic components upholstery fabrics, paint etc.

The dependent pattern of demand for industrial raw material and components is illustrated in the following figure.

Raw materials

↓

Components

↓

Sub-assemblies

↓

Finished product

Demand relevant to industrial raw materials

This inter-dependence among suppliers of a varied assortment of products and services may be used in researching markets. Companies should fully understand their end-use markets and the nature of demand in these, including trends in the final 'consumption markets. The chain of derived demand may have many links, and research may be necessary at several levels.

It may be feasible to develop a consumption indicator for specific suppliers related to the demand experienced by customers for their products. Packing manufacturers, for instance study carefully the trends in food consumption: consumer preferences may mean that glass-bottle manufacturers will experience marked variations in demand for their products.

In some case, it may be difficult to assess the size of a particular industrial market, either because published figures are too general or they do not exist at all. By studying end-use markets it is often possible to collect some useful data to guide production and marketing decisions. Firms in other industries which supply the same end-use market may be willing to share their market knowledge, and mutual exchange of market data among non-competing companies may be very helpful to all concerned.

End-use analysis offers a very effective approach to industrial market research and can lead to profitable market segmentation strategies. Opportunities across market sectors can be evaluated and resources targeted on specific end-use with their distinctive technical and service requirements.

It is desirable to develop a creative research strategy using well-balanced mix of methodologies in order to achieve valid and reliable findings.

Industrial marketing research has a long way to before it is used as extensively as consumer product research. The problems of industry are no less vital than those of manufacturers of consumer products, and in times of difficult trading it is more important than over to assist the process of decision making by gathering accurate information about the problem in hand.

In general, British industry has neglected marketing and has undertaken comparatively little marketing research, perhaps because of some in-built prejudice about using techniques of management which have become closely associated with supermarket trading.

Technical and industrial marketing enquiries are seldom easy; often they are demanding in their complexity and call for the highest skills in research practice. Over 20 years ago, it was said tat British industry suffers from a removable uncertainty-it does not pay sufficient attention to marketing research, there is still a long way to go before there is general acceptance of its vital importance to the successful marketing of industrial and technical goods and services.

Industrial marketing research association

Founded in 1963, IMRA is the principal British organization for those professionally concerned with 'research into the marketing of goods and services to industrial and institutional consumer's.

One of the prime aims of IMRA is 'to create a greater awareness on the part if Industry and the State of the Value of Marketing research and its needs in the way of informations.

It is now accepted as the representative body for industrial marketing research in the UK. Specialized a sectors of IMRA have been developed to study problems of research in specific industries such as construction, electrical engineering, electronics, metals, paper, printing and packaging and chemical.

Twice a year, IMRA runs residential courses, in the fundamentals of industrial marketing research at Birmingham University. A list of publications includes Guide to Industrial Marketing Research Consultancy which gives useful guidelines on the use and selection of consultants.

The European Association for Industrial Marketing Research (EVAF) was founded in 1965, with the following aims:

1. To establish the association as the organization representing industrial marketing research in Europe.
2. To carry out the following activities:
   (a) Liaison with:

   European official, professional, or educational bodies or organizations, European marketing research organizations.

   (b) Promotion of national or industry-based marketing research study groups, etc.

   (c) Encouragement and improvement of contact between European researchers.

3. The establishment of ethical standards in industrial marketing research.

4. The improvement of technical standards and quality in industrial marketing research.

The EVAF organizes seminars and encourages researchers to exchange, on an internal basis, information and experience of professional interest.

The EVAF and IMRA work very closely together, the former being more concerned with the international aspects of industrial marketing research, whereas the latter is more directly interested in the national aspects.